The Flu Epidemic of 1918

In 1918, a devastating worldwide influenza epidemic hit the United States. Killing over 600,000 Americans and causing the national death rate to jump 30 percent in a single year, the outbreak obstructed the country's participation in World War I and imposed terrible challenges on communities across the United States.

This epidemic provides an ideal lens for understanding the history of infectious disease in the United States. *The Flu Epidemic of 1918* examines the impact of the outbreak on health, medicine, government, and individual people's lives, and also explores the puzzle of Americans' decades-long silence about the experience once it was over. In a concise narrative bolstered by primary sources, including newspaper articles, eyewitness accounts, and government reports, Sandra Opdycke provides undergraduates with an unforgettable introduction to the 1918 epidemic and its aftereffects.

Sandra Opdycke is the Associate Director at the Institute for Innovation in Social Policy at Vassar College.

Critical Moments in American History

Edited by William Thomas Allison, Georgia Southern University

The Battle of the Greasy Grass/Little Bighorn
Custer's Last Stand in Memory, History, and Popular Culture
Debra Buchholtz

The Assassination of John F. Kennedy
Political Trauma and American Memory
Alice L. George

Freedom to Serve
Truman, Civil Rights, and Executive Order 9981
Jon E. Taylor

The Battles of Kings Mountain and Cowpens
The American Revolution in the Southern Backcountry
Melissa Walker

The Cuban Missile Crisis
The Threshold of Nuclear War
Alice L. George

The Nativist Movement in America
Religious Conflict in the 19th Century
Katie Oxx

The 1980 Presidential Election
Ronald Reagan and the Shaping of the American Conservative Movement
Jeffrey D. Howison

The Louisiana Purchase
A Global Context
Robert D. Bush

The Fort Pillow Massacre
North, South, and the Status of African Americans in the Civil War Era
Bruce Tap

From Selma to Montgomery
The Long March to Freedom
Barbara Combs

The Homestead Strike
Labor, Violence, and American Industry
Paul E. Kahan

The Flu Epidemic of 1918
America's Experience in the Global Health Crisis
Sandra Opdycke

The Flu Epidemic of 1918

America's Experience in the Global Health Crisis

Sandra Opdycke

 Routledge
Taylor & Francis Group

NEW YORK AND LONDON

First published 2014
by Routledge
711 Third Avenue, New York, NY 10017

and by Routledge
2 Park Square, Milton Park, Abingdon, Oxon OX14 4RN

Routledge is an imprint of the Taylor & Francis Group, an informa business

Library of Congress Cataloging in Publication Data
Opdycke, Sandra.
  The flu epidemic of 1918: America's experience in the global
  health crisis/Sandra Opdycke.
    pages cm
  Includes bibliographical references and index.
  1. Influenza Epidemic, 1918–1919. 2. Influenza Epidemic,
  1918–1919—United States. 3. Influenza—United States—
  Management. 4. Medical policy—United States—International
  Cooperation. I. Title.
  RC150.4.O63 2014
  614.5′1809041—dc23
  2013038142

ISBN: 978-0-415-63684-1 (hbk)
ISBN: 978-0-415-63685-8 (pbk)
ISBN: 978-0-203-07772-6 (ebk)

Typeset in Bembo and Helvetica Neue
by Florence Production Ltd, Stoodleigh, Devon, UK

This book is dedicated to my dear stepdaughters:
Susan, Deb, Meg, Sarah, and Fanny

Contents

Series Introduction

Welcome to the Routledge *Critical Moments in American History* series. The purpose of this new series is to give students a window into the historian's craft through concise, readable books by leading scholars, who bring together the best scholarship and engaging primary sources to explore a critical moment in the American past. In discovering the principal points of the story in these books, gaining a sense of historiography, following a fresh trail of primary documents, and exploring suggested readings, students can then set out on their own journey, to debate the ideas presented, interpret primary sources, and reach their own conclusions—just like the historian.

A critical moment in history can be a range of things—a pivotal year, the pinnacle of a movement or trend, or an important event such as the passage of a piece of legislation, an election, a court decision, or a battle. It can be social, cultural, political, or economic. It can be heroic or tragic. Whatever they are, such moments are, by definition, "game changers," momentous changes in the pattern of the American fabric, paradigm shifts in the American experience. Many of the critical moments explored in this series are familiar; some less so.

There is no ultimate list of critical moments in American history—any group of students, historians, or other scholars may come up with a different catalog of topics. These differences of view, however, are what make history itself and the study of history so important and so fascinating. Therein can be found the utility of historical inquiry—to explore, to challenge, to understand, and to realize the legacy of the past through its influence on the present. It is the hope of this series to help students realize this intrinsic value of our past and of studying our past.

William Thomas Allison
Georgia Southern University

Figures and Tables

FIGURES

TABLES

Acknowledgments

I would like to express my appreciation, first, to the thousands of individuals who have enhanced our understanding of the 1918 flu epidemic by recounting their own experiences with it. Some of them recorded their impressions at the time—in letters, diaries, professional journals, and newspaper interviews—while others unburdened themselves only years later, when revived interest in the epidemic gave them new opportunities to share their memories. We are fortunate indeed to have such a vivid record of what it meant to live through one of the great health crises in American history.

I would also like to pay tribute to Alfred Crosby, who was the first professional historian to give serious study to this long-untold story. His 1976 book, *Epidemics and Peace* (later republished as *America's Forgotten Pandemic*), highlighted a vital event in our history—an event that many other scholars have since explored in productive ways. This volume has benefited from all their work.

For help in the preparation of this book, I am grateful to the staff at the National Archives, to Genevieve Aoki at Routledge, and to my most valued editorial advisers—my sister Karen Smith, my colleague Marque Miringoff, and my cherished husband Leo Opdycke.

Timeline

1510	First well-documented influenza epidemic in history—although descriptions of outbreaks that sound like this disease go back to ancient times.
1557–1891	At least 20 more major influenza epidemics.
August 1914	World War I breaks out in Europe. US proclaims its neutrality.
April 6, 1917	United States enters World War I on the side of the Allies. Over the next 18 months, 4 million American men will be called up for military duty.

FIRST WAVE OF THE 1918 INFLUENZA EPIDEMIC

January–February 1918	Serious flu outbreak in Haskell County, Kansas.
March–May 1918	Soldiers from Haskell County bring the flu to Camp Funston, Kansas. From there, the flu spreads nationwide, infecting both soldiers and civilians. It is very contagious, but cases are generally mild.
April–June 1918	Flu travels to Europe with U.S. troops. By June, it has spread across Europe and around the globe.
June–July 1918	The first wave of the epidemic gradually dies down.

SECOND WAVE OF THE EPIDEMIC

August 4, 1918	Military physicians in France report the rise of a new, more virulent strain of influenza, which soon attacks soldiers and civilians throughout Europe.
August 30, 1918	First major outbreak in the US of the epidemic's second wave—at Commonwealth Pier, a naval base in Boston. The disease quickly spreads to surrounding communities. Meanwhile, the second wave is also moving from Europe into Africa and Asia.
September 11, 1918	Sailors transfer from Commonwealth Pier to training stations near Chicago, Philadelphia, and Seattle. Each of these facilities is soon facing its own epidemic, and within days the disease spreads to civilians in the cities nearby.

mid-September 1918	As flu sweeps across the country, American communities—assisted by the U.S. Public Health Service and the American Red Cross—mobilize whatever resources they can to combat the epidemic.
September 26, 1918	Recognizing that flu is paralyzing America's military training camps, the Army Provost-Marshal cancels the next draft call, which had been scheduled for early October.
October 7–November 2, 1918	Flu mortality peaks in the United States and around the globe, after which the second wave of the epidemic starts to decline.
November 11, 1918	Armistice Day. Large crowds congregate in the streets to celebrate the end of the war.

THIRD WAVE OF THE EPIDEMIC

November 1918–January 1919	In many communities around the world, the number of new flu cases starts to climb again, heralding the arrival of the third wave of the epidemic.
April 1919	Third wave abates.

AFTERWARD

1930s	Scientists identify a direct descendant of the virus that caused the 1918 influenza epidemic.
1941	U.S. Army develops the first effective flu vaccine.
1946, 1957, 1968	A series of global flu epidemics.
1997	Major outbreak of avian flu (H5N1) in Southeast Asia. Few human cases, but a high mortality rate among those affected. Repeated avian flu outbreaks in the years that follow.
2005	Team led by virologist Jeffery Taubenberger works out the entire genetic sequence of the 1918 flu virus.
2009	Flu breaks out in Mexico and the southwestern United States. Although the symptoms are mild, the epidemic spreads around the world, ultimately reaching more than 200 countries.
2013	New strain of avian flu (H7N9) emerges in China. Like H5N1, it is deadly for humans, but does not seem to pass easily from person to person.

Introduction

No one who lived through the 1918 influenza epidemic ever forgot it. Years later, Dan Tonkel, who grew up in North Carolina, vividly recalled the fear of contagion that pervaded his neighborhood:

> I felt like I was walking on eggshells. I was afraid to go out, to play with my playmates, my classmates, my neighbors . . . It was like—don't breathe in my face, don't even look at me, because you might give me germs that will kill me.[1]

The memory that stuck with Francis Russell, who was in third grade at the time of the epidemic, was the sound of hearses going past his school on their way to the graveyard. Day after day, he said, "as we followed the morning routine of multiplication tables, we could hear the carriages passing outside, the clop of horses' hooves in the wet leaves."[2] Anna Lavin, recalling the situation in Philadelphia, summed it up with brutal simplicity: "It was horrible. They died like flies."[3]

There have been many influenza epidemics over the centuries, but the one in 1918 was the worst in history—so pervasive that it touched almost every corner of the world, so fast-moving that it circled the globe three times in a single year, and so destructive that it killed an estimated 50 million people. In most places—including the United States—at least 25 percent of the population got the disease; in some hard-hit areas, the infection rates rose as high as 60 percent.

Although influenza is a highly contagious disease, a major reason this particular epidemic spread so far and so quickly was because it happened during wartime, coinciding almost exactly with the last year of World War I. Because of the war, soldiers and support workers from all over the globe converged on Europe, passing the virus among each other and spreading it to civilians wherever they traveled. But the soldiers did more than carry the virus—they also suffered terribly from it themselves. Indeed, some of the most haunting accounts of the epidemic are descriptions of its impact on the armed forces. An aging veteran exclaimed: "I can to this day see the 'cords' of bodies stacked in the Base Hospital. They were dying faster than the bodies could be taken care of."[4]

Pleading for nursing reinforcements at the height of the epidemic, authorities in Philadelphia pointed out that on any given day, more Americans were dying of flu in just that one city than were dying in combat overseas.[5] Worldwide, in fact, the epidemic killed about five times as many people as the number who died in combat, and in the United States the contrast was even sharper—675,000 flu deaths compared to about 50,000 soldiers killed in combat.[6] And yet for decades thereafter, people remembered the war, while the epidemic was barely mentioned. Only in recent years have we turned our attention again to one of the most dramatic explosions of infectious disease in history: the influenza epidemic of 1918.

When an epidemic as devastating as this one attacks a society, every part of that society is tested—not just its hospitals and doctors and nurses, but its elected officials, public services, newspapers, churches, businesses, and civic organizations. And when the epidemic occurs in wartime, as this one did, then the crisis also places extraordinary demands on the military. One can understand why historian Charles Rosenberg observes that studying how a society responds to an epidemic can provide us with valuable insight into the very nature of that society.[7]

Each country responded to the influenza epidemic of 1918 in its own way. This book focuses on what happened in the United States. It will discuss the scientific challenge that the flu virus represented, but its primary purpose is to explore the epidemic as a human—and a social—experience. What did it feel like to be there? And how did the American people respond when this calamity descended upon them?

In 1918, the U.S. government had no official responsibility for disaster management and (except for the relatively small Public Health Service) had little to do with ensuring the nation's health. In any case, at the time the epidemic struck, the federal government was almost entirely preoccupied with fighting the war. As a result, when we talk about "the American response" to the epidemic, we are not talking about a unified national campaign, but about the way that thousands of different groups and individuals marshaled their resources to meet the crisis.

Of course, not every American took an active public role in this fight. Some were too sick, some were too frightened of contagion, and some were wholly involved in caring for their own ailing family members. Nevertheless, a remarkable number of people did participate in some kind of organized response. In the pages that follow, for instance, we will explore the experiences of Red Cross workers driving ambulances, health officials debating which public gathering places to close, club women establishing emergency referral centers, nurses making their rounds in remote logging communities, doctors—both military and civilian—striving to develop a flu vaccine, and military commanders working to keep contagion under control in bases full of sick and dying soldiers.

Some of these participants were men and some were women; some became involved because of their jobs, while others were volunteers. But what many of these people seem to have shared was a certain outlook on life that influenced how they acted during the epidemic. Key to this outlook was a belief in a better future, and in people's own power to bring that better future about. America's scientific achievements during the early twentieth century, the important breakthroughs that were occurring in medicine, and the array of recent social reforms—all these advances seemed to support the idea that humans in general, and Americans in particular, had the capacity to make the world a better place, through their own clear thinking and organized action.

Organized action was an important part of the picture. Voluntary associations had been a major factor in American life for more than a century (as Alexis de Tocqueville famously observed). But collaborative activity reached a true flowering during the Progressive Era, when innumerable new groups and institutions sprang into existence, many of them focused in one way or another on improving social and economic conditions. This habit of working through organizations proved to be an enormous asset during the epidemic, when charitable societies, settlement houses, women's clubs, civic groups, and religious associations all swung into action. The American Red Cross, in particular, achieved new prominence during the double crisis of war and epidemic, taking prime responsibility for allocating the country's precious supply of nurses, and mobilizing hundreds of thousands of volunteers (mostly female) through its local chapters.

The importance of the Red Cross, and of nursing in general, during the epidemic highlights another legacy of the Progressive Era years—the idea that women had a role to play in public life. Traditionally, most American women had confined themselves to the private world of home and family. But starting in the late nineteenth century, women began to insist that in order to fulfill their *private* obligations to their families, they needed to involve themselves in the *public* sphere, where so many decisions were made that affected their families' well-being. Operating outside the established male-dominated institutions of the day, women built a galaxy of their own clubs, committees, and associations. And the organizational skills and extensive networks they developed during these years would play a central role in combating the flu epidemic. Nor were all these women volunteers. Female social workers and teachers and settlement house workers participated actively in the fight, while nurses made their own hugely significant contribution.

And so in 1918, all these threads wove together—faith in science and progress, commitment to collaborative action, and an expanding role for women—circling around one central idea: that if public-spirited Americans pooled their energies and approached their challenges in a systematic way, they could solve almost any problem they encountered.

Of course, the conditions they were facing were extraordinarily difficult. On the medical side, the frustrating lack of a cure for flu, or an effective vaccine, or even a reliable form of treatment, would bedevil America's caregivers throughout the epidemic. And then there was the war. Because of the war, the country engaged in practices that no society would have permitted if its sole object had been to stop the spread of infection. The crowding together of the troops in barracks and troopships, the frequent transfers of soldiers and sailors from bases with raging epidemics to facilities in other parts of the country that had not yet been exposed, and the constant traffic between flu-ridden military bases and nearby civilian communities—all these activities helped to keep the epidemic going, by continually providing it with new people to infect.

In the face of such obstacles, there was a limit to what rational problem-solving could accomplish. Nevertheless, within the constraints of their situation, great numbers of Americans continued as best they could to confront this crisis in the logical, organized way that had served them so well in the years before the war. And if they did not succeed in stopping the epidemic in its tracks (probably no one could have), they did ease the suffering of many patients, both soldiers and civilians. They also supported stricken families, experimented tirelessly with new ways of attacking the disease, and instituted at least some policies that helped to limit the spread of infection. The epidemic remained a nightmarish memory for everyone who lived through it, but Americans could take some comfort in the energy with which they had worked together in the face of so ferocious an onslaught.

In the chapters that follow, we will explore how—building on their prewar experience—Americans responded to the epidemic of 1918, and how they reacted when the storm had passed. The first two chapters set the stage for the events that follow. Chapter 1, "No Ordinary Flu," provides an overview of the epidemic, and then discusses it in relation to other great epidemics of history and to changing ideas about contagious disease over time. Chapter 2, "America in 1918," provides another kind of context for the epidemic by describing some of the forces that shaped American society in 1918, including the country's impressive economic and scientific progress during the prewar years, the development of local and state public health systems, and the country's decision to enter World War I.

The next three chapters focus on how the epidemic was experienced by different groups of Americans. Chapter 3, "Fighting Two Wars at Once," explores its dramatic impact on every aspect of the American military effort, from recruitment to training camps to troopships to front-line battles. Chapter 4, "A Caregiver's Nightmare," begins by explaining the specific workings of influenza. It then discusses the medical challenges involved in treating the disease, and explores the different ways in which doctors and nurses responded to these challenges. Chapter 5, "Communities on Their Own," describes the epidemic on the home front, where wartime priorities generally trumped civilian needs, leaving each locality to develop its own response to the crisis.

The final three chapters provide a longer perspective on the epidemic experience. Chapter 6, "After the Storm," describes the epidemic's immediate global impact, and then explores the aftereffects—the long-term physical and mental symptoms experienced by some flu victims, as well as the emotional scars carried by millions of Americans who lost people they loved. Chapter 7, "The Long Silence," recounts how for decades after 1918, Americans seemed to suppress all memory of the epidemic—erecting no memorials to the event, passing over it in histories and memoirs, and rarely mentioning it even in family conversation. The possible reasons for this collective silence are explored. Chapter 8, "Feeling Vulnerable Again," traces the recent revival of interest in the epidemic, triggered in part by our growing awareness of the world's continuing vulnerability to infectious disease. This chapter explains what has been learned about influenza over the years, and it ends with a consideration of how the lessons of 1918 can help us in thinking about the possibility of future influenza pandemics.

Finally, the Documents section presents the story of the epidemic as it appeared to those who lived through it, expressed in letters, newspaper articles, official reports, and personal interviews.

★   ★   ★

Once the 1918 epidemic was over, it lived on in the minds of individual survivors, but for many decades it was largely forgotten by historians and scientists. The possible reasons for this collective amnesia will be explored later in this book. Suffice it to say here that it was only during the late twentieth century that people began paying serious attention to the epidemic again. A major contributor to the change was the appearance of a host of diseases—including both HIV/AIDS and avian flu—which have forced us to recognize, just as our great-grandparents did in 1918, that modern medicine has not banished infectious disease after all. Under these circumstances, the 1918 epidemic has received belated recognition as a major event in our country's history, and we study with renewed interest the way those long-ago Americans responded to a crisis that we too may face one day.

NOTES

1. Lynette Iezzoni, *Influenza 1918: The Worst Epidemic in American History* (New York, NY: TV Books, 1999), 154–155.
2. Ibid. 57–58.
3. "'They Were Piling Them in the Streets'; or What Became of the Influenza Pandemic of 1918?," radio show, WHUY-FM (1983), produced and directed by Charles Hardy III. [See Document 8 for full citation.]
4. Nancy K. Bristow, "'It's as Bad as Anything Can Be': Patients, Identity, and the Influenza Pandemic," *Public Health Reports* 125, supp. 3 (2010), 138.
5. John M. Barry, *The Great Influenza: The Story of the Deadliest Pandemic in History* (New York: Penguin 2004, 2005), 324.
6. Flu deaths: Niall P. A. S. Johnson and Juergen Mueller, "Updating the Accounts: Global Mortality of the 1918–1920 'Spanish' Influenza Pandemic," *Bulletin of the History of Medicine* 76 (2002), 111, 114. Worldwide combat deaths: Gina Kolata, *Flu: The Story of the Great Influenza Pandemic of 1918 and the Search for the Virus That Caused It* (New York, NY: Simon & Schuster, 1999, 2005), U.S. combat deaths: Carol R. Byerly, *Fever of War: The Influenza Epidemic in the U.S. Army During World War I* (New York, NY: New York University Press, 2005), 186.
7. Charles E. Rosenberg, *Explaining Epidemics and Other Studies in the History of Medicine* (New York, NY: Cambridge University Press, 1992), 279.

CHAPTER 1

No Ordinary Flu

The Epidemic of 1918

It seems to be a plague, something out of the Middle Ages.
Did you ever see so many funerals, ever?

Katherine Anne Porter[1]

During the last two weeks of October 1918, more than 9,000 people died in New York City from a single cause. During the same two weeks, about 7,500 people died in Philadelphia, and another 4,400 in Chicago.[2] These Americans did not die in fires or floods or earthquakes, but in a different kind of calamity: the great influenza epidemic of 1918.

This epidemic, which peaked during the final months of World War I, swept three times around the globe in just over a year—a relatively mild first wave that began in the winter of 1918, a devastating second wave in the fall, and a third and final wave that started late in the year and ran into 1919. By the time the third wave was over, the epidemic had infected about one-quarter of the world's population and killed an estimated 50 million people. In the United States alone, recent estimates put the death toll at 675,000.[3] That is more than all the U.S. soldiers killed in combat in all the wars of the twentieth century, including World War I, World War II, Korea, and Vietnam.

Any epidemic can be terrible for those who experience it. But the outbreak of 1918 was especially shocking, for two reasons. First, influenza seemed like such a familiar and unthreatening disease. Every year, thousands of people came down with it, and after feeling miserable for a few days, nearly all of them recovered. People did die of the flu, especially the very young and the very old. But no one thought of this disease as one of the great epidemic killers.

The second reason the 1918 epidemic came as a shock was the fact that in the past few decades, great strides had been made in identifying and controlling more than a dozen of the epidemic diseases that had haunted earlier generations, including cholera, plague, typhoid, yellow fever, and typhus. In this heady atmosphere, it was easy to believe that the conquest of all infectious diseases lay just around the corner. So how could influenza, a "garden variety" disease, suddenly be killing millions of people, in defiance of all the tools of modern science? Vincent Vaughan, dean of the University of Michigan medical school, must have spoken for many when he said in 1918:

> We are inclined to boast that the age of pestilence has passed, but . . . I dare say that the world has never before known a pestilence more widespread, more intensive and appalling in its progress, or more destructive to life, than this epidemic.[4]

As influenza swept the country, Americans saw their efforts to prosecute the war disrupted, their communities engulfed by death and disease, and their faith in science and progress severely tested. As long as the experience lasted, it was all-consuming. And yet—as will be discussed in Chapter 7—once the epidemic ended, it seemed almost to vanish from public memory. For decades, historians scarcely mentioned it, few novelists wrote about it, and survivors rarely talked about it with their children. In recent years, the epidemic has begun to receive more attention, but even today many Americans know very little about this monumental event in our history.

THE PATH OF THE EPIDEMIC

When and where did the 1918 flu epidemic begin? Opinions differ on that point, but many authorities trace the start to an outbreak in Haskell County, Kansas, in February 1918. Influenza needs a sizable population to keep it going, and the Haskell population was small. So under ordinary circumstances, the outbreak might have burned itself out right there. But 10 months earlier, the United States had entered World War I, and as the country scrambled to mobilize and train the enormous army it had promised to deliver to the battlefields of Europe, hundreds of thousands of young men were crowded into hastily constructed camps all across the country. As the soldiers moved from home to camp, and then from one camp to another, they created a huge pool of potential victims among whom the flu virus could circulate.

So a few soldiers returning from leave in Haskell County brought the flu to nearby Camp Funston (see Figure 1.1). Influenza is one of the most contagious of all diseases, since for the first several days after being infected, the victims spray flu germs into the air every time they talk or sneeze or cough. Under these circumstances, a crowded army barracks is a near-ideal location for transmitting the disease. And the military policy of frequent transfers from one camp to another, along with the accelerating shipment of soldiers to Europe, only increased the chances for transmitting the disease. Within weeks, the flu spread from Funston to a dozen other military camps around the country, and from these camps to the surrounding communities. Thus began the first wave of the great flu epidemic of 1918.

One would assume that a disease that spread so quickly and so far would generate a lot of public attention. But the outbreak lasted no more than a few weeks in any single locality, and it caused most of its victims only mild discomfort. In fact, many of them probably never even called a doctor. Even if they had, influenza was not a "reportable" disease like tuberculosis or cholera, so doctors had no obligation to notify the local

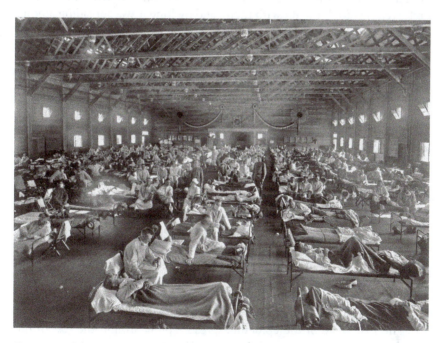

Figure 1.1 A crowded influenza ward at Camp Funston, Kansas, 1918.
New Contributed Photographs, Otis Historical Archives,
National Museum of Health and Medicine.

health department about the cases they saw. Any actual deaths from flu would have been recorded locally, but the country's system for reporting vital statistics to Washington was so undeveloped that it was hard to get a national overview of what was going on.

The result is that much of what we know about the spring wave of the flu epidemic comes from individual institutions that kept good records. For instance, we know that 1,000 workers at the Ford Motor Company got flu in March 1918. So did 500 of the 1,900 inmates at California's San Quentin prison.[5] But little of this information was published at the time. Furthermore, even though so many people caught the disease, their symptoms were too mild to generate much interest in the local press. As a result, many Americans were probably never even aware that an epidemic was happening, and those who did know soon forgot about it.

But though the epidemic was forgotten in the United States, it had not disappeared; it had gone to Europe on the American troopships. Starting at the French port of Brest, where the U.S. soldiers disembarked, the epidemic was soon surging through not only the American Expeditionary Force (the U.S. divisions in Europe), but also through the armies of France, Great Britain, Italy, Austria, and Germany. When soldiers went on leave, they took the flu with them, and by June it was spreading among European civilians as well.

The progress of the disease was not widely publicized at the time, since no belligerent country wanted to announce to the world the vulnerability of its soldiers, or even of its civilians. Thus, during the early summer of 1918, when American newspapers mentioned the flu epidemic at all, they focused almost entirely on how hard it was hitting the enemy. For instance, the *New York Times* explained that the only reason flu was such a problem among the German soldiers was because of their hunger and exhaustion. At the same time, American readers were assured (falsely) that there was, as one newspaper headline proclaimed, "No Influenza in Our Army."[6]

By May 1918, the disease was prevalent throughout the United States and Europe, but thanks to wartime censorship, there were still very few stories about it in the papers. Only when influenza hit neutral Spain in June was it given full press coverage and explicitly acknowledged as an epidemic. As a result, many people got the impression that the epidemic had actually begun in Spain. It was this historical accident that led to its becoming known as "Spanish flu."

The first wave of the epidemic spread rapidly around the rest of the world, but however far it traveled, it nearly always remained as harmless as it had been in the United States. One army doctor at the front described it in his diary as "a mild epidemic of 'three-day fever'."[7] Then something changed. In late August, the *Journal of the American Medical Association* warned its readers that a new "acute influenza-like disease is passing over Europe."[8] Of course, with all the wartime traffic across the Atlantic and around the United States that year, it was inevitable that any new flu strain that established itself in Europe would soon find its way to every corner of the United States. And that is exactly what happened.

> Besides being widely known as Spanish flu or the Spanish Lady, the 1918 epidemic acquired a variety of local names, including La Grippe (France), Blitzkatarrh (Germany), Great Cold Fever (Thailand), Trancaso (meaning "blow from a heavy stick") (Philippines), Coquette (Switzerland), Bombay Fever (Sri Lanka), Bolshevik Disease (Poland), Flanders Grippe (England), Naples Soldier (Spain), the Black Whip (Hungary), and the Blue Death (USA, North Carolina).[9]

The first recorded cases of the epidemic's second wave in the United States appeared on August 27 in a vast navy barracks in Boston called Commonwealth Pier. On that day, two sailors reported sick with what turned out to be influenza. Commonwealth Pier was a perfect place for the disease to multiply, with 7,000 sailors all sleeping and eating in the same crowded, ill-ventilated building. So it is hardly surprising that the day after the first two men developed flu, eight more cases appeared. The day after that, there were 58. Meanwhile, the disease was spreading into the surrounding towns, and soon thousands of flu cases—and several hundred flu deaths each week—were being reported among Boston civilians.[10] Influenza also exploded among the soldiers at Camp Devens, a huge and crowded army camp just outside the city.

Late in September, J. J. Keegan, a navy physician based in Boston, wrote a brief article for the *Journal of the American Medical Association*, alerting doctors around the country to the "severe and rapidly spreading" epidemic in New England. Reminding his readers that "in pandemics of this nature, influenza is the most contagious of diseases," Keegan warned that the flu would probably soon sweep the whole United States.[11]

By the time Keegan's article appeared on September 28, his prediction had already come true. Fostered by the transfers from one infected military camp to the next, and by continual interaction between each camp and its surrounding towns, the flu was racing across the country. By late September, there were at least 20,000 cases of flu in the nation's training camps.[12] At the same time, the epidemic had spread to virtually every American city. And from the cities, it reached outward to the surrounding towns and villages.

In fact, Keegan's only error had been in limiting his predictions to the United States. At almost the exact time that the epidemic was devastating the United States, the same virulent new strain was being carried to countries all around the world. In the African port city of Freetown, a handful of dock workers contracted the disease when a ship from Europe spent a few days in the harbor. Days later, virtually all the workers in the port were down with influenza, and within a week flu was being reported in dozens of inland towns and villages.[13] The same story was repeated on every continent. A few cases would develop, usually around a port or a military camp, and then almost overnight the epidemic would sweep outward. Throughout Europe, all across Asia, and from Iceland to Chile, influenza pervaded the globe.

This second wave of the epidemic had three unusual characteristics. The first was its frightening speed of transmission. "Stated briefly," said one physician, "the influenza has usually occurred as an explosion."[14] The epidemic rarely lasted more than a month or two in any given locality; yet within that brief time perhaps a quarter (and in some places as much as half) of the population would catch the disease, and many of them would become desperately ill. In extreme cases, a person might seem quite healthy in the morning and be dead by nightfall. Other patients would appear to be recovering from a brief bout of flu and then suddenly develop a severe case of pneumonia and be gone within a week.

That was another surprising thing about the second wave—how many patients died of the disease. The death rate was not as high as for some of the traditional "killer diseases" such as cholera or plague. But it was far higher than was usual for influenza, and when such a large share of the population was infected, even a moderate mortality rate could produce hundreds of thousands of deaths.

Still another unexpected aspect of the epidemic's second wave—and in many respects the most unsettling—was the way it affected different age groups. Throughout history (and right up to our own time), the great majority of influenza deaths have occurred among the very young and the very old. On a graph, this produces a U-shaped curve, with high numbers of deaths among children, very few among teens and adults, and then high numbers again among the elderly. Little children continued to be highly vulnerable throughout the 1918 epidemic, but for reasons that are still not entirely understood, the second wave caused remarkably few deaths among the elderly, while it struck young adults with devastating force.

It was this unprecedented impact on people in their twenties that made the epidemic's second wave such a scourge in the armed forces, where several million young men of exactly that age were crowded together under the worst possible conditions for controlling the disease. Civilians in this age group were also hit hard. In his semi-autobiographical novel, *Look Homeward, Angel,* Thomas Wolfe described watching his 26-year-old

Flu at the Front: A Soldier Mourns His Brother's Death[15]

Three brothers—Nathaniel, John, and Willard Simpkins—were all serving in France in 1918. When Nathaniel died of influenza in October, John wrote this letter home.

28 October 1918

Dearest Mother,

It cut me to the heart to send such a dagger thrust as those cablegrams must have been, out of a clear sky, when the general atmosphere was so hopeful. The ways of God are inscrutable, and his wisdom is infinite. I cannot help but believe, with Sir Oliver Lodge, as he writes in "Raymond," that such fine spirits are greatly needed in the next world, where so many unready souls are so suddenly hurled, to straighten out the chaos and perplexity of the new arrivals, and to interpret to them their new sphere. How well Nat would fill that need!

I was lifted right out of myself, and felt as though every one of the family was with me, as I ministered to his last wants and held his hand when his gentle brave spirit was released. It was an inestimable privilege that I can never be sufficiently thankful for, and it was chiefly due to Gen. Edwards who gave me the use of his car to cover the 30 miles . . .

The nurses who took every care of him, and who learned to love his courage and uncomplaining fortitude, are Inez Hatch and Clementine Invernezio, Evacuation Hospital #6, Souilly.

All his baggage and equipment is with Gen. E. I am taking care of the wristwatch Uncle Gorham gave him, and his gold sleeve links. I enclose the paper money (should be 250 francs if someone don't filch it), about $46.00 at the present rate.

I am under difficulties writing this—in a 4 × 8 dugout with five people crowded in, typewriter going, telephone constantly—so forgive any incoherencies. Of this sector I won't speak—let the newspapers do that—but wait.

Today [we face] the Austro-Hungarians—may the whole damned edifice crumble to immediate and quickly forgotten ruin. As for me, let the war go to hell— I am doing two men's job and that is good, for work is our best anodyne—but my chief business in life . . . is to keep well and make no sacrifice that is not for the cause. We have been thru almost what the French went thru in 1914, without rest or leave, and we have earned it surely by now.

Courage, bravest of mothers! We have been strong thru adversities because we all had one another, let us show ourselves not less strong in the real test of such a parting. Remember always that Nat suffered no pain, had no foreknowledge of his end, was cheerful and courageous to the last, and had me with him so as not to feel alone. I will not be able to write much, if at all, until we are relieved from this sector—so tell all inquiries what I wrote you and Olivia [Nathaniel's wife]. My dearest love to Father and Faith [sister] and Tudor [younger brother]—I think of you all more and more daily, and am inexpressibly nearer to you, as you are dearer to me.

Devoted love, JOHN

For God's sake stay in the country, even in overcoats, rather than risk Boston while the epidemic is on. It is the only safe place—in the open, away from people—and keep Tudor away from school. A month's education is nothing in a lifetime.

brother die a painful death from flu, while his elderly, cancer-stricken father lived on, untouched. Sharing his family's bewilderment over this unnatural turn of events, Wolfe wrote, "They all felt the grim trickery of Death, which had come in by the cellar as they waited at the window."[16]

Assaulted by this wave of sickness and death, Americans began looking for a cause. Some people blamed the epidemic on the alignment of the planets—echoing medieval Italians, who gave the disease its name when they attributed it to the "influenza" (influence) of the stars. Others maintained that the epidemic must be a punishment from God. But most of all, people's thoughts turned to the war. There had been reports of something like influenza in China earlier that year; perhaps the many Chinese laborers who had been transported to France to work for the Allies had brought the disease with them. Or perhaps all the chemical weapons and the innumerable tons of munitions that had been exploded by both sides over the past four years had poisoned the atmosphere. Or had the air been poisoned by all the putrefying corpses in the battle-scarred territory between the opposing lines?

Speculating about the war as a cause of the epidemic led naturally to speculating about enemy action. One government official insisted that the flu had been disseminated by German spies put ashore by U-boats. Others agreed, suggesting that the germs had been sprayed into the air over Boston, or injected into (German-made) Bayer's Aspirin.[17] There was a logical difficulty with blaming the Germans for the epidemic, since their soldiers and civilians were also suffering terribly from the flu, as were neutral countries such as Sweden and Switzerland. But in an atmosphere that was already pulsing with hostility toward all things German, the rumors received wide coverage in the press, and were believed by many Americans.

Amid all these speculations, the government journal *Public Health Reports* offered another theory, reminding its readers of the "mild epidemic" of influenza that had swept the United States that spring. "Is it possible," asked the editors, "that there is a direct relation between these outbreaks?"[18]

This theory is the one that most scholars today tend to favor. But in the fall of 1918, it was only one of many explanations being discussed and debated. Indeed, in trying to make sense of the catastrophe that had befallen them, Americans were carrying on a struggle that had been going on for thousands of years—the effort to survive epidemics and to understand why they happened.

EPIDEMICS OVER TIME

As long as there have been crowds of people living together—in villages, towns, and cities—there have been "crowd diseases," that is, ailments that perpetuate themselves by passing from one person to the next. The hunter-gatherer groups that existed in prehistoric times were too small to keep such diseases active; the germs would soon run out of new people to infect, and so die off. Mankind's history with epidemics really began about 10,000 years ago, with the rise of agriculture, because that is when people started living together in settled communities. As towns grew larger, and as networks of trade and travel connected them with each other, the pool of potential victims expanded, thus increasing the opportunities to transmit infection from one person to the next. In these societies, by the time a disease had run through the local population, there would be more people to infect—in the next town down the road, or among newcomers who had not been exposed to the disease before.

Newcomers not only caught the local diseases; they also brought unfamiliar germs with them from wherever they had been before. And not all the newcomers were human. For example, the waves of plague that visited Europe over many centuries are generally thought to have been triggered by the arrival of ship-borne rats. These rats carried fleas, which in turn carried *Yersinia pestis*, the bacterium that causes plague. Periodically, it is thought, the rats themselves would suffer an epidemic of plague, and when they died, the fleas would migrate to the nearest humans and start infecting them. We see the start of this grim cycle in the very first pages of Albert Camus' novel *The Plague*, when, leaving his office one morning, Dr. Rieux accidentally treads on something soft, and discovers he has stepped on a dead rat.[19]

One of the first historical accounts of this kind of epidemic is Thuycidides' description of the Plague of Athens in 430 BC. He found the outbreak deeply troubling, both because of the suffering it caused and because, he said, when people realized that life could end so suddenly and so randomly, they abandoned themselves to a wave of crime and loose living.[20] In AD 541, another major epidemic, the Plague of Justinian, spread through the eastern end of the Mediterranean, devastating both the Byzantine and Persian Empires. The disease continued to flare up periodically over the next two centuries, and then sank virtually out of sight for almost 600 years. Then came the Black Death, which spread from China to Europe in the mid–1300s, causing mass casualties wherever it went.

The Black Death: The First Great Pandemic

The pandemic known as the Black Death is thought to have started in China around 1330. Coupled with civil war, it killed almost half the Chinese population. It then traveled westward along the trade routes, reaching Italy in 1347 and spreading out from there into the rest of Europe. The term "Black Death" only emerged in later years; at the time, people called the pandemic the "Great Pestilence," the "Great Mortality," or the "Great Plague." In fact, scholars debated for years whether the disease involved actually was the plague, but recent DNA analyses of Black Death victims have confirmed that it was.[21]

Agnolo di Tura del Grasso, an Italian chronicler who survived the Black Death himself but lost all five of his children to the disease, wrote this description of the pandemic's impact in his native town of Siena:

> The victims died almost immediately. They would swell beneath their armpits and in their groins, and fall over dead while talking. Father abandoned child, wife husband, one brother another; for this illness seemed to strike through the breath and sight. And so they died . . . And in many places in Siena great pits were dug and piled deep with the multitude of dead. And they died by the hundreds both day and night, and all were thrown in those ditches and covered over with earth. And as soon as those ditches were filled more were dug.[22]

Faced with this horror, people tried every rational—and irrational—thing they could think of to stop the onslaught of disease. They engaged in prayer and fasting, in penitential rituals such as whipping themselves, and they adopted community measures such as isolating the sick and barring their city gates against strangers. In addition, building on centuries of anti-Semitism—aggravated in this case by allegations that Jews had caused the epidemic by poisoning local wells—Christians in Spain, France, Germany, and Switzerland turned on their Jewish neighbors, killing thousands of them, burning many of them alive, and entirely wiping out more than 200 Jewish communities.[23] But the plague continued.

By the early 1350s, the Black Death had penetrated virtually every part of the Eurasian continent. It is estimated to have killed one-third of the people in Europe, while in some parts of the world the death toll reached 50 or even 60 percent.[24] It remains one of the most devastating pandemics in human history.

Even after the Black Death subsided, in the late 1300s, plague continued to haunt Europe for the next three centuries, and it flared up periodically thereafter. In his *Journal of the Plague Year*, which described an outbreak in London in 1665, Daniel Defoe wrote:

> The Contagion despised all Medicine. Death rag'd in every Corner; and had it gone on as it did then, a few Weeks more would have clear'd the Town of all, and every thing that had a Soul: Men every where began to despair, every Heart fail'd them for Fear, People were made desperate thro' the Anguish of their Souls, and the Terrors of Death sat in the very Faces and Countenances of the People.[25]

In among the plague epidemics, there were many influenza epidemics as well—one historian counts 23 major flu outbreaks in Europe and North America between 1500 and 1918.[26] A few of them were quite severe, but most were like the first wave of the 1918 epidemic—spreading widely but doing relatively little damage. Writing to a friend in 1562, a British nobleman said that the recent flu outbreak in Edinburgh had spared "neither lordes, ladies nor damoysells" and that the queen herself "had kept her bed six days." Nevertheless, he wrote, "There was no appearance of danger, nor manie that die of the disease, except some olde folks."[27]

Partly because influenza rarely had a high mortality rate and partly because it reappeared regularly with cold weather, even in non-epidemic years, it was not considered a very frightening disease. Plague was the disease that evoked the greatest fear, and after plague became less common, the new terrors, especially in the cities, were diseases such as cholera, typhus, typhoid, diphtheria, and yellow fever. Year after year, societies strained to deal with these epidemic diseases. And at the same time, they struggled to understand where they came from and why they happened.

Starting in the 1300s, people began to distinguish between endemic diseases, which simmered permanently in a given region, and epidemic diseases, which burst out from time to time with sudden intensity. This distinction is one we still make today. The most notable characteristic of an epidemic is not which particular disease it involves, or how much damage it does, but how dramatically its behavior differs from the usual behavior of that disease in that particular region.[28]

In most years in most communities, then as now, endemic diseases took many more lives than epidemics did, but it was the epidemics that struck terror in people's hearts. After all, when a disease is endemic, it seems to require no more explanation than any other familiar part of the landscape. But when a sudden scourge of plague or cholera bursts upon a community, it is natural to feel that the event must carry some meaning. Why now? Why here? Where did it come from? Who is to blame? The blaming has often come first, and nearly every marginalized group can point to some period in its history when it was accused of causing or spreading disease. In the United States, for instance, Jews, Italians, Chinese, African-Americans, and gays have all had their turn in the spotlight, and sometimes they have been cruelly punished for it.

But throughout history, there have also been continuing efforts to understand the actual process of disease—how it starts and what to do about it. And in that age-old search, few thinkers have had more impact than the Roman physician Galen of Pergamon, who first came to prominence about AD 150. Building on the earlier work of Greek physicians such as Hippocrates, Galen maintained that the key to good health was to maintain a proper balance among the four "humors" in the body: blood, black bile, yellow bile, and phlegm.

According to Galen, each individual lived in a continual process of adjustment, as the humors within his or her body reacted to each other and to the surrounding environment. When people got sick, it meant that their internal balance had been disrupted by forces inside or outside them. It was the task of the physician to assess both the patient and the environment, and to restore the patient's internal harmony—by bleeding, causing the patient to sweat profusely, administering a laxative, or perhaps using a cathartic to induce vomiting.

Galen's theories are no longer accepted today, but he commanded a huge following for many centuries, and it is not hard to understand why. Even after the precise model of the four humors lost currency, Galen's stress on the interaction between the patient and the environment addressed one of the enduring puzzles of medicine—why do some people catch a disease while others, equally exposed, do not? Moreover, both patients and doctors wanted to feel that *something* was being done in the face of suffering, and it was reassuring that all of Galen's major interventions—including bleeding, sweating, and laxatives—"worked," in the sense that they produced immediate and visible results. Since a person's own internal constitution was an essential factor in his or her disease, it was to be expected that not everyone would recover. But of course there were patients who did get better, and that happened often enough to sustain widespread faith in the value of Galenic medicine.[29]

Galen was not the only medical thinker who believed that the environment played a role in disease. Starting in ancient times, another school of thought blamed sickness on miasmas (Greek for "bad air")—poisonous vapors that were thought to emanate from rotting vegetation in dirty streets and fetid swamps. The miasma theorists argued that diseases such as cholera, plague, and yellow fever were not passed from person to person, but were spread when many people inhaled the same polluted air.

Like Galen, the miasma theorists have no followers today. But although they were mistaken about how epidemic diseases are transmitted, they were correct that unclean conditions can be unhealthy. In fact, such conditions are associated with a good number of serious diseases, including typhus from lice, typhoid and cholera from contaminated water, plague from the rats that thrive on urban garbage, and a variety of disorders that are either caused or aggravated by chemical pollutants in the air. In any case, the harsh light that the miasmatists cast on urban living conditions helped buttress the drive for cleaner streets and purer water in the world's increasingly crowded cities.

One weak point in the teachings of both Galen and the miasmatists was their inability to explain why, during epidemics, hundreds and sometimes thousands of people suddenly got sick at once. If, as Galen taught, sickness was the result of a unique interaction between the individual patient and his or her environment, why, in an epidemic, did so many people suddenly exhibit the same symptoms at the same time? On the other hand, if the miasmatists were correct that disease was caused by poisonous vapors, why did epidemics begin and end so abruptly, even when there had been no change in the environment?

Most ordinary citizens had believed for centuries that epidemic diseases were transmitted from person to person. Many city officials thought so too, which is why, in times of plague, they often imposed what we would call "social distancing" measures—regulations designed to separate those with the disease from those who might catch it. For instance, our term "quarantine" comes from the French practice of requiring incoming ships to wait 40 ("quarante") days in the harbor before their passengers disembarked, so as to be sure that any diseases they carried had run their course. Some cities tried to wall themselves off from disease by barring their gates against strangers whenever there was plague about. Others, focusing on their own infected citizens, built separate isolation hospitals for plague victims.

Interestingly, most established physicians at that time were quite skeptical of "contagionism," as it came to be called. They maintained that diseases nearly always resulted from multiple causes and that external influences affected different patients differently. In fact, they viewed the belief in a

> By the late 1500s, London had 21 different laws for controlling contagion during epidemics; they included rules for street-cleaning, prohibition of public gatherings, and placing warning signs on patients' houses.[30]

single cause—contagion—as naive and unscientific. They acknowledged that some ailments, such as syphilis and smallpox, were passed from person to person. But the learned doctors scoffed at the idea that major epidemic diseases such as cholera and plague could be explained so simplistically.[31]

Over time, however, the idea of contagion as the sole cause of epidemic disease did begin to attract some scientific support. Among the new "contagionists" was John Snow, a British physician who is remembered today for his pioneering work on cholera. In that era, the established wisdom was that people caught cholera by breathing bad air. But since cholera affected the digestive tract, not the lungs, Snow thought that it might instead be caused by drinking water that had been contaminated by other people who already had the disease.

To test his theory, during the cholera epidemic of 1854 Snow mapped the distribution of cases in one hard-hit London neighborhood—Soho.[32] His "disease maps" made it clear that most of the cases in Soho clustered around a single water source—the Broad Street pump. He presented his findings to the local authorities, and after some debate, they agreed to disable that pump by removing its handle. Snow's intervention did not bring the epidemic to a sudden halt, as legend has it—the outbreak had already started to wane by the time the pump handle was actually removed. But by demonstrating the connection between a large cluster of cholera cases and a single water source, he dramatized his theory and encouraged other scientists to take his work further. (Today there is a plaque in Broad [now Broadwick] Street where the pump once stood, and you can see a model of the original pump handle in a nearby pub, which is appropriately named the John Snow.)

Many "anti-contagionists" remained unconvinced by Snow's findings. As established physicians, these men had some personal motives for resisting the idea of contagion, since it tended to devalue their own specialty of assessing the interaction between individual patients and their environments. But whatever their personal motives, they also identified some logical problems with the ideas advanced by Snow and his allies. For instance, Snow maintained that people "caught" cholera from contaminated water. But if cholera was essentially a chemical, why was it not diluted by the water? On the other hand, if it was, as Snow speculated, an "animacule," where was the proof of his claims?

Scientists had been observing microbes ever since the late 1600s, when Antonie van Leeuwenhoek first reported seeing them with his microscope. But one might easily accept the existence of such creatures without believing that their passage from one person to the next was the sole cause of cholera. And contagionism seemed like an equally shaky explanation for diseases such as plague, typhus, and yellow fever. "What about these diseases?," the anti-contagionists asked. How was it possible to be infected by people one never even met face to face? Today we know that these diseases are carried by insects that act as "vectors," transmitting the infection from one human to the next. But until that was understood, it seemed illogical to suggest that you could catch a disease from someone you never saw.

Besides the physicians, other social groups had their own reasons for opposing contagionism—primarily because they associated the theory with the coercive regulations that had so frequently been imposed in its name. For instance, in an era when the ideal of individual liberty was inspiring revolutions from the United States to France to Chile, many liberals objected to the constraints on freedom of movement and public assembly that were often imposed in the name of controlling contagion. And since the same constraints were terrible for business, commercial interests also often aligned themselves with the anti-contagionists. In any case, the explanations offered by Galenic medicine and miasma theory struck many people as at least as compelling as the arguments of the contagionists.

Thus, as late as the middle of the nineteenth century, there were a number of widely accepted explanations for disease, among which contagionism was only one contender. But that situation was about to change.

GERM THEORY SHEDS NEW LIGHT

The intellectual revolution that transformed modern medicine can be said to have begun with the work of two scientific pioneers: Louis Pasteur and Robert Koch. Pasteur, a French chemist, helped make the germ theory plausible in 1860, when he demonstrated that fermentation in beer, wine, and milk was caused by microscopic living organisms. Then in 1879, working with colleague Pierre-Paul-Emile Roux, he dramatized the practical applications of germ theory by isolating the bacterium that caused chicken cholera, a serious poultry disease, and using the isolate to create a vaccine.

Meanwhile, Robert Koch, a German physician still in his twenties, isolated the bacillus that caused anthrax in cattle, and proved the potency of the germ by injecting it into healthy cattle and giving them the disease. Then in 1882, Koch managed to isolate the germ that causes tuberculosis. Here was a disease that killed not animals, but people—hundreds of thousands of them every year. Koch had not found the cure for TB—that lay decades ahead, with the discovery of antibiotics. But in demonstrating the microbial basis of a disease that was grimly familiar to every one of his contemporaries, Koch galvanized public interest in the germ theory.

The following year, 1883, Koch traveled to Egypt and isolated the germ that was causing an outbreak of cholera. The contagionists had argued for years that epidemic diseases such as cholera *must* be caused by microbes traveling from one individual to the next, but Koch provided visible evidence of how the contagion worked. With cholera, as with anthrax, he identified which microbe was involved, and with anthrax he also proved his claims by transmitting the disease from sick to healthy animals.

Next, building on Koch's work, Pasteur produced an anthrax vaccine that was so widely accepted that in 1885 it was administered to 438,000 cattle and 3.3 million sheep. That same year, Pasteur made international headlines by injecting his new rabies vaccine into the arm of a boy who had been bitten by a rabid dog. The boy survived, and Pasteur was hailed as a hero.

Koch and Pasteur did more than identify the causes of a few specific diseases. They offered a sweeping vision of what the field of bacteriology might achieve in the future. As a guide toward those achievements, Koch laid out a series of "postulates" that defined the precise steps necessary to prove that a given bacterium caused a given disease. First, he said, the bacterium must be found in every single patient who had that disease. Second, bacteria drawn from these patients must be cultured and injected into healthy animals. Third, these animals must then develop the same disease. And fourth, specimens drawn from these animals must contain the same kind of bacteria that were drawn from the original patients.[33]

These postulates were important because they provided a kind of gold standard for experimental work in bacteriology that guided medical researchers for generations thereafter. Moreover, inherent in these postulates was the central principle that contagionists had been trying to establish for years. The idea was this—as inelegantly expressed by epidemiologist Philip Alcabes—"one bug causes one disease."[34]

No longer was sickness to be attributed to an undefined sea of environmental influences that might produce different diseases in different individuals. According to germ theory, each infectious disease was caused by a unique type of microbe, which had been transmitted from another animal or person who had that disease. And the only way to acquire the disease yourself was to absorb that bacterium into your body—through the air in the case of tuberculosis or influenza, through the bite of a flea carrying

> The microbe causes the illness. Look for the microbe and you will understand the illness.
>
> Louis Pasteur (1900)[35]

infected blood in the case of the plague, through eating food or drinking water contaminated by fecal matter from infected people in the case of cholera and typhoid. One bug, one disease. It was a revolutionary concept.

The emergence of germ theory added a new chapter to the age-old debate about whether disease was best understood as a matter of interaction or invasion. Galen, as we have seen, stressed interaction, emphasizing the continual dialogue between each individual and his or her surrounding environment. The miasmatists, on the contrary, pictured the body as more of a fortress, which periodically was invaded by polluting elements from outside. The contagionists also, of course, stressed disease as invasion. And as germ theory took hold in the late 1800s, it reinforced that view of disease even more strongly.[36]

Nevertheless, these contrasting views of disease—interaction and invasion—should not be thought of as mutually exclusive, either in time or in individual people's minds. Throughout most of history, both ideas have played a role in the way people thought about disease, although the emphasis between the two has varied from one period to the next.[37]

A vivid example of how people have managed to embrace multiple, sometimes apparently contradictory, explanations of disease can be seen in a pamphlet written by a London physician, Francis Hering, during a plague outbreak in 1652. Hering begins by explaining that since the current pestilence is a sign of God's displeasure, the only sure remedy is "general humiliation of the people by prayer and fasting." He then moves into miasma territory, recommending that plague victims be buried well outside the city, since the vapors that emanate from their graves are "very dangerous for spreading the contagion and poisoning the whole city." He next recommends a program of street-cleaning, sewer-scrubbing, and air-purifying that probably has its roots in miasma theory but also sounds very much like nineteenth-century urban sanitation campaigns (although those would probably not have included his proposal to ring the city bells frequently and shoot off large guns, so as to purify the air).[38]

Having incorporated divine punishment, miasma theory, and urban sanitation, Hering's next recommendation—a light diet, moderate exercise, and occasional sweating—injects a touch of Galen into his program. And finally, he offers a series of suggestions for avoiding contact with victims of the plague that seems to come straight from the contagionists. For instance, he urges the authorities to close down "stage-plays, wakes or feasts, and Maypole-dancing," because, he says, they dishonor God *and* they spread contagion. Similarly, he urges each community to care for its poor inhabitants, even when they are sick. If you turn them out, he says, they will only wander the countryside spreading the disease further.[39]

Did Hering believe that plague could be prevented by propitiating God? By avoiding foul gases from victims' graves? By cleaning the city streets and sewers? By proper diet and exercise? By staying away from infected people? The answer to all these questions seems to be yes. And this capacity to embrace competing explanations of disease remains a very human characteristic. Thus—as we will see in the response to the 1918 flu epidemic—long after the basic concepts of germ theory had been intellectually accepted, echoes of Galen and the miasma theory continued to linger in the popular imagination.

But even if germ theory was still only partially accepted by the general public, it inspired an explosion of pioneering work among the new generation of medical researchers. Within two decades of Pasteur and Koch's breakthroughs, scientists had isolated the bacteria responsible for more than a dozen additional diseases, including syphilis, gonorrhea, typhoid, pneumonia, meningitis, plague, and tetanus.

Most of these important discoveries were made by scientists in France and Germany, with some participation from Britain and Japan. During this period, there was just one notable American contribution to the study of infectious disease: the series of experiments begun in 1900 under the auspices of the U.S. Army, in which Walter Reed and his Cuban colleague, Carlos Finlay, demonstrated the role of mosquitoes in transmitting yellow fever. That landmark achievement aside, the Europeans had the field of bacteriological research almost entirely to themselves during the early development of scientific medicine.

Among the Europeans' achievements, as we have seen, were vaccines for a number of diseases, including anthrax, chicken cholera and rabies. The function of such vaccines was to prevent infectious disease, not to cure it once it started. But a few important cures were also developed during these years. In the 1880s and 1890s, for instance, antitoxins were produced for both tetanus and the dreaded childhood disease of diphtheria. And when Salvarsan, a cure for syphilis, was produced in 1910, it quickly became the most widely prescribed drug in the world.[40]

It was in this exciting atmosphere, when every few months seemed to bring another scientific breakthrough, that a new influenza epidemic burst upon the world. Racing across Europe in 1889, the epidemic reached the United States by the end of the year, and then spread to Latin America and Asia in 1890. A second wave in 1891 hit many parts of the world even harder, and some regions experienced a third wave in 1892.

As in most flu outbreaks (other than 1918), only young children and old people suffered many deaths during this epidemic. But even a disease with a relatively low death rate can cause a great many fatalities if it infects enough people. And that is what happened in the 1890s. Although scientists did not know it at the time, this epidemic involved a new strain of flu against which hardly anyone in the world had immunity. So even though the *percentage* of flu patients who died in the 1890s epidemic was quite low, the disease infected so many people that it still killed an estimated 250,000 people in Europe, and probably many more elsewhere (although the precise totals are not known). In Chicago, more people died of influenza, pneumonia, and bronchitis in 1891 than in any other year between 1867 and 1918.[41]

The epidemic of 1889–1892 was the first such outbreak since the germ theory revolution, and scientists immediately began trying to identify the bacterium that was causing the disease. In 1892, Richard Pfeiffer, one of Koch's best students, who had now become a renowned scientist in his own right, claimed that he had isolated the bacterium that caused influenza. In fact, as we know now, flu is caused by a virus, not a bacterium, and viruses are so tiny that they can only be seen with an electron microscope—which was not invented until the 1930s. But the 1890s outbreak was virtually over by the time Pfeiffer made his announcement, so "Pfeiffer's bacillus," as it came to be called, was not seriously explored until epidemic influenza returned to the world in 1918.

One might think that a global phenomenon such as the epidemic of 1889–1892 would have lingered in people's minds. But as soon as it passed, people seem to have reverted to their customary view of influenza as no more than a routine seasonal ailment. It is true that the collective fear of epidemics lived on, rooted in centuries of experience going back to the Black Death and beyond. But it was scourges such as cholera and plague that evoked that fear, not flu. So throughout the early days of the 1918 epidemic, American officials continued to insist that this disease was nothing to worry about, because after all, it was "just influenza."

Once Americans recognized the seriousness of the threat in 1918, many of them pinned their hopes on the new powers of scientific medicine. But as we have seen, influenza turned out to be one disease that contemporary researchers could not penetrate with the methods then at their disposal. Accordingly, Americans generally fell back on "social distancing" methods that would have been familiar to residents of medieval Florence or seventeenth-century London—isolating patients, closing schools and theaters, and quarantining military camps. Despite scientists' tireless efforts to isolate the flu microbe and produce an effective vaccine, it was old-fashioned social distancing that dominated America's public response to the epidemic in 1918.

Of course, social distancing as a way of limiting the spread of disease was quite consistent with modern theories of contagion, even if it had been used for centuries. But look closer at American behavior in 1918 and you can recognize the influence of much older beliefs as well. Clearly, many Americans still believed in their hearts that certain remedies—civic cleanups and vigorous housekeeping, healthy bowels and plenty of sleep— were good for virtually any kind of epidemic. These beliefs, too, were a social legacy, going all the way back to Galen and the miasma theorists, and they surfaced continually during the 1918 epidemic.

All these traditions helped to shape Americans' behavior in 1918— the terror of past epidemics, the disinclination to worry about influenza, the Galenic stress on internal balance, the miasmatists' emphasis on the link between dirt and disease, the scientific breakthroughs of the late nineteenth century, and the time-honored methods of social distancing. Weaving these traditions together with the political and social circumstances of their own time, Americans produced their own distinctive response to the flu epidemic of 1918.

NOTES

1. Katherine Anne Porter, *Pale Horse, Pale Rider* (New York, NY: Harcourt Brace, 1939), 158.
2. "Deaths from Influenza and Pneumonia in Cities of the United States, 1918–1919," *Public Health Reports* 34 no. 6 (February 7, 1919), 226.
3. Niall P. A. S. Johnson and Juergen Mueller, "Updating the Accounts: Global Mortality of the 1918–1920 'Spanish' Influenza Pandemic," *Bulletin of the History of Medicine* 76 (2002), 111, 114. See full article for discussion of changing estimates over time.
4. Carol R. Byerly, *Fever of War: The Influenza Epidemic in the U.S. Army During World War I* (New York, NY: New York University Press, 2005), 69.
5. Dorothy A. Pettit and Janice Bailie, *A Cruel Wind: Pandemic Flu in America 1918–1920* (Murfreesboro, TN: Timberlane Books, 2008), 48; Lynette Iezzoni, *Influenza 1918: The Worst Epidemic in American History* (New York, NY: TV Books, 1999), 25.
6. Debra E. Blakely, *Mass Mediated Disease: A Case Study Analysis of Three Flu Pandemics and Public Health Policy* (New York, NY: Lexington Books, 2006), 23–24; Pettit and Bailie, *Cruel Wind*, 72–73.
7. Byerly, *Fever of War*, 97.
8. "Spanish Influenza" (Editorial), *Journal of the American Medical Association* 71 no. 8 (August 24, 1918), 660.
9. Iezzoni, *Influenza 1918*, 35, 91; Pete Davies, *The Devil's Flu: The World's Deadliest Influenza Epidemic and the Scientific Hunt for the Virus that Caused It* (New York, NY: Henry Holt, 2000), 58–59; Robert Mason, "Surviving the Blue Killer, 1918," *Virginia Quarterly Review* 24 no. 2 (Spring 1998), 343; Tom Quinn, *Flu: A Social History of Influenza* (London, UK: New Holland Publishers, 2008), 144.
10. Alfred W. Crosby, *America's Forgotten Pandemic: The Influenza of 1918*, 2nd ed. (New York, NY: Cambridge University Press, 2003), 39–40.

11. John J. Keegan, "The Prevailing Pandemic of Influenza," *Journal of the American Medical Association* 71 no. 13 (September 28, 1918), 1051.

12. Crosby, *America's Forgotten Pandemic*, 47.

13. Quinn, *Social History of Influenza*, 135.

14. Byerly, *Fever of War*, 90.

15. Reprinted by permission of John Simpkins' daughter, Mabel Simpkins Stoneman.

16. Thomas Wolfe, *Look Homeward, Angel* (New York, NY: Scribner's, 1929, 1957), 469.

17. John M. Barry, *The Great Influenza: The Story of the Deadliest Pandemic in History* (New York, NY: Penguin Books, 2004, 2005), 343; Iezzoni, *Influenza 1918*, 67.

18. "Epidemic Influenza among American Soldiers Abroad," *Public Health Reports* 33 no. 47 (November 22, 1918), 2037.

19. Albert Camus, *The Plague*, translated by Stuart Gilbert (New York, NY: Vintage, 1948, 1972), 7.

20. Gina Kolata, *Flu: The Story of the Great Influenza Pandemic of 1918 and the Search for the Virus That Caused It* (New York, NY: Simon & Schuster, 1999, 2005), 37.

21. Nicholas Wade, "Scientists Solve Puzzle of Black Death's DNA," *New York Times* (October 12, 2011).

22. Agnolo DiTura del Grasso, "The Plague in Siena: An Italian Chronicle," at www.u.arizona.edu/~afutrell/w%20civ%2002/plaguereadings.html (accessed August 16, 2013).

23. Diane Zahler, *Black Death* (Minneapolis, MN: Twenty-First Century Books, 2009), 63–67.

24. John Kelly, *The Great Mortality: An Intimate History of the Black Death, the Most Devastating Plague of All* (New York, NY: Harper, 2005), xii.

25. Daniel Defoe, *A Journal of the Plague Year* (Oxford, UK: Basil Blackwell, 1928), 298.

26. Pettit and Bailie, *Cruel Wind*, 21.

27. Beveridge, *Last Great Plague*, 25.

28. "Epidemic" in John M. Last, Ed., *A Dictionary of Epidemiology*, 3rd ed. (New York, NY: Oxford University Press, 1995), 54.

29. Charles E. Rosenberg, *Explaining Epidemics and Other Studies in the History of Medicine* (New York, NY: Cambridge University Press, 1992), 15, 19.

30. Philip Alcabes, *Dread: How Fear and Fantasy Have Fueled Epidemics from the Black Death to Avian Flu* (New York, NY: Public Affairs, 2009), 43.

31. Stephen Kunitz, "Explanations and Ideologies of Mortality Patterns," *Population and Development Review* 13 no. 3 (September 1987), 380.

32. Sandra Hempel, *The Strange Case of the Broad Street Pump: John Snow and the Mystery of Cholera* (Berkeley, CA: University of California Press, 2007), esp. 137–141, 204–218, 223–224.

33. Crosby, *America's Forgotten Pandemic*, 265.

34. Alcabes, *Dread*, 88.

35. Cited in Fred R. van Hartesveldt, "Doctors and the 'Flu': The British Medical Profession's Response to the Influenza Pandemic of 1918–1919," *International Social Science Review* 85 no. 1–2 (2010), 29.

36. Rosenberg, *Explaining Epidemics*, 295–296, 299.

37. This point is explored in Rosenberg, *Explaining Epidemics*, 296.

38. Francis Hering, *Certaine Rules, Directions, or Advertisments for This Time of Pestilentiall Contagion* (London, 1625), pages unnumbered. Note that for ease of reading, I have updated Hering's spelling.

39. Hering, *Certaine Rules*.

40. Amanda Yarnell, "Salvarsan," *Chemical & Engineering News*, at http://pubs.acs.org/cen/coverstory/83/8325/8325salvarsan.html (accessed August 16, 2013).

41. George E. Dehner, *Influenza: A Century of Science and Public Health Response* (Pittsburgh, PA: University of Pittsburgh Press, 2012), 39–41; "Report of an Epidemic in Chicago Occurring During the Fall of 1918," in *Octennial Report of the Department of Health, City of Chicago, 1911–1918* (Chicago Department of Health, 1919), 43–44.

CHAPTER 2

America in 1918

The Epidemic's Social Context

*We believe that this new century will develop a progress and
an achievement and a splendor of greatness such as it does not
now enter into the mind of man to conceive.*
New York Tribune, *January 1, 1900*[1]

The sunlight is sparkling on Tampa Bay; a blue Florida sky arches
overhead. Down the street toward the St. Petersburg waterfront comes
a jubilant parade, brass band blaring. And there to greet the marchers are
thousands of ecstatic citizens, crowding the shore by the boat basin. It is
January 1, 1914—the day the world's first commercial airline will launch
its maiden flight from this very city. At the dock sits the plane that will
make the flight—a handsome flying boat, shipped in especially for this
venture. It will carry only one passenger per trip, just two round trips a
day, and the flight will be short—about 20 minutes to cover the 23 miles
across the bay to Tampa. But the same trip takes 12 hours if you go all
the way around the bay by train, and the prospect of making the trip so
quickly, and in such elegant style, has created a stampede of would-be
passengers.[2]

As the festive crowd looks on, the first passenger ticket is auctioned
off to the former mayor of the city for the astronomical sum of $400.
Percival Fansler, the businessman who organized this enterprise, makes a
celebratory speech, the passenger climbs into the waiting plane, the pilot
revs the motor, and off they fly into the sky, with Fansler's jubilant words
echoing in their ears: "What was impossible yesterday is an accomplishment
today, while tomorrow heralds the unbelievable."[3]

As it turned out, carrying paying passengers was not as profitable as
Fansler and his backers had hoped, and the St. Petersburg-Tampa Airboat

Line lasted only one season. But the promise of commercial air travel lived on in people's minds, and that landmark flight became part of local legend. More than that, it stands as a symbol of a self-confident and optimistic era. If we want to understand the atmosphere in America in the years leading up to the epidemic, then an important part of the story is the sense of unlimited possibilities that was reflected in that flight across Tampa Bay in 1914.

A WORLD OF POSSIBILITIES

New ideas, new inventions, new century. These phrases were repeated again and again in the period between 1900 and 1918. Among the wonders achieved during these years were the first mass-produced automobile, the first airplane flight, the opening of the Panama Canal, and the creation of the world's largest corporation (U.S. Steel). Best of all, for a country that had long thought of Europe as the center of scientific and technical innovation, it was the United States that achieved each one of these marvels.

The transformation of the United States into a major industrial power began in the years following the Civil War, but the pace of change seemed to accelerate with every decade. Thus, any American over the age of 30 at the time of the 1918 flu epidemic would have witnessed remarkable changes just within his or her own lifetime. Since 1890, the country's population had grown from 63 million to 100 million, augmented by the addition of six new states and the arrival of nearly 18 million immigrants from overseas. Moreover, the nation's power now extended even beyond North America. In 1898, the United States had annexed Hawaii, and a few months later, having won the brief Spanish-American War, it seized Spain's former possessions: Puerto Rico, Guam, and the Philippines. By 1900, one could, for the first time, speak of the United States as an imperial power.

As America's population and territory expanded, so did its economy. Even discounting for inflation, the country's gross domestic product nearly doubled between 1890 and 1920. The expansion of the transcontinental railroad, combined with the settling of the Great Plains, produced a bonanza of agricultural goods. Besides helping to feed America's growing cities, these products provided the country with a valuable source of exports. The railroads also brought vast quantities of minerals from the western mines to the nation's factories, where they gave a massive boost to America's industrial development. By 1913, the United States was producing more manufactured goods than any other country in the world.

Despite the country's impressive achievements, a great many of America's problems remained unsolved in the early years of the twentieth century—including, to name just a few, poor working conditions, child labor, racial discrimination, and unsafe housing. How could the country have remained so optimistic in the face of these problems? Clearly, one reason was the fact that these issues affected primarily those at the bottom of the social and economic ladder. But if this were simply one more society in which the well-off ignored the sufferings of the poor, there would have been nothing to set prewar America apart from all the other prosperous and unequal societies in history. What made the United States in the early twentieth century different was its sense of democratic promise—a promise so compelling that during these years, it attracted millions of immigrants to American shores. However hard their lot once they got here, these new arrivals recognized that the United States provided more opportunity than Europe, and that fact made it possible to believe that in this new land and this new century, everyone had at least a chance of achieving his or her dreams.

Besides these dreams of individual success, American life in the early twentieth century was enlivened by an unusual number of reformers and activists who were convinced that the whole country could and should be made better. Labor leaders, socialists, anarchists, suffragettes, prohibitionists, and many more—all chimed in with their own versions of how the country should be improved. The heated debates and protests generated by these groups have been interpreted by some historians as evidence of social disintegration. But another way to look at all this agitation is to recognize the thread of hope that ran through so much of it—the conviction that America really could be made into a better and more democratic society.

One of the most significant sources of pressure for social change during these years was the wave of reform activity known as progressivism, which was so influential that the whole prewar period (roughly 1890–1914) is often called the Progressive Era. Although progressives disagreed among themselves on many key issues of the day, they were united by their conviction that in a complex industrial society, the demands of private individuals and businesses had to be tempered by concern for the public interest. They also believed that the government had an obligation to protect that public interest, both by preventing the most dominant groups from abusing their power, and by ensuring certain minimum living conditions for all Americans. At the federal level, little social legislation was enacted during the Progressive Era; that would have to wait for the New Deal of the 1930s. But by 1918, the reformers had managed to enact many of the regulations they sought at the state and local level.

Given the expansion of governmental power and responsibility during the progressive years, it is not surprising that when the flu epidemic struck in 1918, state and local officials played a major role in the response. Historian Nancy Tomes has noted that public officials took almost no action during the flu epidemic of the 1890s, leaving the response to individual physicians.[4] The fact that in 1918, mayors and especially public health officers were dominant figures in the fight against influenza is one notable indication of the changes that occurred during the Progressive Era.

Selected social reforms initiated by U.S. cities, counties, and/or states during the Progressive Era:

- minimum wage;
- prohibition of child labor;
- food and drug standards;
- housing construction codes;
- juvenile courts;
- public pensions for widows;
- occupational safety laws;
- women's suffrage; and
- workmen's compensation.

Another important legacy of the prewar years, as we noted in the Introduction, was psychological—the conviction that intelligent, public-spirited Americans could surmount any obstacle, conquer any challenge. This was, of course, the message that echoed throughout the national experience during this period—in the United States' soaring economy, in its victory over the crumbling Spanish empire, in the conquest of so many infectious diseases, and in achievements from the Model T Ford to the completion of the Panama Canal to that flight over Tampa Bay.

So we can understand how upsetting—even shocking—it was for Americans raised in this optimistic era to confront the epidemic of 1918, and to watch the efforts of modern medicine (in the words of one physician) being "swept away as chaff before a mighty tempest."[5] As we will see, people rallied bravely to the challenge, but the pains and setbacks of the epidemic made a sharp contrast with the expansive future that everyone had been predicting.

INVESTING IN PUBLIC HEALTH

Watching the inability of modern medicine to stop the onward march of influenza in 1918 was a particularly bitter blow to Americans because of the important advances in public health that had been achieved during the Progressive Era. These advances were, of course, linked to the bacteriological revolution of the late nineteenth century, but they incorporated other elements as well. Indeed, as we trace the evolution of public health programs between 1900 and World War I, we can see the continuing interaction of new and old ideas about disease.

Public health leaders of the Progressive Era carried into the twentieth century three major approaches to controlling infectious disease: social distancing, public sanitation, and the germ theory. As we have noted, social distancing—the practice of separating infected people from healthy ones—had been common practice since at least the Middle Ages, and it was still a well-established response to communicable disease during the Progressive Era. Social distancing has rarely been 100 percent effective, because it is hard to enforce, and because many diseases are transmitted by insects or contaminated water, even when the victims never meet face to face. Furthermore, infected people can spread some diseases, such as influenza, for several days before they show any signs of being sick. Nevertheless, social distancing has remained a standard way of dealing with epidemics—partly because it does offer some protection, and partly because, at a more visceral level, it expresses people's instinctive desire to wall themselves off from disease. During the 1918 epidemic, social distancing regulations of one kind or another were established in most military camps, and many civilian communities as well.

The second of the three established approaches to disease, public sanitation, can be traced back to miasma theory and the ancient belief that filth causes disease. But this idea took on new urgency during the Industrial Revolution, when both European and American cities became so dirty and crowded that urban mortality rates began to soar. In response, a new army of social reformers called "sanitarians" began agitating for urban improvements that would create a healthier environment and slow the spread of epidemics.

The sanitarian movement began in England in the late 1700s, where industrialization first took hold, and by 1850, when America's manufacturing cities had become just as dirty, crowded, and unhealthy as England's, the movement gained ground here as well.[6] Preaching the value of cleanliness, fresh air, and pure water, the sanitarians threw themselves into the task of making cities healthier. In particular, their successful crusades

"*Bad air, bad water, or bad habits.*" This was how one nineteenth-century sanitarian explained why epidemics tended to hit urban slums the hardest. His comment reminds us that sanitary reformers frequently combined genuine concern over the conditions in poor urban neighborhoods with rather moralistic attitudes toward the people who actually lived in those neighborhoods.[7]

to clean up urban water systems virtually stopped the spread of cholera in the United States and Europe after the 1860s. They also campaigned for cleaner streets, safer food and milk supplies, and stricter standards for plumbing, density, and ventilation in tenement housing.

How much impact did these efforts have on the health of the American people? During the latter part of the nineteenth century, when epidemics began to wane and overall death rates declined, the sanitarians took credit for the change. After all, social distancing measures had been around for centuries; the sanitarians insisted that it was their own recent campaigns to clean up the cities that had turned the tide.

Or had the introduction of the germ theory been responsible for the change? When researchers such as Robert Koch and Louis Pasteur first demonstrated the role of germs in causing disease, their findings electrified research-minded physicians. And by the early 1900s, their ideas were starting to percolate more widely through American society. For many laypeople, the idea that germs caused disease simply became synonymous with the familiar idea that dirt caused disease, justifying the same kind of civic cleanups that the sanitarians had long promoted. (This approach lived on into the 1918 flu epidemic, when efforts to control the disease frequently included the sanitation of public and private spaces.)

More committed disciples of the new bacteriology had little use for this approach to curing disease. For instance, Rhode Island public health official Charles V. Chapin, scoffed at the days when "warfare was waged against everything decaying and everything which smelled bad."[8] The job of public health, he insisted, was not to scour every street and alley, but to find the specific germs that were making people sick. For Chapin and those who shared his views, it was the microscope, not the scrub brush, that held the key to ending infectious disease.

In fact, it would be some years before the principles of bacteriology made a real difference in day-to-day medical practice. And few people would claim that social distancing alone could have caused the drop in urban death rates. So if we are looking strictly at the improvements that had happened by 1900, it is probably accurate to give the sanitarians a good share of the credit. But the important thing to remember is that all three of these approaches—social distancing, sanitarianism, and the germ theory—represented important legacies from the nineteenth century to the twentieth, and that all three would continue to influence public health policies during the 1918 epidemic.

What the progressives added to these ideas was organization. The changes came slowly in rural areas, but between 1890 and 1918 nearly all American states and most cities expanded their public health capacity significantly. Seeking—as they usually did—to keep public administration free of party politics, the progressives did their best to ensure that the expanding departments were staffed with professionally trained experts—a goal that was easier to achieve because of the growing prestige of scientific medicine. The old sanitarians had helped to set the public health agenda, with their concerns about the quality of the food Americans ate, the water they drank, and the air they breathed. But the germ theorists provided new tools for addressing these concerns, and they gave the public health enterprise a scientific aura that helped to win broad support for its programs. Now there was a compelling new symbol of public health: the bacteriologist—who, as one admirer explained, "bending over the microscope in the quiet laboratory . . . stands between death and the children."[9]

The Progressive Era health officials also gained new legal powers to enforce their recommendations, because they could now document the presence of disease, whether in individual people or in environments such as dairies and reservoirs. For instance, it was only after laboratory studies showed incontrovertibly that tuberculosis was contagious that public health leaders in a number of states won passage of laws making TB a "reportable" disease—meaning that doctors were required to notify the health department whenever they encountered a new case.[10]

Perhaps the classic example of laboratory findings and legal enforcement going hand in hand is the case of "Typhoid Mary"—a cook who was imprisoned for years by order of the New York City health authorities because of her status as a "carrier" of typhoid. Mallon's treatment by the city raises provocative questions about her civil rights, but it also dramatizes the increased power of public health officials during the Progressive Era, and the role of germ theory in enhancing that power. When we see the sweeping orders that health officials were able to issue in 1918—closing down public gathering places, setting curfews, requiring people to wear face masks —we are witnessing the operation of a much more muscular public health authority than the one that existed in 1890.

Who was "Typhoid Mary"? She was Mary Mallon, an Irish-born resident of New York City. Mallon, who made her living as a cook, had the misfortune of being a lifetime "carrier" of typhoid, capable of transmitting the disease to others, even though she herself never got typhoid. After laboratory analysis traced a serious outbreak—including at least three deaths—to Mallon in 1907, she was incarcerated on an island in the East River for three years. She was released when she promised to stop working as a cook, but a few years later she secretly returned to her occupation. When another fatal outbreak was traced to her in 1916, she was sent back to her island prison, where she remained until her death 22 years later.[11]

Besides increasing their legal power, public health departments also increased their visibility in Americans' daily lives—particularly in the lives of school children. The progressives paid special attention to improving the lives and prospects of the next generation, and the schools played a central role in that effort. In terms of public health, this meant hiring nurses and doctors to do regular health monitoring in the schools, so that sick children could be identified and follow-up care could be arranged. By 1913, 443 American cities and towns had teams of doctors making regular rounds in the local schools. Besides what this "medical inspection" system did for individual children, health officials were convinced that it was a good method for spotting the emergence of contagious diseases.[12] In fact, when flu struck in 1918 and several major cities (including New York and Chicago) chose *not* to close their schools, they based their decision on the importance of the medical inspection systems that had been instituted during the previous decade.

Another way that Progressive Era public health departments reached into people's daily lives was through extensive campaigns to educate the public about sanitation and personal hygiene. Once it was understood how many diseases were caused by the transmission of germs from one person to the next, health officials began placing new emphasis on each individual's responsibility for preserving the public's well-being—by avoiding infection, and by taking care not to pass infection onto others. This information was widely disseminated, in advertisements, news articles, pamphlets, and lectures. Schools reinforced the message with health education courses, and the Red Cross enrolled thousands of women around the country in its classes on Elementary Hygiene and Home Care of the Sick. Nor was the general public the only audience. Health educators also reached out to practicing physicians, many of whom had trained in earlier times and knew scarcely more about germ theory than their patients did.

If we were talking about fighting infectious disease in the United States today, we would certainly include the role of the federal Centers for Disease Control and Prevention (CDC) and the U.S. Public Health Service (PHS). But during the Progressive Era, the CDC did not yet exist and the Public Health Service was considerably less active than it is today. Although the PHS had a respected research laboratory and was responsible for quarantine arrangements in American ports, it was by no means a significant factor in the nation's overall approach to public health. The agency's responsibilities expanded somewhat after the United States entered World War I in 1917, but throughout these years—as became strikingly clear during the flu epidemic—it was state and local officials, not the federal government, who carried primary responsibility for ensuring the health of American communities.

Fighting Tuberculosis: Preparation for 1918

By the beginning of the twentieth century, tuberculosis had declined significantly, but it was still a leading cause of death. Contrary to earlier times, when many people had attributed TB solely to patients' weak constitutions, by 1900 it was generally understood that the disease was contagious.

Large numbers of American adults had only "latent" cases of tuberculosis. This means that TB germs had settled in their lungs, but their immune systems were managing to keep the bacilli inactive. "Latent" individuals remain healthy and non-contagious, sometimes for a lifetime. But in perhaps 10 percent of these cases, the bacilli ultimately defeat the immune system and produce "active" tuberculosis. When that happens—and it can occur months or even years after the initial exposure—people become visibly ill, while also becoming contagious to others. Nowadays, a case of active TB can be controlled with a few months of antibiotics. But in that pre-antibiotic era, patients could remain actively sick with TB—and actively contagious—for months or years. If they were too weak to leave their beds, then the danger was primarily to their immediate caregivers. But if they were well enough to walk around, then they could spread the TB germs wherever they went.

One option for dealing with active TB was to send the patient away to a sanitarium. But the number of cases was so enormous that the cost would have been prohibitive, especially since some patients might need months or even years of care. Moreover, few TB sufferers wanted to spend such long periods away from home, and a considerable number of them could not afford to do so. The alternative therefore was to care for TB patients in the community, while teaching both them and the people around them to prevent the spread of the disease.

Between 1900 and 1910, working with voluntary groups such as the National Association for the Study and Prevention of Tuberculosis, local health departments developed a whole array of materials designed to educate doctors and the general public about how to control the spread of TB. These campaigns leaned heavily on the importance of "respiratory etiquette"—that is, the need to avoid spreading germs when people coughed and sneezed. Or spat. Anti-spitting campaigns were a major element in the war against TB, involving the dissemination of pamphlets in four languages, the posting of placards in public places, as well as fines and arrests for those who violated the anti-spitting regulations. The scale of the effort may seem extreme, but as a leading physician observed in 1918, the United States was "a spitting nation."[13] It would remain one, and many cities' campaigns against spitting during the 1918 flu epidemic were taken wholesale from the fight against tuberculosis before the war.

Of course, TB was a very different disease from influenza, but the fact that it was spread by droplet infection and nose/mouth/hand contamination meant that by the time the flu epidemic came along in 1918, health officials had accumulated a good deal of experience in tracking the spread of respiratory diseases, and a strong background in teaching the public how to avoid them (see Figure 2.1).

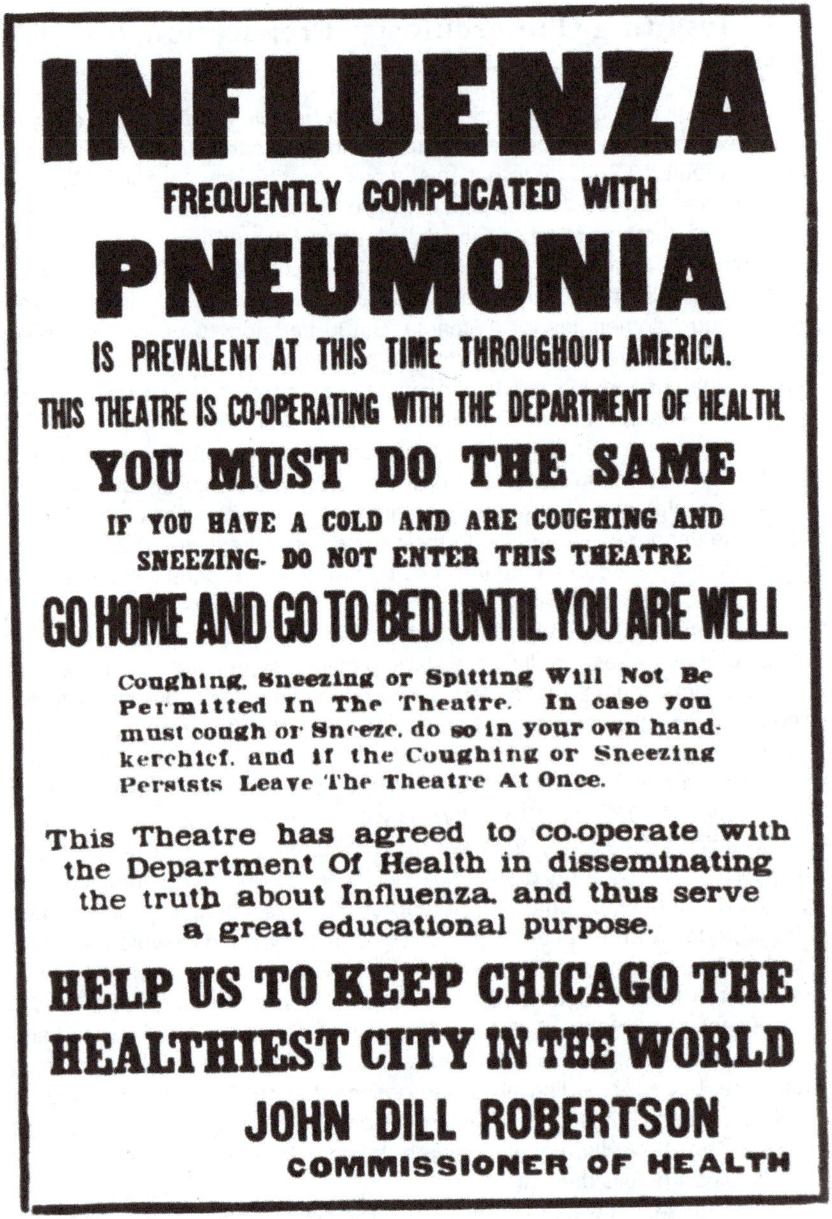

Figure 2.1 Signs such as this one, which was posted in Chicago theaters during the 1918 flu epidemic, drew on the legacy of public instruction about health issues that began during the Progressive Era. National Library of Medicine, AO29485.

MAKING THE WORLD SAFE FOR DEMOCRACY

Perhaps if the federal government had had no other major preoccupations in 1918, it might have played a larger role in fighting influenza. But by the time the epidemic began, the government was devoting every ounce of its energy to the military and political challenges of fighting World War I. As it turned out, influenza killed far more Americans than the war did. But prosecuting the war represented a more tangible and inspiring challenge, and for President Woodrow Wilson and the men around him, it outranked every other task on the national horizon.

When World War I began, in August 1914, there seemed to be 100 good reasons for the United States *not* to get involved. Pacifists argued against wars of all kinds; Irish-Americans opposed any action that would help Great Britain, their hereditary enemy; German-Americans were reluctant to fight against their homeland; progressives worried that war would distract the country from social reform; and labor militants called it a rich man's fight in which poor men would do the dying. In general, there was more public sympathy for the Allies (Britain, France, Russia, and later Italy) than for the Central Powers (Germany, Austria-Hungary, the Ottoman Empire, and Bulgaria). And certainly the Allies, primarily Britain, received the lion's share of U.S. assistance. But we can deduce Americans' reluctance to send troops overseas when we recall that one of the most popular songs of 1915 was "I Didn't Raise My Boy to Be a Soldier." Understanding the public mood, President Wilson swept to re-election in 1916 under the reassuring slogan, "He Kept Us Out of War."

Two circumstances increased the pressure on the United States to intervene. The first was the bleak situation on the Western Front, where as early as the spring of 1915 the two sides had settled into a grim stalemate, entrenched along a line that extended for several hundred miles. All through 1915, 1916, and into 1917, the war dragged on in a succession of gigantic battles that gained hardly an inch of ground while slaughtering hundreds of thousands of soldiers. It seemed increasingly clear that only the entry of U.S. troops could break the stalemate.

At the same time, America's insistence on its neutral status was being continually challenged by Germany. Besides claiming the right to keep shipping supplies to Great Britain, President Wilson insisted that as citizens of a neutral country, Americans should be free to travel on any vessel they chose. This doctrine was severely tested in May 1915, when a German submarine sank a British ship, the *Lusitania*, killing nearly 2,000 passengers, including more than 100 Americans. Battered by a storm of international criticism and eager to keep America from entering the war on the side of the Allies, Germany promised to scale back its submarine attacks on merchant and passenger ships.

But by the winter of 1917, 18 months later, the situation had changed. German leaders decided that if they could cut off all supplies to Britain, they could starve the country out and force the Allies to sue for peace. Accordingly, Germany announced in January 1917 that it was going to resume unrestricted submarine warfare, gambling that even though this would probably draw the United States into the war, the Allies could be forced to surrender before the US could mobilize its forces and get them to Europe.

Within weeks of this announcement, the story of the "Zimmermann Telegram" hit the American newspapers, revealing that the German Foreign Minister had been secretly encouraging Mexico to attack the United States. This was the final straw, and on April 2, 1917, President Woodrow Wilson went before Congress to ask for a declaration of war. The congressional response was not unanimous (50 representatives and 6 senators voted no), but the declaration passed by a wide margin, and was signed by Wilson on April 6. After resisting intervention for more than two and a half years, the United States had finally entered World War I. As President Wilson explained, "The world must be made safe for democracy."

Once the decision to enter the war was made, it seemed to evoke much the same "can-do" spirit that had enlivened American society during the prewar years. There was pride in being called to the aid of the country's Old World allies, and many Americans seemed to believe that now the "Yanks" had entered the fight, victory was just around the corner. In fact, the war would last for 18 more months, and during that time, over 50,000 U.S. soldiers would be killed in combat, while hundreds of thousands of Americans would die of flu, in an epidemic that the war would play a major role in spreading. But in April 1917, all those events lay in the future.

In taking the country to war, the Wilson administration was committing itself to two significant kinds of mobilization—military and political. Recruiting and training the necessary number of troops was a monumental task, because the country's initial force levels were so low. As soon as the United States entered the war in April 1917, President Wilson named General John J. Pershing to command the American Expeditionary Force (the U.S. troops in Europe). Pershing immediately set the goal of getting 1 million U.S. soldiers to Europe within a year. A draft was enacted, and on June 5, more than 10 million young men between the ages of 21 and 30 showed up to register. A few weeks later, 687,000 of them were selected for the first call, and many thousands more were called up during the months that followed.[14] Meanwhile, military camps were hastily constructed around the country to accommodate them.

So close was the timing that throughout the fall, new recruits often had to sleep in tents because their barracks were still being built.

Training all these soldiers took time, as did finding enough shipping to transport them to Europe. And so, despite sustained efforts, only about 400,000 U.S. troops (less than half of Pershing's goal) had reached France by the target date he had set, April 1918. Over the following summer, however, draft calls picked up, more ships were made available, and American soldiers started sailing to Europe at the rate of 250,000 to 300,000 per month. That meant that at the height of the flu epidemic in the fall of 1918, literally millions of American soldiers were crowded together in training camps, on troopships, and in overseas bases, ideally situated to catch the disease from each other and pass it on.

Along with the task of mobilizing the troops, President Wilson faced another crucial challenge: mobilizing public opinion. Wilson knew that prosecuting the war would require public sacrifice, and he was convinced that the most democratic way to achieve it—and the most likely to succeed, given the American character—was to use persuasion rather than coercion. For instance, he chose to finance the war not by taxes, but primarily through periodic Liberty Loan drives, during which all Americans were encouraged to contribute whatever they could. Wilson even managed to add a touch of voluntarism to the draft, by insisting that it was "in no sense a conscription of the unwilling." Rather, he said, it was simply a "selection from a nation which has volunteered in mass."[15] The same philosophy shaped the way that Americans were encouraged to conserve food and gas, knit socks for soldiers, and help in the fields at harvest time— all voluntary, all done to support their country in time of war.

There is a dark side to relying on voluntarism, however, and that is the temptation to manipulate the public so that it will "volunteer" to do the tasks that are needed. At its most extreme, this drive to control public opinion was embodied in the Espionage Act of 1917, which empowered the authorities to arrest almost anyone who spoke out against the war. Meanwhile, local vigilantes frequently took the matter further, beating and in some cases murdering those whom they suspected of being disloyal.

Most Americans escaped this kind of overt coercion. But all of them were exposed to the government's relentless psychological campaign to generate support for the war. Much of this effort was organized by a new federal agency known as the Committee on Public Information, which worked tirelessly to publicize the nobility of the Allied cause, the importance of doing one's share on the home front, and the wickedness of those who obstructed the war effort. When, in the next chapter, we discuss the reluctance of President Wilson and other national leaders to deal with, or even acknowledge, the influenza epidemic, we need to remember that their silence was designed to serve the very same goal as the work of the Committee on Public Information—to keep the American people focused on one topic, and one topic alone: winning the war.

As we review America's participation in World War I—both in the military sphere and on the home front—we are reminded over and over how strongly the war influenced the course of the 1918 epidemic. To begin with, it is important to remember that unlike any other influenza virus ever recorded, this one tended to target young adults—exactly the age group that the war gathered up by the millions and brought together under conditions of crowding and physical exhaustion that maximized the

The Committee on Public Information: Selling the War

When the United States entered World War I in 1917, the federal government established the Committee on Public Information (CPI). Its official purpose was simply to disseminate news about the war, but its true mission was to "sell" the war to the American public—an effort that the director, journalist George Creel, proudly described as "the world's greatest adventure in advertising."[16]

The Wilson administration always stressed the need for *voluntary* support of the war effort, and the CPI ensured that this voluntarism was forcefully encouraged with all the modern tools for building unanimity of opinion—press releases, ads in newspapers and magazines, conferences and speaking campaigns, posters and billboards, cartoons, slides, movies, exhibitions, pageants, and parades. It has been estimated that by the end of 1917, the CPI was sending each newspaper in the country an average of six pounds of material a day.[17]

The central message behind this tsunami of publicity was the idea that every loyal American must provide unquestioning support for the war—not only through contributing to Liberty Bond drives and performing other war-related tasks, but also, more broadly, by accepting the nobility of America's role in the war and the bestiality of the enemy. The CPI also continually suggested that anyone who obstructed the war effort was a traitor—from the "slackers" who avoided the draft to "hyphenated Americans" (especially those of German ancestry) who might be foreign spies.

The CPI director, George Creel, sometimes talked as if his agency's only role was to keep the public informed. But at other times, he was more explicit, explaining that the CPI's real mission was to turn Americans into "one white-hot mass."[18] When questions arose about the accuracy of some of the material the agency was circulating, another CPI official explained: "The force of an idea lies in its inspiration value. It matters little if it is true or false."[19]

chances for spreading infection. The Western Front was a particular hot spot, because the give and take of germ transmission there involved not only Americans and Europeans, but also soldiers and laborers from European colonies all over Asia and Africa. It is hard to think of a situation better calculated to get a contagious disease going and then spread it around the world.

In addition, as we have noted, the war affected how the country's leaders talked about the epidemic. Resisting unpleasant facts is a very human failing, and perhaps there would have been a certain level of denial no matter what else was happening at the time. But during World War I, public morale was regarded as an essential resource, like oil or steel. Accordingly, the nation's leaders seem to have concluded that to acknowledge the seriousness of the epidemic would undermine the single-minded focus on the war that they were working so hard to establish. The reality of day-to-day conditions soon forced most camp commanders and local officials to drop their denials and start responding to the epidemic, but President Wilson and those around him resolutely kept their distance. Americans' upbeat confidence in their own powers must not be shadowed, even for a moment, by the fear and uncertainty associated with a massive outbreak of disease.

★   ★   ★

This, then, was the atmosphere in the United States in 1918. Here was a society still energized by the scientific and social achievements of the Progressive Era—with the nation's aspirations now expanded to include the even grander task of saving the world for democracy. A noble challenge, indeed! And yet, at the same time, with much less fanfare, the American people soon found themselves caught up in a another conflict, fought against an even more implacable foe: the influenza epidemic of 1918. In the next three chapters, we will explore this struggle in three different arenas of American life—within the military, among doctors and nurses, and in communities on the home front.

NOTES

1. "From Century to Century" (Editorial), *New York Tribune* (January 1, 1900), 8.
2. Carroll V. Glines, "St. Petersburg Tampa Airboat Line: World's First Scheduled Airline Using Winged Aircraft," *Aviation History* (June 12, 2006). To be precise, this was the world's first *scheduled* commercial airline using *fixed-wing* aircraft.
3. Glines, "St. Petersburg Tampa Airboat Line"; Warren J. Brown, *Florida's Aviation History* (Largo, FL: Aero-Medical Consultants, 1994), 68.

4. Nancy Tomes, "'Destroyer and Teacher': Managing the Masses During the 1918–1919 Influenza Pandemic," *Public Health Reports* 125, supp. 3 (2010), 50.

5. Nancy K. Bristow, "'You Can't Do Anything for Influenza'," in Howard Phillips and David Killingray, Eds., *The Spanish Influenza Pandemic of 1918–1919: New Perspectives* (New York, NY: Routledge, 2003), 62.

6. John Duffy, *The Sanitarians: A History of American Public Health* (Champaign, IL: University of Illinois Press, 1990), 175–183.

7. Philip Alcabes, *Dread: How Fear and Fantasy Have Fueled Epidemics from the Black Death to Avian Flu* (New York, NY: Public Affairs, 2009), 80.

8. Paul Starr, *The Social Transformation of American Medicine: The Rise of a Sovereign Profession and the Making of a Vast Industry* (New York, NY: Basic Books, 1982), 190.

9. Cited in Naomi Rogers, *Dirt and Disease: Polio Before FDR* (New Brunswick, NJ: Rutgers University Press, 1992) 17.

10. Duffy, *Sanitarians*, 197–199.

11. Judith Walzer Leavitt, *Typhoid Mary: Captive to the Public's Health* (Boston, MA: Beacon Press, 1996).

12. Alexandra Stern, et al. "'Better Off in School': School Medical Inspection as a Public Health Strategy During the 1918–1919 Influenza Pandemic in the United States," *Public Health Reports* 125, supp. 3 (2010), 65–66.

13. Allison Bell, "1918 Flu Pandemic Hit Insurers Hard," *National Underwriter, Life & Health* (March 31, 1997), 46.

14. David M. Kennedy, *Over Here: The First World War and American Society* (New York, NY: Oxford University Press, 1980), 154, 169.

15. Ronald Schaffer, *America in the Great War: The Rise of the War Welfare State* (New York, NY: Oxford University Press, 1991), 176.

16. Ibid. 5.

17. Ibid. 5.

18. "Press Lessons from the 1918 Pandemic Flu," *Nieman Report* 61 no. 1 (Spring 2007), 60.

19. Ibid. 60.

CHAPTER 3

Fighting Two Wars at Once

Flu in the Military

> *One day 50 were admitted; the next day 300, then the daily average became 500; into a 2,000-bed hospital 6,000 patients crowded . . . Three miles of hospital corridors were lined on both sides with cots.*
>
> Chief Nurse Jane Malloy, Camp
> Devens, Massachusetts[1]

On September 20, 1918, Private Roscoe Chittim sat in his barracks at Camp Dix, New Jersey, writing a letter to his wife Vera. "Dearest Baby," he began, "Well, we have all been in since Wednesday but are slowly recovering from the awful disease. We had eighty-three men in bed at same time and I was one of them." A few weeks earlier, influenza had broken out at Camp Dix, and once the epidemic began rampaging through the base, the authorities had shut the whole place down (see Figure 3.1). As Roscoe explained, "We haven't done a thing in the way of work, just sticking in our barracks under guard and quarantine." Until the epidemic passed, these soldiers would be fighting just one enemy: influenza. But that was battle enough. As Roscoe wrote, "There could be no war so bad as this."[2]

Despite the ferocity of the epidemic, Roscoe seemed hopeful that the worst was over; he was feeling better, he told Vera, and they might be leaving for France as early as the next week. "I think everyone will be over this stuff by then." But his next letter sounded much gloomier: "We will be here for some time," he wrote, "that is a cinch . . . May be all winter we don't know." The rapid change in his mood reflected the increasing inroads the epidemic was making in his own company. "We had four die today and there will be more tomorrow they say." At one

Figure 3.1 Soldiers at Camp Dix, New Jersey, dutifully gargle salt water—a treatment that was thought (incorrectly) to prevent influenza. National Archives, 165-WW-269B-6.

point, Roscoe himself had become so sick that he had one of his friends wire Vera in Texas, telling her to be ready to travel, in case he needed her at his side. Writing the next day, he was able to assure her that his own danger had passed. But even as he was finishing that sentence, he got news of another death in the company. "That is five and they are all the nicest boys we had and the boys are all heartbroken."[3]

A day later, Roscoe sounded even more discouraged: "This is getting to be simply awful. Our men getting worse again and deaths all around us and the awful nights . . . There is nothing going on in camp no drill or anything just tending the men." He insisted he was getting better, but his tone kept changing from dark to light and back again: "Just now this is a blue bunch," he wrote. "We all hate to die in a hospital sick. It doesn't seem so bad over there, but here I can't see much fun in that. Of course myself I am not thinking of that, but some do, because I am not going to die either place."[4]

Roscoe Chittim did recover from flu, and on October 21—about a month later than originally planned—his company sailed for Europe. They arrived just weeks before the armistice, too late for much involvement in the fighting.[5] And so, as happened with thousands of other American soldiers, Roscoe's most life-threatening experience during World War I turned out to be his battle with influenza. No monuments would be erected to that battle, nor would future historians of the war devote much attention to it. Nevertheless, the epidemic would kill almost as many U.S. soldiers as died in combat. And the memories it left with the survivors would last a lifetime (see Table 2, p. 60).

FROM HASKELL COUNTY TO FRANCE

The flu epidemic in the United States began seven months before Roscoe Chittim's encounter with it at Camp Dix, and 1,400 miles away. As was noted in Chapter 1, the first sign of it was a flurry of flu cases in Haskell County, Kansas, in February 1918. Local soldiers then carried the disease to Camp Funston, which soon developed its own mini-epidemic. From there, influenza spread rapidly across the country, facilitated by the continual transfer of soldiers among the various training camps. Over the next several months—the period that is now considered the first wave of the 1918 epidemic—it affected a good number of the country's military camps, and many civilian communities as well. But this mild first phase of the epidemic attracted relatively little attention.

Then the epidemic moved onto Europe. By this time (spring 1918), the United States had been in the war for almost a year. But because mobilizing and training the troops had taken so long, American soldiers were only just beginning to cross the Atlantic in significant numbers. Week after week, all through the spring months, the U.S. troops marched off the ships onto European soil. And they brought the virus with them.

Some authorities believe that a related strain of the influenza virus may already have been lurking in Europe. For instance, virologist John Oxford points to widespread pneumonia and "purulent bronchitis" at certain military bases in France and England in 1916 and 1917. He believes that these incidents included early, undiagnosed cases of the 1918 influenza virus. Other authorities disagree, arguing that the disease in 1918 was caused by a different viral strain from those earlier outbreaks. They believe that the primary source of the epidemic was the virus that was carried to Europe by American soldiers.[6] In fact, despite all the research that has been done on this subject, scientist Edwin O. Jordan may have been correct when he observed in 1927: "It will probably never be possible to fix one definite starting point for the 1918 pandemic, if indeed a single starting point existed."[7]

However much these scholars may disagree about the epidemic's precise point of origin, nearly everyone agrees that the explosion of influenza across Europe in 1918 was set off by the arrival of U.S. troops that spring. Cases multiplied rapidly in the ports where the Americans landed, such as Brest and Bordeaux. And as British, French, and American troops moved in and out of the port areas, they picked up the disease and spread it further. Between March and May, influenza swept through every army in Europe, and through civilian communities as well. But even though this first wave of the epidemic traveled with remarkable speed, it was not widely commented upon—largely because wartime censorship discouraged the publication of any news that could be interpreted as evidence of national weakness. (As we have noted, influenza's arrival was covered much more freely by the press in neutral Spain, thus giving rise to the name by which the epidemic is still known: "Spanish flu.")

Besides the constraints of censorship, there was another reason the first wave of influenza did not attract widespread attention in Europe, and that was because the war overshadowed everything else. Both sides had been bled white by almost four years of slaughter, but Germany was at a particular disadvantage because of the effectiveness of the British blockade. By the spring of 1918, Germany's soldiers were hungry and its civilians were starving. Germany was also facing another threat: the American troops were finally on their way. Back in 1917, German leaders had gambled that they could defeat the Allies before the United States completed its mobilization. But now, after a year of preparation, American forces were starting to arrive in force. Several hundred thousand soldiers had already landed in Europe, and the pace of shipments was increasing every week. The clock was ticking; if Germany was going to deliver a knockout blow to the Allies, it had better come soon.

And so in late March, General Erich Ludendorff launched a series of major offensives against the Allies. Within days, his army broke through the French lines and started using a formidable long-range gun to bombard Paris, 75 miles away. For the next three months, battle followed battle, causing huge casualties on both sides.

As the fighting intensified, the Allies called with growing desperation for reinforcements from the United States. "A terrible blow is imminent," wrote the French prime minister to Woodrow Wilson. "Tell your Americans to come quickly."[8] But so far, even the

Germany benefited considerably from the Russian Revolution in 1917, because the Bolsheviks, who soon seized power, were determined to take their country out of the war. Germany's "separate peace" with Russia, which was formalized in the Treaty of Brest-Litovsk (March 3, 1918), enabled the Germans to take all the troops that had been fighting the Russians and shift them to the Western Front, just as General Erich Ludendorff was preparing his big spring attack there.

U.S. soldiers who had already arrived were not of much help to the Allies, because rather than parceling them out to fill gaps in the French and British lines, the American commander, General John J. Pershing, insisted on holding them in reserve until there were enough of them to fight as a unit. Only late in the spring, under extreme pressure, did Pershing finally release about 70,000 of his soldiers to fight under British and French command.

Gradually, the great German offensive faltered, and by July it was over. Perhaps the Americans' participation had helped to turn the tide. More likely, it was the Germans' own terrible casualties during the offensive— estimated at 900,000.[9] And there was another important factor: influenza, which had hit the underfed and exhausted German soldiers particularly hard. General Ludendorff later recalled: "It was a grievous business having to listen every morning to the chiefs of staff's recital of the number of influenza cases, and their complaints about the weakness of their troops."[10] For a weakened army, struggling to advance against fierce opposition, the debilities of influenza must have been a significant added handicap.

As the German offensive ground to a halt, so did the first wave of the 1918 epidemic. Although it had not affected the Allies as severely as the Germans, the disease had spread throughout Europe, giving huge numbers of soldiers and civilians at least mild cases of flu. As for other parts of the globe, there were reports that the first wave of the epidemic had reached as far as China and Brazil. But by the summer of 1918, it seemed to have sputtered out.

Then, without warning, disease rates suddenly began to pick up again. Starting in August, U.S. commanders in Europe started getting reports of a new kind of flu, "of a very fatal variety." And on August 17, a military surgeon who just a few months earlier had casually described the disease as "three-day fever" made a new entry in his diary: "Influenza increasing and becoming more fatal." We can track the transition from the first wave of the epidemic to the second by following the experience of three infantry brigades that were based at the Valdahon training camp in France one after the other. In the first brigade, which stayed through most of June and July, there were only 77 mild cases of flu—presumably the last stages of the spring wave. During the month of August, when the second brigade was stationed at the same camp, there were 200 quite serious cases. And in September and October, when the third brigade was at the camp, there were more than 1,600 cases, with 151 deaths.[11] What happened at Valdahon was repeated all through the region. The second wave of the 1918 influenza epidemic had begun.

This new wave of the epidemic had several unusual features that scientists are still trying to explain. The first conundrum was the timing.

In the northern hemisphere, influenza typically appears late each fall, with the cold weather. But in 1918, the first wave spread across the United States and Europe as the weather was getting warmer, not colder, and the second wave started in the heat of summer. Moreover, both the first and second waves of the epidemic traveled speedily around the whole world and through both hemispheres, regardless of what the weather was doing.

It is also puzzling how rapidly the second wave followed the first. To understand what a departure this was, we need to consider the way viruses reproduce. When a flu virus attacks a patient, it hijacks the individual cells' machinery for producing more cells and uses it instead to produce copies of the virus. Thereafter, each time the patient talks or coughs or sneezes, millions of these new virus copies are expelled into the air, ready to be inhaled by the next victim. Inevitably, with so many copies being produced, not all of them are identical to the original. Most of these imperfect copies—or mutations—are less effective than the original and they quickly die off. But occasionally a mutation is so effective that it out-produces and ultimately replaces the earlier strain.

This process of "viral *drift*," as it is called, occurs gradually, so the immunity you get after a case of flu is likely to protect you for two or three years. That is because, despite some drift, your immune system will continue to recognize the virus you inhale as the same one that infected you before. But over time, the virus will keep drifting further from the strain that originally infected you, and ultimately it will become so different that your immune system will not recognize it. At that point, you will become susceptible again.

In 1918, the change in the virus was much faster and more dramatic. The second wave of the epidemic started less than two months after the first wave ended—a pattern that had never been seen before. How did that happen? One possible theory is that the second wave was caused by an entirely different flu virus, which had already been present somewhere in Europe. An alternative theory is that it might have been produced by a type of viral change called viral *shift*. Sometimes, instead of changing gradually over a period of years (viral *drift*), a virus goes through a "reassortment event," during which it swaps some of its genes with another virus, producing a brand new third strain. Because people's immune systems do not recognize this new strain, nearly everyone in the population will be vulnerable to it. This kind of reassortment event (or viral *shift*) is what causes most epidemics.

The problem with both these hypotheses—the appearance of a second virus, or a reassortment event—is that in 1918, people who had had flu during the first wave of the epidemic seemed to be at least somewhat less susceptible to the second wave.[12] The pattern was by no means universal, but if infection during the first wave offered any level of protection against the second wave, then it was not likely that the second wave represented an entirely new strain of flu. Accordingly, most historians today subscribe to a different scenario. They believe the viral strain that caused the first wave of the epidemic simply went through an extraordinarily rapid process of mutation over the summer. As we have noted, mutation goes on all the time, but it usually takes many months, or even years, to achieve a change as significant as the one that occurred during the summer of 1918. This is because, in any given community, before the virus has mutated enough to become widely contagious again, it has run out of new people to infect. It then goes underground (often in an animal or avian host) until the next flu season. But wartime Europe in 1918 offered the virus a uniquely hospitable environment.

To begin with, the soldiers' poor living conditions—crowded barracks, rain-sodden tents, and muddy trenches—made them unusually susceptible to respiratory disease. More important, the continual introduction of new troops (particularly the hundreds of thousands of American soldiers who kept arriving in Europe during the spring and summer of 1918) meant that there was a never-ending supply of new people for the virus to infect. And so, instead of burning itself out, the virus lived on, becoming more and more skillful at evading the human immune system. The result was that the process of viral drift, which would ordinarily have taken several years before producing a significant new outbreak, was accomplished much faster.

That could explain the *speed* with which the second wave followed the first. But what about the spike in *virulence*—that is, its harmfulness to humans? Among other things, there was a dramatic increase during the second wave in the proportion of flu patients who developed secondary complications such as pneumonia. The death rate was also much higher. In fact, according to microbiologist Paul Ewald, within a few months the virus had become 10 times more virulent than in the spring.[13] This feature, too, is generally attributed to the special conditions of wartime Europe. Researchers hypothesize that in passing so rapidly through so many people, the virus dramatically increased its severity. It was this combination of being unusually *virulent* and unusually *contagious* that made the second wave of the 1918 epidemic so memorable.

While the second wave was picking up steam in Europe, the summer went by in the United States with hardly a cloud on the medical horizon. The spring wave of influenza was over, the health of the soldiers still in the United States was generally good, and, although periodic reports filtered back from Europe, army physicians seem to have paid little heed to the new phase of the epidemic that was emerging there.

IN THE TRAINING CAMPS

Then, in the last days of August 1918, sailors returning from Europe brought influenza to Commonwealth Pier, a big navy barracks in Boston. Within days, the whole facility was full of coughing, sneezing men, many of whom became desperately ill. And thus began the second wave of the 1918 epidemic in the United States. The infection spread outward from Boston into the surrounding communities, and on September 8, Camp Devens (30 miles away) had its first case of flu. The virus may have been transmitted directly to the camp by someone connected with Commonwealth Pier, but it is worth noting that just four days before its first flu case, Devens had taken in 1,400 recruits from all over the state. So it is also possible that as the infection spread out from Commonwealth Pier, it reached the hometown of one of Devens' recruits, who picked the infection up there and brought it to camp with him.

For the next several weeks, every day at Devens was worse than the one before. By September 22, almost 20 percent of the camp had influenza, with most of the soldiers so weak they had to be hospitalized. On the single worst day, medical officers identified 1,543 new cases of flu. And while these cases multiplied, there was also a spike in the number of flu patients who developed pneumonia. On a typical fall day, the camp usually had about 25 cases of pneumonia. But on September 24, there were 342 cases. By September 30—just three weeks after the first soldier got sick—Devens had had 10,000 cases of flu, 2,000 cases of pneumonia, and 500 deaths.[14]

In many respects, Devens was an epidemic waiting to happen. Built for 35,000 soldiers, the camp in September held 45,000, with half the extra men crowded into the barracks, while the rest were housed in tents on the grounds. When the United States first entered World War I, in April 1917, a panel of doctors had drawn up a list of recommendations for maintaining the soldiers' health in the training camps—good ventilation, plenty of space between beds, and adequate hospital facilities. But with the rush to house the troops as they assembled that fall, few of these recommendations were followed. Instead, around the country three dozen huge military camps were thrown together in furious haste, even as the newly mobilized soldiers were arriving for training. In Camp Devens' case, the builders managed to turn out an average of 10 buildings a day, and the pace was similar at other camps.[15]

In part because of the rush, the completed buildings tended to be crowded and poorly ventilated. As for the medical facilities, a physician later observed: "A farmer who gave no more thought to the planning of his milking barns than was given to the planning of Army hospitals in

World War I would go broke in a month." In fact, the conditions were so bad that when an epidemic of measles with pneumonic complications broke out in the camps in the fall of 1917, it triggered a round of congressional hearings and bitter criticism of both the War Department and the Medical Corps.[16]

A few months later, when concern was expressed over the number of pneumonia cases in the army, a commander at Camp Dix told the head of the Medical Corps: "We know perfectly well that we can control pneumonia absolutely if we could avoid crowding the men, but it is not practicable in military life to avoid this crowding."[17] The principle he was enunciating would continue to dominate military leaders' thinking throughout the war: that whenever health measures conflicted with military priorities, the latter would always come first. So it is perhaps not surprising that, despite the complaints, conditions in the training camps had improved only slightly when influenza descended on them in the fall of 1918.

The crowding in the camps would probably have helped to spread the flu epidemic in any case, but in 1918 it also mattered *who* was being crowded. The young men in these facilities belonged to an age group that during this particular epidemic was one of the most vulnerable in the population. Children, too, died in considerable numbers in 1918, but while their mortality rate from flu and pneumonia increased by a factor of five or six compared to an ordinary year, the death rate from these diseases among young adults was 22 times higher than usual.[18]

In an era when one out of every 10 babies died before its first birthday, people had become sadly accustomed to seeing children struck down by disease. But no one could get used to an epidemic that was just as deadly for strong, healthy young men. Shaken by the incongruity of seeing "these well-developed and well-nourished bodies" laid out on the autopsy table, a navy doctor observed that they "made a spectacle sad beyond description." Similarly, when an army doctor at Devens described the "long lines of dead soldiers all dressed and laid out in double rows" in the camp morgue, he evoked both the pathos of the sight before his eyes and the eerie parallel with the way one expected to see young soldiers: marching smartly on parade. As the doctor observed, the array of bodies beat "any sight they ever had in France after a battle."[19]

Given the crowded conditions in the camps and the special vulnerability of the soldiers' age group, it is not hard to see why any individual camp might have experienced a flu epidemic. But the fact that the disease swept across the country so quickly requires a bit more explanation. The key here is the military practice of continually transferring groups of soldiers and sailors from one camp to another—for extra training, to consolidate or restructure military units, or to prepare for shipment overseas. The transfer process itself perpetuated the close quarters the men had experienced in camp—on the crowded troop trains, they often had to sit three across in a double seat, or sleep two to a berth. But even more harmful was the extent to which the transfers moved the virus around the country.

The men who were scheduled for transfer to other camps were always examined before they left. But because flu victims show no symptoms for the first several days after they have been infected, and because they can start passing the virus on to others during this period, it was inevitable that soldiers and sailors who looked perfectly healthy would bring the flu with them to camps that had not yet been infected. For instance, in early September, when Commonwealth Pier in Boston was already engulfed by flu, the facility shipped 300 sailors to the Philadelphia Navy Yard. Within four days of their arrival in Philadelphia, 19 of these men wound up in the hospital. Meanwhile, Commonwealth sent another group of sailors to the Great Lakes Naval Training Station outside Chicago. And at about the same time, some of the men who had been sent from Commonwealth to Philadelphia were shipped out again, this time to a navy base near Seattle. By the time they arrived, 11 of them were so sick they had to be carried off the ship on stretchers.[20] Predictably, the receiving camps all rapidly

Table 1 Spread of epidemic through selected U.S. military camps, Fall 1918

First case	State	Camp
September 8	Massachusetts	Devens
September 9	New Jersey	Dix
September 13	New York	Upton
September 13	Virginia	Humphreys
September 16	Kansas	Funston
September 16	South Carolina	Jackson
September 18	Florida	Johnston
September 18	Louisiana	Beauregard
September 18	Iowa	Dodge
September 19	Texas	Travis
September 20	Alabama	McClellan
September 21	California	Kearny
September 21	Illinois	Grant
September 22	Kentucky	Taylor
September 23	Arkansas	Pike
September 23	Michigan	Custer
September 24	Ohio	Sherman
September 26	Texas	Bowie
September 26	New Mexico	Cody
September 28	Alabama	Sheridan
September 28	Georgia	Hancock
September 30	Texas	MacArthur
October 8	California	Fremont
October 9	Washington	Lewis

Source: Vincent Vaughan[21]

developed their own flu epidemics, and within a short period thereafter, so did Philadelphia, Chicago, and Seattle. [*See a firsthand account of one troop transfer, Document 3.*]

Military commanders were well aware that the transfers helped spread the disease, and medical officers frequently urged them to suspend these moves. But the transfers were seen as an essential part of mobilizing and training the forces needed in Europe, so they continued to take place, and the virus continued to travel. Within a month of the first case at Commonwealth Pier, the epidemic had reached all but a few of the army's 39 camps, as well as most of the navy's training stations. Table 1, reflecting the experience of selected camps, shows the progression of influenza through the system, based on the date on which each camp had its first hospital admission for flu. It can be seen that camps on the east coast were hit the earliest, but that thereafter, long-distance transfers often leapfrogged across the country, bringing the epidemic with them.

Every time influenza hit another camp, it rapidly overwhelmed whatever arrangements had been established for healthcare. As public health expert George Soper observed in November 1918, "The disease never spreads slowly and insidiously. Wherever it occurs its presence is startling."[22] Within days of the first case, base hospitals would start running short of beds and medical supplies, barracks would have to be converted to sick wards, and doctors and nurses would find themselves working around the clock. A decade later, writing his memoirs, physician Victor Vaughan could still recall the look of the wards at Camp Devens at the height of the outbreak there:

> I see hundreds of young, stalwart men in the uniform of their country coming into the wards of the hospital in groups of ten or more. They are placed on the cots until every bed is full and yet others crowd in. The faces soon wear a bluish cast; a distressing cough brings up the blood stained sputum.[23]

Many of the ailing soldiers—at Devens and elsewhere—did recover, but death rates were shockingly high compared to an ordinary flu out-break. A nurse recalls: "An ambulance would arrive, carrying four litters. It would bring us four live soldiers, and take away four dead ones." And where were the "dead ones" going? To the morgue, where, as the nurse explained, "the morticians were working day and night."[24]

In the next chapter, we will explore in greater detail the precise nature of influenza as a disease, and the challenges doctors and nurses faced in trying to deal with it, in both military and civilian settings. But right now, let us look at the specific efforts that camp commanders made to control

Camp Grant: Balancing Priorities[25]

In August 1918, an army medical officer named Joe Capps published an article in the *Journal of the American Medical Association* suggesting how respiratory diseases such as influenza could be prevented and controlled in a military setting. Among other things, he recommended that all new arrivals (whether transfers or recruits) should be kept quarantined from the rest of the camp for three weeks, to ensure that they were clear of disease. He also proposed reducing cross-infection in the barracks by placing the beds further apart, and erecting cloth partitions between one bed and the next.[26]

Capps had had direct experience with the problems he was discussing. His own facility—Camp Grant in Illinois—was so overpopulated that in order to avoid extreme crowding in the barracks, many of the men were sleeping in tents. But more soldiers kept arriving; between June and August 1918, the number of troops at the camp rose from 30,000 to 40,000. Then, in the same August week that Capps' article was published, Camp Grant received a new commander, Colonel Charles Hagedorn. The new man in charge was not indifferent to public health concerns, but he believed there was greater danger in letting his men suffer through a chilly Illinois autumn living under canvas. So, against his medical officers' advice, he decided to crowd all the soldiers into the barracks. Within a few weeks, virtually all of them were back indoors. This left the barracks so packed with men that there was no possibility of setting aside a separate quarantine space for new arrivals, even if Hagedorn had wished to do so.

In mid-September, a group of transfers arrived from Camp Devens in Massachusetts, which had been one of the first facilities to be hit by the epidemic. Not long after, on the morning of September 21, the first few soldiers at Grant came down with flu. By midnight, there were 108 cases. Within two days, influenza was all over the camp. Admissions to the base hospital soared, peaking at 788 on the day of September 29. On October 4, the daily death toll broke 100.

As the situation deteriorated, supplies of everything ran low—ambulances, sheets, beds, drugs, disinfectant, sputum cups, and thermometers. Almost 100 doctors, nurses, and orderlies got sick themselves. Soon, desperate relatives were offering bribes to the remaining medical staff, trying to get decent care for their family members. Meanwhile, the reeking wards were packed with coughing, bleeding, delirious, and dying soldiers.

On October 8, Colonel Hagedorn got the latest mortality figures. Then he sent his sergeant out of the room and shot himself through the head.

the epidemic. Following "social distancing" principles, just like the plague cities of old, they often shut down public gathering places on their bases, set up sheet partitions between hospital beds, and moved the beds in the barracks further apart. Some facilities (such as Camp Dix, where Roscoe Cottims served) completely dispensed with training and confined the soldiers to their barracks. Others required the wearing of gauze masks, either by healthcare providers or by everyone. In addition, most military camps worked hard to eliminate dirt and dust, since both were seen as possible sources of infection. And by late September, an increasing number of camps were put under total quarantine, with no one allowed in or out.

Did these efforts make a difference? It is certainly true that no camp completely escaped influenza, however energetically its leaders worked at prevention. It was hard to react fast enough; often, preventive measures did not begin until after the infection had already taken hold. Nevertheless, historians have noted that in the camps that moved quickly and aggressively to control the spread of infection, the epidemic was often somewhat milder, even if it lasted longer. In the end, these camps may have had almost as many flu cases, but because fewer men were sick at a time, the burden on the available resources was lighter, and the overall experience was somewhat less traumatic.[27]

Whatever the various preventive efforts did to control influenza, they also dramatically curtailed the camps' capacity to accomplish their fundamental mission—which was to train soldiers and ship them overseas. By late September, American forces in Europe were moving into their first major military engagement, and once again General Pershing was calling for reinforcements. The next draft call—for 142,000 more men—was scheduled for early October. But by now all the camps to which these new recruits would have been sent for training were under quarantine. So the authorities in Washington made the dramatic decision to cancel the October draft, and to put on hold an additional 78,000 men who were about to report for duty. The army Chief of Staff, Peyton March, followed up with an explanatory cable to General Pershing: "Influenza not only stopped all draft calls in October but practically stopped all training."[28]

HEADING FOR EUROPE

Throughout the summer and fall of 1918, while the second wave of the epidemic was making its way across the Atlantic and through the U.S. training camps, the shipment of troops to Europe continued uninterrupted. Back when America first entered the war in April 1917, General Pershing had set a target of getting 1 million U.S. soldiers to Europe within a year.

By the following spring, less than half that number had crossed the ocean, but the pace of troop shipments increased considerably from then on, rising from about 120,000 per month in April to about 250,000 in September. By the end of that time, there were more than 2 million American soldiers in Europe, with another 2 million in the training camps at home.[29] And still the troopships kept sailing.

The trouble was that as the influenza epidemic swept through the United States, a growing number of the American soldiers who landed in Europe were in no condition to help the Allied cause. Military authorities had instituted a system of pre-embarkation physicals, to make sure no one who was obviously suffering from influenza got on the ships. But doctors could not possibly predict who might come down with the disease after the ship left port. And once even a few cases developed on board, an epidemic was all but inevitable.

The journey to Europe by troopship had never been a picnic. Even refitted luxury liners could become highly disagreeable when they were crammed with anxious, unwashed, and seasick soldiers. As for the old freighters that were frequently pressed into service, one soldier described the one he had sailed on as "the blackest, foulest, most congested hole that I ever set foot into."[30] But however bad conditions were before, they turned far worse once influenza joined the crew.

Since none of the troopships had enough designated hospital space to accommodate hundreds of patients at a time, the sick and the dying soon filled the regular bunks—coughing and vomiting, bleeding from the nose and mouth—while dead bodies piled up on deck. Dealing with the bodies became a particular problem. Sometimes room was found for them in the ship refrigerators, but often there were too many, and they had to be buried at sea. A sailor on the *U.S.S. President Grant* described working "till my fingers bled" during his off-duty hours, sewing dead flu victims into their shrouds.[31] And from a nearby ship in the same convoy, a soldier watched the bodies being dropped over the *Grant*'s side. "It was death," he said, "death in one of its worst forms, to be consigned nameless to the sea."[32]

Just as medical officers had tried fruitlessly to stop the transfers from camp to camp, so they also urged military authorities to cut back on troop shipments to Europe—at least from the camps with influenza. However, the Army Chief of Staff, General Peyton March, insisted that the shipments had to continue. Nor would he accept the proposal that all soldiers headed for Europe undergo a one-week quarantine before leaving. He ordered some reduction in crowding and increased the medical staff assigned to the troopships; otherwise, the program went on as before.

President Woodrow Wilson had been extraordinarily close-mouthed about the epidemic from the first—so much so that historians have been

The Voyage of the *Leviathan*: The Epidemic at Sea[33]

The *S.S. Leviathan* started life in 1914 as the *Vaterland*, a German passenger liner. She happened to be in New York when World War I broke out, so she stayed there, to avoid being sunk by the British. Then when the United States entered the war in 1917, the ship was seized, renamed the *Leviathan*, and refitted to carry U.S. troops. One of the biggest liners in the world, the *Leviathan* was a valuable resource for troop transport. But, packed with 9,000 soldiers lodged in bunks tiered four levels high, she was the worst possible place for an influenza outbreak.

In late September 1918, when the *Leviathan* started loading troops for her next trip to Europe, one of the units that came on board was the 57th Pioneer Infantry from Vermont. The Vermonters' troubles had begun several days earlier, when flu began circulating in the New Jersey camp where they were based. Their march to the port on the day before embarkation was a disaster, with dozens of men collapsing along the road, more succumbing during the ferry ride to the ship, and another 120 put back on shore after they had boarded because they were too sick to travel. Nevertheless, the *Leviathan* set sail as planned on September 29.

By the next day, the ship's hospital was full of flu patients, and by nightfall there were 700 cases. Each day brought more. The Vermonters' commander wrote in his journal that as the number of sick men increased, "Washington was apprised of the situation, but the call for men for the Allied armies was so great that we must go on at any cost." Meanwhile, scores of doctors and nurses came down with flu themselves, leaving the dwindling staff to struggle with a caseload that ultimately totaled 2,000 patients.

As conditions grew worse, the environment below decks became increasingly grim, especially at night. One of the officers reported:

> The conditions during the night cannot be visualized by anyone who has not actually seen them. Pools of blood from severe nasal hemorrhages of many patients were scattered throughout the compartments and the attendants were powerless to escape tracking through the mess, because of the narrow passages below the bunks. The decks became wet and slippery, groans and cries of the terrified added to the confusion of the applicants clamoring for treatment, and altogether a true inferno reigned supreme.

The first death of the voyage took place three days after the ship set sail, and from then on, the deaths kept mounting: 30 one day, 45 the next. Since the *Leviathan* had neither the staff nor the supplies to keep up with the embalming, some of the corpses started to decompose, which added to the accumulating stench of blood, vomit, and human waste that pervaded the ship.

The *Leviathan* finally pulled into the French port of Brest on October 7, but the deaths continued. Thirty-one more patients died before they could go ashore, and there were hundreds of additional deaths among the almost 1,000 soldiers who were taken straight to hospitals on land. No one knows exactly how many of the *Leviathan*'s passengers died, but the voyage stands as a nightmarish testament to the destructive power of the 1918 epidemic.

unable to find a single occasion on which he mentioned it in public. Nevertheless, the president was troubled by the reports of deaths on the troopships, and on October 7 he called General March in and asked him whether it would not be wise to suspend the shipments until the epidemic had subsided. March held firm. He explained the screening procedures that were in place, warned that any letup in the shipments would give a boost to German morale, and assured the president: "Every such soldier who has died just as surely played his part as his comrade who died in France." The president sighed and let the shipments continue.[34]

In fact, the situation did ease a little during October. The military reduced the crowding on the ships by 10 percent, and then another 10 percent. And by mid-October, the training camps that had been hit first by the epidemic were seeing a significant drop in new cases, so troop shipments could be drawn from them. Nevertheless, few of the camps sending soldiers overseas were wholly free of the disease, even if the number of new cases was declining. So influenza continued to travel with the U.S. troops on every ship that crossed the Atlantic. And all fall, sick and dying American soldiers continued to stumble off the ships onto European soil.

The most debilitated men were taken straight to U.S. military hospitals. As for the soldiers who had had flu on the way over and were now judged strong enough to report to their new European bases, some were loaded onto crowded troop trains, while others were required to march to their destinations, often in the driving rain. This latter group made a pitiful sight as they tottered along, many of them so weak they fell by the side of the road and had to be carried on stretchers. And marching along beside them—or perhaps even carrying their stretchers—were other soldiers who had only recently been infected and were at that moment passing the virus on to those around them.

FLU IN THE AMERICAN EXPEDITIONARY FORCE

From the moment the second wave of the flu epidemic emerged in France in late August 1918, it moved outward in every direction, propelled by wartime shipping and population movements. This chapter discusses its sweep through the American army, and in Chapter 5 we will look at how it affected America's civilian communities. But, as has been noted, the United States' experience is part of a much larger story. During the same months that the epidemic was laying Americans low, it was also spreading to every other part of the world, bringing with it an avalanche of death and disease; India alone lost nearly 20 million people.[35] Meanwhile, the virus was also continuing to circulate in Europe. The French and British armies had thousands of cases, and the exhausted German army was devastated by the disease.

As for the Americans, in the staging areas around the ports, the pool of susceptible people was continually renewed by the influx of new troops from the United States. By September, they were coming in at the rate of 60,000 a week. Some of these new arrivals had had flu in their training camps at home or on the voyage over, and were now supposedly on the road to recovery, although they were still very weak. Unfortunately for the many who had escaped flu so far, the epidemic was well established in and around the French ports, and—just as in the training camps back home—the soldiers' crowded, ill-ventilated barracks helped to keep the virus spreading from one person to the next.

Closer to the front, ill-ventilated barracks were hardly the problem, since most of the soldiers were living in tents or drafty farm buildings. But this kind of existence had its own health hazards, as we can see in Roscoe Chittim's letters home. By the time Chittim reached France, he had recovered from his own case of flu, but his letters provided a vivid picture of life in and around the front lines that rainy autumn. He wrote, for instance:

> I am laying on my stomach in a bunch of straw, soaking wet and so am I. My shelter tent is leaking all over and I have about two inches of candle for my heat. It has been raining for two days and nights so you can possibly imagine some of the pains we have
> . . . You have read of sunny France well it isn't.[36]

One can understand how vulnerable the American soldiers must have been to influenza, living as they did in an environment where the greatest conceivable luxuries were a warm bed and a pair of dry socks.

Until the fall of 1918, the U.S. troops did not spend much time right on the front lines. When the first detachments of the American Expeditionary Force (AEF) had begun arriving in Europe earlier that year, the soldiers were disheartened to discover that their main job was to wait for the rest of the U.S. army to assemble. Except for the few units that were released to fight with the Allies during the Germans' spring offensive, most of the AEF soldiers spent the spring and summer of 1918 well behind the lines, grousing under their breath about the long marches and make-work exercises that were devised to keep them busy. But come fall, the situation changed. The Americans were given their own sector of the battle line, and by then they finally had enough troops to man it—in September, the number of U.S. soldiers in Europe topped 2 million. And so at last, after almost 18 months of preparations, the AEF was ready to join the fight.

Of course, September 1918 was also the month when the second wave of the influenza epidemic really took off in Europe, as well as everywhere else. The AEF's first offensive—the successful capture of the St. Mihiel area from the Germans—was not seriously affected by the epidemic, because the action came early in the month. But by the time the Americans began their great Meuse-Argonne offensive on September 26, conditions had grown much more severe. From a few thousand cases of flu in the week before the battle began, the numbers kept climbing until, in just seven days in early October, the AEF had 16,000 new cases. On October 3, Pershing wired Washington that "influenza exists in epidemic form among our troops," and demanded 1,500 more nurses to deal with the crisis. A week later, he cabled again, urgently requesting more medical staff and equipment.[37] But by then, the epidemic was also reaching a crisis point at home, and it would take time to fill Pershing's requests. Meanwhile, the AEF would have to face the epidemic with the resources it had on hand.

It was no small achievement that America's leading medical schools, working with the Red Cross, had set up and staffed 50 fully equipped base hospitals to serve in Europe, each with 500 to 1,000 beds. But once the Meuse-Argonne offensive began and thousands of combat injuries and flu cases started pouring into the few hospitals closest to the battle area, these facilities were rapidly overwhelmed. During a desperate period in mid-October, one field hospital near the front reportedly had an admission every one and a half minutes. There were so many patients, recalled one nurse, "it took a tight-rope walker to move among them without hitting arms, legs, or heads."[38]

At first, medical officers tried to set up separate facilities for the flu cases, so as to prevent the spread of infection. But space was so tight that patients were constantly being squeezed in wherever there was a bed. As a result, the virus kept spreading, even in the hospitals. And not only to the patients; dozens of doctors and nurses also came down with flu, further aggravating the workload for those who remained healthy. And still the patients kept coming. A surgeon working near the front wrote in his diary: "Everything is overflowing with patients. Besides wounds, there is rain, mud, 'flu,' and pneumonia." He summed up the whole situation: "Rain, rain; mud, blood; blood, death!"[39]

It was a daunting task to deal simultaneously with a full-blown epidemic and a large-scale military offensive. The unfortunate combination of the two presented AEF commanders with a huge logistical challenge: the need to move thousands of sick soldiers to the rear on the same narrow roads that were being used to bring forward equipment and supplies for the fighting. In addition, fresh troops continually had to be brought up to the front to replace the sick and wounded soldiers heading for the rear. The demands of this two-way traffic strained the army's transport resources, and caused monumental jams on the roads leading to the front.

Meanwhile, the troops who were actually doing the fighting were not in particularly good condition either. Among them were a sizable number of soldiers who were still weak and shaky from having had flu during the previous month. In addition, there were hundreds—perhaps thousands—of men who had come down with the disease but had chosen not to report their conditions—whether from pride or misguided optimism or distrust of army hospitals. And then there were many more who were feeling a little "off" but did not yet realize that they too were coming down with flu. Altogether, including those who were shipped to the rear, it has been estimated that nearly 70,000 AEF soldiers were suffering in one way or another from influenza during the Meuse-Argonne campaign.[40]

Besides the problems associated with the epidemic, the military situation itself presented a number of challenges. On the plus side, the Americans greatly outnumbered the German forces in their sector. Moreover, they were not in this effort alone. A unit of the French army was also attacking the Argonne Forest, and the whole Meuse-Argonne campaign was part of a much larger Allied campaign known as the Hundred Days Offensive—a coordinated series of assaults on the German lines along the whole length of the Western Front.

On the negative side, most of the American troops were brand new to combat. General Pershing had hoped to give all his soldiers at least eight months of training and then a month in a quiet sector of the line before they saw combat. But because of the tremendous push to get the troops to Europe in the summer of 1918, many soldiers had received only a few weeks' training; some arrived without ever having handled a rifle. As for the U.S. soldiers who had been waiting in Europe for the rest of the troops to arrive, they had had more training than the newcomers, but scarcely more battle experience.

Another challenge the Americans faced during the Meuse-Argonne offensive was the difficult terrain. Most of the great battles in this war involved mass attacks across broad, flat fields. But the Germans' position on the high ground of the Meuse was hard to approach, and the Argonne Forest, densely wooded and broken up by streams, provided endless obstacles to the army's advance. Also, as usual that fall, the weather was cold and rainy. The result was that at the end of the fifth day of the offensive, the American army was still trying to reach the objective planned for day two.[41] Throughout the rest of the month, the AEF's progress continued to be slower than Pershing had hoped.

By the end of October, all up and down the Western Front, the Allies had managed to push the Germans back behind their defensive Hindenburg Line. The Americans contributed to that victory, since by then they and their French allies had finally achieved their own objective, which was to drive the Germans out of the Argonne Forest. The success of the Hundred Days Offensive is generally seen as the final blow to Germany's military fortunes, leading directly to the armistice only two weeks later, on November 11. Pershing did take up the offensive again on November 1, but by then the German soldiers were already heading for home. For them—if not quite yet for their leaders in Berlin—the war was over.

Because the Meuse-Argonne campaign contributed to the Allies' successful last great offensive against Germany, and because the AEF did ultimately achieve its objective there—and perhaps also because this battle was the AEF's only major engagement during World War I—it has often been portrayed in popular histories written by Americans as an unambiguous victory. But more skeptical historians (as well as some European commanders at the time) have raised a number of questions about the Americans' performance during the campaign. These queries have been directed not so much at the individual soldiers as at the AEF as a military organization. Critics point to the Americans' inexpert leadership, their slow progress, their scrambled communications, and their inefficient supply lines.[42]

Part of the reason for these problems, surely, was the Americans' inexperience. After all, this was the first battle many of these soldiers had ever seen, whereas the Europeans had been at this brutal business for four long years. But inexperience was not the whole story. There was also influenza. For instance, a good number of the Americans' problems with communications and supply were clearly attributable to the chaos on the roads behind the lines, as hundreds of vehicles carrying sick soldiers to the rear collided with relief troops and trucks and messengers trying to reach the front.

Historians have also identified another weakness in the Americans' performance: the extraordinary number of soldiers who left their units and gravitated to the safer area behind the lines. One commander estimated that there may have been as many as 100,000 of these "stragglers" (a term of disgrace, although not as serious as "deserter," which means someone who definitely *intends* not to return to duty). During the Meuse-Argonne battle, the problem of stragglers became so acute that scouting parties were sent to the rear to round up the men and send them back to their posts, sometimes with the shameful word "straggler" written on their backs.[43] Moving away from the front in this way has generally been interpreted as dereliction of duty, and no doubt some of the stragglers were simply hiding out from the fighting, as critics have claimed. But historian Carol Byerly reminds us that others may well have been so disabled by influenza that they were physically unable to keep pace with their units, or so lightheaded with fever that they simply lost their bearings.[44] Thus, as we assess the AEF's performance in the Meuse-Argonne—whether in terms of leadership, communications, logistics, or the problem of stragglers— we need to remember that throughout this battle, the Americans were fighting not only the Germans, but also influenza.

★   ★   ★

In later years, when there was time to analyze the military implications of the epidemic more systematically, certain patterns could be identified that had not been so clear at the time:

- Every army that participated in World War I was affected by the epidemic, but the German army seems to have been hit the hardest, probably because of the soldiers' poor physical condition by 1918. Some historians argue that the Germans' problems with influenza helped speed their final surrender, but they acknowledge that so many things were going wrong for the Germans in the fall of 1918 that it is hard to say exactly how great a role the epidemic played.[45]
- By the time the second wave of the epidemic hit, in the fall of 1918, the U.S. army was about evenly balanced between the number of troops overseas and the number in the training camps at home. However, disease rates and death rates were both considerably higher among the soldiers still in U.S.-based camps than among those overseas. This is probably because the intensity of the epidemic at any given military location tended to be directly related to the proportion of new recruits there. So the training camps lost more soldiers to flu than the American Expeditionary Force in Europe, and within the AEF, soldiers in the rear areas had higher flu death rates than those in the front lines.[46]
- The U.S. navy's experience was one that still puzzles historians. Even though *soldiers* on the troopships to Europe caught flu in droves, the

sailors manning those ships seemed remarkably resistant to the disease. Yet the navy as a whole had extremely high infection rates, particularly on its battleships and in its onshore training stations. One sailor, asked for his war memories, summed them up this way: "Mostly flu. Men were dying every day."[47]

Overall, it is estimated that about 1 million U.S. soldiers (roughly 25 percent of the army) got flu at some point during the epidemic, along with more than 100,000 sailors. (The navy's cases, though much smaller in number, are thought to have represented nearly 40 percent of its total forces.) As for deaths, the army lost nearly 40,000 soldiers to flu and pneumonia in 1918, while the navy lost about 5,000.[48]

When the United States entered the fighting in 1917, Army Surgeon General William Gorgas set himself the goal of making this the first war in American history in which there were fewer deaths from disease than from combat. If one counts only deaths in the army, he almost achieved his goal—the number of soldiers who died from all diseases was just a fraction higher than those killed in combat. But if the navy is included in the total, then deaths by disease did predominate, since the navy had relatively few combat deaths (see Table 2).[49]

Still, it was a near miss. And it was true that World War I death rates among U.S. soldiers for diseases *other* than influenza or pneumonia were the lowest in history. So one can understand why, in later years, top military physicians often chose to focus almost exclusively on this positive aspect of the record, and treat the epidemic as if it were an irrelevant sideshow. Of course, it is hardly rational to discuss deaths from disease in wartime while ignoring the one disease that accounted for 80 percent of those deaths. But the temptation to do so was a very human one.

Some medical caregivers seemed more willing than the military doctors to acknowledge the impact of the epidemic. But all of them—both nurses and doctors—were shaken by their encounter with a disease that so effectively resisted the powers of modern medicine. The experience of these caregivers is the subject of the next chapter.

Table 2 Deaths in the U.S. military, by cause, World War I[50]	
Battle deaths	50,280
Deaths from disease	57,460
Deaths from influenza and pneumonia	*43,000*
Deaths from other causes, such as accidents	7,920
TOTAL DEATHS	115,660

NOTES

1. Mary T. Sarnecky, *A History of the U.S. Army Nurse Corps* (Philadelphia, PA: University of Pennsylvania Press, 1999), 120–121.
2. Roscoe Chittim, letter to Vera Chittim, in Paul Spellman, "'A Million Kisses': Love Letters from a Doughboy in France," *Southwestern Historical Quarterly* 114 no. 1 (July 2010), 39, 41.
3. Spellman, "Million Kisses," 39–41.
4. Spellman, "Million Kisses," 41–42.
5. Spellman, "Million Kisses," 44–45.
6. John S. Oxford, et al., "World War I May Have Allowed the Emergence of 'Spanish' Influenza," *Lancet Infectious Diseases* 2 (February 2002), 111–114; Jeffery Taubenberger and David M. Morens, "Influenza: The Once and Future Pandemic," *Public Health Reports* 125, supp. 3 (2010), 19–20. See also: Christopher Langford, "Did the 1918–1919 Influenza Pandemic Originate in China?," *Population and Development Review* 31 no. 3 (September 2005), 488–490, 493–495.
7. Edwin O. Jordan, *Epidemic Influenza: A Survey* (Chicago, IL: American Medical Association, 1927), 60.
8. Pete Davies, *The Devil's Flu: The World's Deadliest Influenza Epidemic and the Scientific Hunt for the Virus that Caused It* (New York, NY: Henry Holt, 2000), 57.
9. Carol R. Byerly, *Fever of War: The Influenza Epidemic in the U.S. Army During World War I* (New York, NY: New York University Press, 2005), 98.
10. John M. Barry, *The Great Influenza: The Story of the Deadliest Pandemic in History* (New York, NY: Penguin Books, 2004, 2005), 171.
11. Carol R. Byerly, "The U.S. Military and the Influenza Pandemic of 1918–1919," *Public Health Reports* 125, supp. 3 (2010), 86.
12. See, for instance, John M. Barry, et al., "Cross-Protection between Successive Waves of the 1918–1919 Influenza Pandemic: Epidemiological Evidence from US Army Camps and from Britain," *Journal of Infectious Diseases* 198 (November 15, 2008), 1427–1434.
13. Paul Ewald, *Evolution of Infectious Disease* (New York, NY: Oxford University Press, 1994), 112–113.
14. Barry, *Great Influenza*, 187; Col. Deane C. Howard, "Influenza—U.S. Army," *Military Surgeon* 46 (1920), 526–527.
15. Barry, *Great Influenza*, 185.
16. Alfred W. Crosby, *America's Forgotten Pandemic: The Influenza of 1918*, 2nd ed. (New York, NY: Cambridge University Press, 2003), 6; Byerly, *Fever of War*, 54–60.
17. Byerly, *Fever of War*, 14.
18. U.S. Bureau of the Census, *Mortality Statistics 1918* (Washington, DC: Government Printing Office, 1920), 32.
19. Navy doctor's quote: Crosby, *America's Forgotten Pandemic*, 215–216. Army doctor's quote: Tom Quinn, *Flu: A Social History of Influenza* (London, UK: New Holland Publishers, 2008), 129; for full letter, see Document 2.
20. Barry, *Great Influenza*, 192, 200, 225.
21. Vincent C. Vaughan, cited in Jordan, *Epidemic Influenza*, 128.
22. George Soper, "The Influenza-Pneumonia Pandemic in the American Army Camps, September and October 1918," *Science* 48 no. 1245 (November 8, 1918), 454, 456.

23. Victor C. Vaughan, *A Doctor's Memories* (Indianapolis, IN: Bobbs-Merrill, 1926), 383–384.

24. Iezzoni, *Influenza 1918*, 121.

25. Barry, *Great Influenza*, 210–219.

26. Joe Capps, "Measures for the Prevention and Control of Respiratory Disease," *Journal of the American Medical Association* 71 no. 6 (August 10, 1918), 448–449.

27. Howard, "Influenza—U.S. Army," 531; Byerly, "U.S. Military and the Influenza Pandemic," 90.

28. Crosby, *America's Forgotten Pandemic*, 49; Edward M. Coffman, *The War to End All Wars: The American Military Experience in World War I* (New York, NY: Oxford University Press, 1968), 82.

29. David M. Kennedy, *Over Here: The First World War and American Society* (New York, NY: Oxford University Press, 1980) 169.

30. Ibid. 189.

31. William Still, "'Everybody Sick with the Flu'," *Naval History* 16 no. 2 (April 2002), 37.

32. Barry, *Great Influenza*, 306.

33. Crosby, *America's Forgotten Pandemic*, 125–135.

34. Ibid. 307–308.

35. Niall P. A. S. Johnson and Juergen Mueller, "Updating the Accounts: Global Mortality of the 1918–1920 'Spanish' Influenza Pandemic," *Bulletin of the History of Medicine* 76 (2002), 112.

36. Spellman, *Million Kisses*, 44–45.

37. Crosby, *America's Forgotten Pandemic*, 156–157.

38. Ibid. 162; Anne Frances Hardon, *43 bis* (privately printed, 1927), 313.

39. Crosby, *America's Forgotten Pandemic*, 166.

40. Byerly, *Fever of War*, 110.

41. Ibid. 109.

42. Ibid. 110–111; Kennedy, *Over Here*, 200–203.

43. Ronald Schaffer, *America in the Great War: The Rise of the War Welfare State* (New York, NY: Oxford University Press, 1991), 167.

44. Byerly, *Fever of War*, 117–118.

45. See, for instance, Crosby, *America's Forgotten Pandemic*, 160.

46. Ibid. 153; Howard, "Influenza—U.S. Army," 528–529.

47. Still, "'Everybody Sick with the Flu'," 36–39.

48. Byerly, "U.S. Military and the Influenza Pandemic," 83; Crosby, *America's Forgotten Pandemic*, 206.

49. Crosby, *America's Forgotten Pandemic*, 206

50. Flu deaths: Crosby, *America's Forgotten Pandemic*, 206. Other deaths: U.S. War Department (1919), cited in Byerly, *Fever of War*, 186. For slightly different figures, see Anne Leland and Mari-Jana Oboroceanu, "American War and Military Operations Casualties: Lists and Statistics" (Washington, DC: Congressional Research Service, February 26, 2010), 2.

CHAPTER 4

A Caregiver's Nightmare

Trying to Treat Influenza

Never again allow me to say that medical science is on the verge of conquering disease.

Vincent Vaughan, MD[1]

When the full force of the influenza epidemic hit New York City in September 1918, one of the many people whose lives it affected was Dorothy Deming, a student nurse at Presbyterian Hospital. Besides taking classes, Deming was assigned to a regular 12-hour stint on the night shift, where she and a fellow student were in charge of a female medical ward. The hours were long, but many of the patients were convalescing and the duties were not too heavy. Then suddenly, Deming recalls, "almost overnight, the hospital was inundated by flu victims." Immediately, nursing classes were suspended, vacations were canceled, the less critical patients were discharged, and extra beds were set up all over the hospital, even in the halls.[2]

Deming and her coworker found themselves in charge of more patients, and sicker patients, than ever before. Few of them could sit up, and nearly all required a high level of care. Furthermore, there was constant turnover on the ward. Some of it occurred when patients got well enough to go home, but all too frequently it was death, not discharges, that created the vacancies. "A night without a death became an exception," Deming recalls, "and our heart-breaking report one morning was seven deaths in eight hours."

The epidemic was transforming doctors' lives as well as nurses'. Instead of making regular afternoon rounds, the doctors now hurried in and out of the ward at all hours. "It was quite usual to see a haggard doctor come in long after midnight to make a last examination of his patient before staggering home to bed." The doctors prescribed a variety of medications and treatments, which the two student nurses duly administered. In addition, the young women fed and bathed their patients, monitored their conditions, sat up with them through the long nights, and comforted their families when they died.

Deming and her coworker (who was also named Dorothy) took pride in meeting this professional challenge. "Reassure them, ease them, help them, watch over them, carry out every order, and comfort them . . . This was nursing as I had dreamed of it," writes Deming. Even so, the emotional strain of dealing with so much suffering was sometimes hard to bear. "One dawn, after a particularly sad death," writes Deming, "I knew the tears I had been shedding inwardly must find outlet. I rushed to the linen closet, always our place of refuge, and there ahead of me, was Dorothy, sobbing her heart out."

While Deming and the rest of the staff were combating the epidemic in New York City, other doctors and nurses were fighting the same fight in homes and hospitals around the country, as well as in military facilities in the United States and overseas. Like Deming, these caregivers experienced the frustration of dealing with a disease for which there was no cure, but they threw themselves into the challenge with all the energy and skill they could muster. In order to understand what they were dealing with, let us start by looking more closely at the actual workings of the disease.

INFLUENZA UP CLOSE

No one has written more eloquently about coming down with flu than Katherine Anne Porter, who based her novella *Pale Horse, Pale Rider* on her own experience during the 1918 epidemic. As the story begins, the main character, Miranda, is waking up for the third day in a row with a "burning slow headache." She tries to pass it off as the result of too many late nights, but the symptoms keep piling up. She feels "odd," she has spells of lightheadedness, she is shaky on her feet, and the sun hurts her eyes. "There's something terribly wrong," she says to her boyfriend. "I feel too rotten. It can't just be the weather and the war."[3] Within a few days, she is desperately ill with influenza.

Other people had different initial symptoms from Porter's. Some began with a sore throat; others had muscle pains so acute that, as a doctor observed, "the patient feels as though he had been beaten all over with a club." For a young man named Franklin Martin, the first sign of illness was 24 hours of feeling cold all the time. Then his temperature started to climb, and by midnight, "I was so feverish I was afraid I would ignite the clothing." Meanwhile, he developed "a cough that tore my very innards out." By the next morning, says Martin, "I was some specimen of misery —couldn't breathe without an excruciating cough and there was no hope in me."[4]

However people's illnesses began, within a few days they were nearly all in a similar state: coughing and sneezing, weak and achy, and burning up with fever. It was a miserable condition to be in, but medically it was only a little worse than the familiar seasonal flu that came round every year. And if the patients did not develop complications, their illnesses tended to follow more or less the usual course. A young soldier described the experience as follows:

In 1918, Katherine Anne Porter was living in Denver, working as a reporter on the *Rocky Mountain News*, and going out with a young soldier. That fall, she came down with a severe case of influenza and spent many weeks in a delirious state, coming so close to death that the newspaper got her obituary ready to print. When she recovered, she learned that while she was ill, her soldier boyfriend had caught flu and died. In the years that followed, Porter established herself as a writer of fiction, but it was not until 1936 that she sat down and—in just nine days—wrote her famous short novel, *Pale Horse, Pale Rider*, based on her experience during the epidemic.[5]

It hits suddenly and one's temperature nearly chases the mercury out thru the top of the MD's thermometer, face gets red, every bone in the body aches and the head splits wide open. This continues for three or four days and then disappears after considerable perspiration, but the "hangover" clings for a week or two.[6]

If cases like these had happened one by one, or even 10 by 10, they would not have presented a significant problem for their communities. What changed them into a social crisis was the fact there were so many of them in so short a period of time. Influenza is always difficult to contain, because flu patients are at their most contagious before they show any symptoms of the disease. Furthermore, people can "carry" the flu virus and transmit it to others even though they never get sick themselves. For these reasons, it is extremely hard to identify and isolate the people who are spreading the disease. But however difficult it is to control influenza under normal circumstances, the situation in 1918 was much worse. The population movements associated with the war kept introducing the virus to new localities, and the particular viral strain that was circulating during the fall appears to have been unusually infectious. The speed with which the epidemic spread in 1918 is suggested by the fact that the United States had its first major outbreak of the epidemic's fall wave at Commonwealth Pier in Boston in early September 1918, and three weeks later sailors in Seattle were dying of the disease. At the same time, the epidemic was also racing across Europe, Asia, and Africa.

In the United States, it is estimated that approximately one out of every four people—a total of about 25 million—got the flu at some point during the epidemic, with the great majority falling sick between September and December 1918. These statistics are only approximations, however, because the country's national health records were extremely rudimentary at the time; 18 states did not even report mortality data to the federal government, and information on disease rates was even sketchier. Nevertheless, the institutions that did keep good records, such as the larger city health departments and the military, give us the flavor of what was happening. For instance, in Chicago the number of new cases of flu and flu-related pneumonia rose from about 350 during the last week of September 1918 to about 14,000 in the third week of October. As for the military, new cases among the nearly 2 million soldiers still based in the United States rose from about 12,000 a week in mid-September to more than 75,000 a week in mid-October.[7]

The unprecedented number of patients needing care would have been enough to make the epidemic a severe challenge in 1918, however mild the individual cases were. But this outbreak was also notable for the unusually large number of patients who started out with ordinary flu and then developed serious secondary infections—especially pneumonia. Often people would have just come through a bout of flu and be starting to feel better again, when suddenly their temperatures would skyrocket, and they would be back in bed, sicker than ever.

When pneumonia followed flu, it was usually because the flu virus had defeated the immune response in the patients' upper respiratory tracts, opening the way for pneumonia bacteria to move down into the lungs. The resulting "bacterial pneumonia" could make people desperately ill, and many people died of it. In fact, most historians attribute the majority of deaths during the epidemic to bacterial pneumonia. Furthermore, with the immune system not doing its job, patients were vulnerable to other infections as well. The author John Dos Passos wrote a friend after recovering from his own siege of illness: "I think I've had symptoms of all known diseases: pneumonia, T.B., diphtheria, diarrhea, dyspepsia, sore throat, whooping cough, scarlet fever and beriberi, whatever that is."[8]

Bouts of pneumonia could last for weeks, and when they were over, many patients had only the foggiest memory of the days that had passed. "Time was a blur," writes one patient. "I had no sense of day and night." Another says: "I think what happened was that I slept and slept and slept and slept."[9] But health workers observed that during these lost weeks, the disease often seemed to affect patients' minds as well as their bodies, causing violent outbursts, delusions, and hallucinations. Katherine Anne Porter is one of the few flu survivors to portray these mental disturbances from the inside. Some of the most remarkable passages in *Pale Horse, Pale Rider* are the ones describing Miranda's mental state during her illness—her confusion at hearing herself babble incoherently, her conviction that her doctor was a German spy, her sense of observing herself and everyone else from a great distance, and—most memorably—her recurrent vision of herself on horseback, desperately trying to outrun Death.[10]

As debilitating and disorienting as bacterial pneumonia could be, some patients in 1918 experienced an even more destructive secondary infection. This occurred when the flu virus itself entered the lungs, causing "viral pneumonia"—described by one doctor as "the most vicious type of pneumonia that has ever been seen."[11] With viral pneumonia, a person could be perfectly healthy in the morning, and by nightfall be weak and delirious and racked by coughing. As the patients' lungs filled up, simply coughing or changing position could make blood pour out of their noses and mouths. Meanwhile, in a process known as cyanosis, the patients' faces often turned blue from lack of oxygen—not a faint bluish tint, but, in the words of one observer, "as blue as huckleberries."[12]

One thing every observer remembered about this form of the disease was the speed with which it killed. In San Francisco, a woman spent the evening playing bridge at a friend's house. Everyone seemed to be fine. But by 8:00 the next morning, she writes, "I was too ill to get out of bed, and the friend at whose house we played was dead."[13] An insurance agent says: "The deaths were so sudden it was unbelievable. You would be talking to someone one day, and hear about his death the next day."[14]

The condition these patients were suffering from—in which the air sacs in the lungs fill with fluid so that they can no longer transmit oxygen to the bloodstream—is known today as acute respiratory distress syndrome, or ARDS. It can be caused by a variety of infections or injuries, and medical historians are still trying to understand exactly how influenza triggered ARDS in some patients in 1918.

One recent theory is that the immediate cause was not exactly the flu virus, but rather the immune system's overreaction to the virus. When someone gets an infection, the immune system launches a counterattack; indeed, many of the symptoms we associate with illness, such as coughing, runny nose, and fever, are really part of the immune system's effort to expel the invaders. The immune system is alerted to the need for this counterattack by molecules called cytokines. Ordinarily, the body shuts down the cytokines' activity once the danger is over, and then the immune response stops. But sometimes, especially if the invader is very aggressive, these controls fail and a "cytokine storm" breaks out. In these cases, the immune system keeps on destroying whatever it encounters, including the body's own cells. The result, especially in the case of lung infections, can be fatal. Is this what happened in 1918? Scholars are still not certain, but if it is, it would help explain why young adults—who have the strongest immune systems—were hit so hard by the epidemic.[15]

Only about 15 percent of all influenza deaths in 1918 were caused by viral pneumonia, but the results when they occurred were so shocking that they haunted the memories of everyone who witnessed them—the families who saw their loved ones sicken and die overnight, the health workers who tried in vain to save them, and the pathologists whose autopsies revealed lungs so damaged that they looked as if the patients had inhaled poison gas.

Taken all together, the incredibly fast spread of influenza in 1918, the large number of secondary infections, and the particularly grim effects of viral pneumonia made the epidemic a compelling challenge to all caregivers—especially those who had believed that the new scientific medicine was on its way to conquering all infectious disease.

NO TRIUMPH FOR SCIENCE

For America's medical leaders, the years leading up to 1918 had been a period of exhilarating progress. Many of these doctors were old enough to remember the exciting days in the late nineteenth century when the grand potential of the germ theory was first revealed to the world. In the years since then, they had seen tremendous advances in identifying and controlling infectious diseases. Perhaps scientific medicine was still better at diagnosing illness than at curing it, but there had been enough successes on both fronts to make the future conquest of all infectious disease seem like a real possibility.

Furthermore, after more or less cheering from the sidelines during the early days of the medical revolution, Americans were now in a position to play a more dominant role. The war had put severe constraints on the European research institutes that had led the way in the past, and the United States' own research capacities had improved a good deal since the early days. If, as America's medical leaders expected, scientific medicine was heading for a glorious future, it seemed certain that they themselves would have a place in the vanguard.

In 1916, a year before the United States entered World War I, a group of the country's leading physicians began planning the medical programs and resources that would be needed if America did enter the war. Interestingly, they focused primarily on treating disease, not combat injuries. That was because in past wars, disease had been the principal killer of American soldiers. During the Civil War, for instance, twice as many soldiers had died of disease as were killed in combat. The imbalance was even greater during the Spanish-American War, when there were six deaths from disease for every combat death. The planners knew that even familiar illnesses such as measles and mumps could take epidemic form when the military brought together large numbers of young men, especially when they included recruits from rural areas who had had little previous exposure to contagious diseases.

Once America entered the war in April 1917, military physicians periodically found themselves recommending disease-control measures that were overruled because they might obstruct the war effort. Nevertheless, they did succeed in getting soldiers vaccinated against a number of diseases, and the vigorous delousing procedures they instituted kept typhus to a remarkably low level. As we have noted, an epidemic of measles did sweep through the training camps during the fall of 1917, and no amount of moral or medical instruction seemed to stop the soldiers from contracting syphilis. But overall, as the United States approached the first anniversary of its entry into the war, the Medical Corps had good reason to take pride in the relative healthiness of U.S. soldiers, both at home and abroad.

And then came influenza. When the second wave hit the United States in the fall of 1918, some members of the public seemed certain that this scourge would succumb to modern medicine as so many other "killer diseases" had done in recent years. For instance, one newspaper editorialized: "There seems to be no occasion for special alarm or panic about the matter, for the disease is evidently one which the American medical profession is perfectly able to handle."[16]

But the doctors themselves were not so sure. Indeed, there was considerable debate among them at first about whether influenza was even the correct diagnosis for what they were seeing. Influenza is always tricky to diagnose, because its symptoms resemble those of several other diseases, including scarlet fever and meningitis. But the task was especially hard in 1918, when secondary complications such as viral pneumonia attacked patients far more viciously than was usual with influenza. William Welch, confronted with a ward full of sick and dying soldiers, could only exclaim to his colleagues that the disease "must be some new kind of infection or

In November 1918, two navy doctors established a research station on an island in Boston Harbor and brought in 62 naval prisoners who agreed to serve as human subjects in exchange for pardons. Over the next few weeks, doctors took mucus from patients who were sick with flu and put it up the volunteers' noses, into their eyes, and down their throats. The men spent time in close contact with flu patients, and inhaled as instructed while the patients coughed in their faces. But not one of these sailors became ill. Nor did the prisoners enrolled in a similar trial at Yerba Buena naval base in San Francisco. The failure of these experiments has never been entirely explained.[18]

plague."[17] Doctors did gradually come to agree that this was simply an unusually virulent form of influenza. But recognizing the disease was not nearly so important as stopping it, and how was that to be done?

According to the principles of scientific medicine, the first task was to identify the germ that was causing the disease. Some researchers set about narrowing the field of possibilities by trying to give healthy people influenza —injecting them with material from patients who already had the disease. The human guinea pigs in these trials were technically volunteers, but since nearly all of them were people in subordinate roles (such as soldiers and prisoners), medical ethicists today would surely raise questions about the experimental subjects' freedom to refuse. Ethics aside, the most puzzling thing about these experiments was that not one of them managed to pass influenza from a sick person to a healthy one.

Historians are still not sure why these experiments failed. It has been suggested that the researchers may have used faulty techniques, or perhaps the sick patients had already passed the contagious stage of their illness, or perhaps the recipients did develop "subclinical" cases of flu that showed no symptoms. All these are possibilities, but none has been confirmed.

Most researchers took the more classic approach used by pioneers such as Koch and Pasteur, which began by using laboratory analysis to identify the causative germ. Dozens and then hundreds of medical researchers threw themselves into this task. Thanks to the work of their predecessors, they knew how to search patient specimens under a microscope for the specific bacterium that was common to all cases of a given disease, how to strain the material through a porcelain filter so fine that it caught the bacteria like a sieve, how to grow bacteria in a culture, and how to use that culture to produce vaccines and antitoxins. But what these researchers did *not* know was that the crucial first step—identifying the key bacterium under a microscope—was going to be impossible for them, because influenza is not caused by a bacterium. It is caused by a virus, which is far too small to have been visible under the microscopes that were available in 1918.

Medical researchers of that era did sometimes use the term "virus" in speaking of disease-causing germs, but to them the word seems to have meant just a very small bacterium. They often spoke, for instance, of a "filterable virus," meaning a microorganism so small that it could slip through the porcelain filters that were used to strain out bacteria. But in their search for the cause of influenza, they were concentrating on the bacteria they caught with their filters, whereas the actual cause—the virus—was in the material that passed through them.

It will be remembered that during the last major flu pandemic, in the 1890s, a German scientist named Richard Pfeiffer reported finding a bacterium that he said caused influenza. In the years that followed, various researchers questioned that claim, but it was only in 1918 that scientists began testing large numbers of influenza patients for the presence of "Pfeiffer's bacillus." Their findings were not encouraging. Although investigators did find the bacillus quite often in their flu patients, not one of them found it in every case. And in some studies, the bacillus appeared in hardly any patients.

These findings did not necessarily mean that Pfeiffer was wrong; technical problems could explain some of the negative results. But as the months went by and not one experiment decisively confirmed Pfeiffer's theory, a general air of skepticism began to prevail. By October 1918, an editorial in the *Journal of the American Medical Association* spoke for most of the research community when it said, "The 'influence' in Influenza is still veiled in mystery."[19]

Despite these setbacks, the need for a medical response to the epidemic was so great that researchers began producing vaccines based on any and all bacteria—including Pfeiffer's—that might conceivably help protect people. Many investigators made great claims for the effectiveness of their vaccines, and because there were no established standards for testing those claims, dozens of different vaccines were administered to the public—18 different kinds in Illinois alone.[20] In many military camps, vaccinations were either required or so "strongly advised" that it amounted to the same thing. Civilians' participation was voluntary, but many of them, too, lined up for their shots (see Figure 4.1). In San Francisco, for instance, more than 30,000 residents came forward to be vaccinated.[21]

Unfortunately, as the data began to accumulate, it became clear that none of the current vaccines was offering consistent protection against influenza. Some officials insisted that they were worth continuing anyway, simply because of the reassurance they provided. In Chicago, for instance, the health commissioner argued that any intervention was better than none

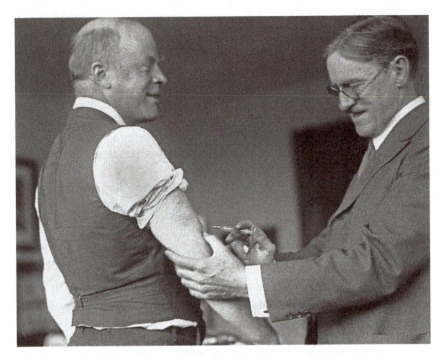

Figure 4.1 The mayor of Boston receives a flu shot—one of the many experimental vaccines that were tried out in 1918. © Bettmann/ CORBIS.

since "fear was getting aroused so that you could not keep the policemen on the wagons." Vaccines were good, he said, "because when I injected vaccine into those policemen they stayed on the job." In Philadelphia, a health official defended the use of vaccines because they "at least do no harm, and . . . possibly do good."[22]

Nevertheless, by early November the U.S. Public Health Service's journal, *Public Health Reports*, laid out a bleak analysis of the whole vaccine situation: "Despite exaggerated and in some respects misleading statements, the evidence that has been presented thus far does not warrant the reposing of confidence in any influenza vaccine."[23] Some preparations did seem to offer some protection against the bacterial infections that often accompanied flu, but this was far less than had been promised, and far less than was needed. The situation was clear: none of the vaccines developed so far was going to defeat the epidemic.

Nor was germ theory in general. In January 1919, a New York State health official wrote an article entitled "What We Really Know About the Epidemic." He started by listing the established facts: that the disease had invaded the country and was still not entirely gone; that it had an unprecedented mortality rate; that many of the associated deaths were caused by secondary infections; that it was particularly hard on young adults; that the only effective treatment seemed to be to go to bed and stay there; and that strict quarantine was often helpful. There was not a single additional theory, he concluded, no matter how eminent the authority who offered it, that had not been disproved by some other equally eminent authority.[24] In combating the influenza epidemic of 1918, the scientific revolution had met a very visible defeat.

But medicine had two roles to play during this difficult time. So while some doctors sought the key to defeating influenza in the laboratory, thousands of others were spending their days and nights in sickrooms and hospitals and camp infirmaries, trying to defeat the disease patient by patient.

In terms of medical care on the home front, the greatest problem was the simple fact that there were not enough qualified doctors to go around. Once the military had recruited almost 40,000 of the country's younger and better-trained doctors, civilian communities were left with far fewer than they had had before, and with a much higher percentage who were either aging or underqualified, or both.[25]

In January 1918—about eight months after the United States entered the war, and shortly before the flu epidemic began—the government established the Voluntary Medical Service Corps (VMSC), which was designed to function for the duration of the war as a reserve unit of civilian physicians. More than 70,000 doctors signed on, pledging to go anywhere in the United States that the Public Health Service might send them. When the second wave of the epidemic hit that fall and the need for civilian doctors escalated, Congress granted the agency an extra $1 million to finance the extra salaries, as well as to support various other flu-related activities. Unfortunately, when the Public Health Service tried to assign the VMSC members to duty in other parts of the country, most of them were already needed so badly where they were that they could not go anywhere else. In the end, about 1,000 VMSC physicians were sent to the highest-need areas, but that was all. The *Journal of the American Medical Association* advertised continually for doctors to help in underserved places, and medical students and even dentists were sometimes called in to lend a hand. But for the most part, the doctors in each community carried the burden as best they could.

Because many of these physicians had trained in an earlier time—and because in any case modern medicine had little to offer for this disease— they tended to dispense what they were accustomed to dispensing. A Georgia woman recalls: "No matter what you had, you got Dr. Clark's

Given the lack of effective medical treatments available for influenza in 1918, many Americans developed their own home remedies. These included: herbs, groundhog grease, onion poultices, mustard packs, turpentine fumes, smoke from burning straw, orange peel, camomile tea, and zinc painted on the inside of the nose.[27]

Medicine, and then you prayed for the best."[26] Most of the interventions these physicians recommended had been in use for generations: a light diet and fresh air, hot water bottles and warm milk, laxatives and towels soaked in hot vinegar, bed rest and good nursing. In addition, alcohol was widely prescribed, along with an astonishing range of narcotics, including heroin, codeine, cocaine, and morphine.

The better-trained physicians in the military seem to have had a somewhat lighter hand with narcotics, and they experimented with a wider variety of other medications. They also initiated many of the experimental vaccination programs undertaken during the epidemic. This was obviously more feasible for them than for civilian doctors because of the military hierarchy within which they operated. Military doctors were also in a stronger position to impose their treatment recommendations. So, for instance, throat sprays and gargles, which were dispensed to civilians in some cities, were administered by the carload to soldiers on both sides of the Atlantic (see Figure 3.1, p. 40).

Gradually, however, it became clear that none of these interventions was doing much good. For example, when a Philadelphia physician dutifully presented the list of available treatments to a group of medical students who were about to go out on house calls, it soon became clear, as one of the students later recalled, that "he had no confidence in any of the remedies."[28] At best, some doctors felt that some interventions made the patients more comfortable; others found various treatments to be helpful with some secondary infections. But nothing could touch viral pneumonia, and as for influenza itself, the U.S. Surgeon General put the matter succinctly on October 27, 1918: "There is as yet no specific cure for influenza." Moreover, he added, many of the common treatments "do more harm than good."[29]

How does it feel to be a trained provider of care when there is no effective care to provide? Imagine that you are a young army doctor. When you answered the call to service, you probably pictured yourself using the wonders of medical science to heal soldiers wounded in battle. But here you are, working around the clock in an overcrowded camp infirmary in Pennsylvania or Texas or Iowa, watching young soldiers cough their lives away without even leaving the country. Bitter for them! And profoundly frustrating for you, to be so helpless in the face of such a familiar illness! [*See camp physician's letter, Document 2.*]

Or imagine that you are an older physician on the home front, perhaps someone who reluctantly came out of retirement when half the doctors in town went off to join the military. Just resuming your old practice was a strain, and now that the epidemic has arrived, the burden is enormous. There are the hospital patients to visit, and then hours and hours of house calls. "I can still see the old doctor's face," recalls one flu survivor. "He made rounds all night long."[30] A New Jersey doctor says:

> There was no need to make appointments. You walked out of your office in the morning and people grabbed you as you walked down the street. You just kept going from one patient to another until late in the evening.[31]

It is one thing to wear yourself out performing a useful service; it is quite another to work just as hectically and question whether you are doing any good. Recalling his endless house calls during the epidemic, one doctor said gloomily: "The main thing about visiting every day was to find out who was dead, and then bury them." Another commented: "One almost came to the conclusion that our struggle against the epidemic [was] futile."[32] Nevertheless, the doctors soldiered on. One discovered he could save time if he rode on the running board of a friend's car, and jumped off at each house. Another limited his sleep to the hasty naps he could catch as his buggy drove from one house to the next.[33] They worked tirelessly, and they were certainly in demand, but few of them took much satisfaction in what they were accomplishing. A leading Los Angeles physician probably spoke for many of his medical colleagues when he said: "I think of the days of our epidemic as one long nightmare."[34]

HOLDING DEATH AT BAY

Throughout the epidemic, one group of health workers was in even greater demand than doctors, and that was nurses. When a hard-pressed hospital in Maine wrote the U.S. Public Health Service to ask for extra staff, the regional director wired him back: "Can send all the Doctors you want, but not one nurse."[35] In fact, as we have seen, extra doctors were not so easy to come by either, but nurses were valued most highly of all. The truth was that in the absence of a medical breakthrough, about the most useful service anyone could offer was the supportive care that nurses specialized in providing—keeping the patients warm, feeding them and

The Nurse: Inventing the Angel of Mercy

Until well into the nineteenth century, nursing was seen as a low-level branch of domestic service. The transition to higher public regard began in 1854 during the Crimean War, when an Englishwoman, Florence Nightingale (1820–1910), traveled to Turkey with a corps of 38 volunteer nurses, and organized changes in the army medical services that dramatically improved the care being provided to wounded British soldiers. She had originally assumed that better nutrition and more medical supplies would make the greatest difference to the soldiers' recovery, but her experience in the Crimea convinced her that sanitation, fresh air, and dedicated nursing were far more important.

Returning to England a media celebrity because of her service to the soldiers, Nightingale articulated her new philosophy in a book, *Notes on Nursing*, and in 1860 she put her ideas into practice when she founded the world's first professional nursing school at St. Thomas' Hospital in London. Within a few years, Nightingale's visionary eloquence began to reshape public ideas about the value of nursing and the importance of cleanliness and good ventilation in hospitals.[36]

Nightingale's approach took root in the United States in 1873 at Bellevue Hospital, when a group of New York City society women founded the first American nursing school organized around Nightingale's principles. Like Dorothy Deming, the Bellevue students learned nursing by doing it, working on the wards 12 hours a day, six days a week, with lectures and homework squeezed into their off-duty hours. The tasks they performed were nearly the same as those performed by their low-status predecessors, but the Nightingale style of training infused the work with new meaning, giving cleanliness, order, and fresh air an almost sacred significance. The new approach to nursing spread like wildfire, and by 1910 there were more than 1,000 Nightingale-inspired training schools across the United States. And in the process, the angel of mercy replaced the drunken harridan as the archetypal nurse.[37]

Once the young women completed their training, a few of the best graduates became hospital supervisors, managing the nursing services and overseeing the next generation of students. Most of the rest of the graduates went into private duty, providing individual care to middle- and upper-class patients. In addition, some graduates became public health nurses, serving primarily poor and working-class patients.

This was an era when career women were still regarded with some ambivalence, but the nursing profession managed to escape that categorization because of its strong identification with "feminine" virtues such as order, nurture, and self-sacrifice. For their part, women had good reason to choose this profession. Their wages were low, and their independence hedged about with the need to defer to physicians, hospital managers, and private patients. But as Barbara Melosh has observed, "few other occupations in the early 20th century could provide young women with a comparable experience of female autonomy."[38]

bathing them, giving them plenty of fluids, making them comfortable, and treating them kindly.

When the United States entered World War I, the American Red Cross was designated to recruit the thousands of nurses who would be needed for military service. Primary responsibility for this task fell on Clara Noyes, a former nursing supervisor who was now director of the Red Cross Bureau of Nursing. Noyes found herself balancing two priorities. On the one hand, she needed to recruit as many workers as possible. But on the other hand, she and her fellow nursing leaders were convinced that if they allowed the ranks to be filled with inexperienced amateurs, it would undermine the quality of the care provided and devalue the professional image of nursing that they had worked so hard to establish. Accordingly, the Red Cross limited eligibility for military service to graduate nurses who were unmarried, ages 25 to 35, and who had trained in hospitals with at least 50 beds. Trained nurses who did not meet these criteria could enroll as "Home Defense Nurses" and be available for civilian service.[39]

In August 1918, with America's intensive involvement in the fighting about to begin, the Army Surgeon General began shipping large numbers of nurses to Europe, and requesting more and more replacements from the Red Cross. In response, the Red Cross put increasing pressure on stateside nurses to leave their jobs and join the military. One recruiter wrote on September 5 that they were searching "from one end of the United States to the other to rout out every possible nurse from her hiding place . . . There will be no nurses left in civil life if we keep on at this rate." In the end, the Red Cross managed to recruit 24,000 young women for the Army Nurse Corps.[40] There were never quite enough of them to meet the need, but they provided invaluable service in military camps around the country, as well as in the 50 base hospitals that the Red Cross helped support in Europe.

At first, it seemed that the nurses sent overseas were getting all the drama. At the front, as one of them poetically wrote home, "we can hear the artillery talk, the shells sing overhead and the sky one mass of bright light."[41] But once the influenza epidemic struck with full force in the fall of 1918, nurses faced plenty of challenges no matter where they were based. One woman assigned to a military hospital in New England wrote to the *American Journal of Nursing* describing how gallantly the nurses there had been carrying on. She praised their dedication, noted their killing work schedules, and concluded: "I do not believe any hospital in France had anything on this hospital during the last two weeks."[42]

On the civilian side, the Red Cross assigned its Home Defense nurses as needed to local hospitals and defense plants. In addition, 200 public health nurses were sent to cover the "Extra-Cantonment Zones"—the

The American Red Cross: Help in Peace and War[43]

In 1862, a Swiss businessman named Jean-Henri Dunant (1828–1910) wrote *A Memory of Solférino*, in which he described the horrors he had witnessed at the recent Battle of Solférino. To improve battlefront conditions in the future, he called for the creation of national organizations dedicated to nursing wounded soldiers, as well as an international treaty to protect the caregivers. Dunant's book led to a flurry of international activity, and in 1864, representatives from 16 countries met in Switzerland to draw up the first Geneva Convention "for the Amelioration of the Condition of the Wounded in Armies in the Field." The red cross was adopted as a symbol of the movement, and within the next few years, nearly every country in Europe formed a national Red Cross society and signed on to the Geneva Convention.

The Red Cross movement soon caught the attention of an American woman named Clara Barton (1821–1912). Barton had first won public recognition during the Civil War, when her exemplary performance as a nurse earned her the title of the "Angel of the Battlefield." She became interested in the Red Cross when she was traveling in Europe in 1869, and after serving with the organization as a volunteer during the Franco-Prussian War (1870), she spent the next decade advocating for the United States to join the Red Cross movement. At last, in 1881, she and a circle of friends formed the American Association of the Red Cross (later, the American Red Cross), and in 1882 the United States signed on to the Geneva Convention.

At that time, the International Red Cross focused almost exclusively on wartime service. The American Red Cross did serve at the battlefront during the Spanish-American War (1898), sending staff to Cuba to care for soldiers, prisoners of war, and civilian refugees. But well before that, Barton had concluded that the organization should also be serving the country during peacetime. Indeed, the first relief effort of the American Red Cross—responding to a Michigan forest fire—was undertaken just three weeks after the organization was incorporated. In the years that followed, the Red Cross provided assistance to the survivors of many disasters, including the Johnstown, Pennsylvania, flood (1889) and the Galveston, Texas, tidal wave (1900). There was some dissension within the International Red Cross about whether the organization should move in this direction, but at the Geneva conference of 1884, Barton (the only female delegate) advocated her view with such eloquence that the "American amendment" was passed, adding disaster relief to the organizational mission.

Barton led the American Red Cross for 23 years. Unfortunately, over time her personalized management style proved less effective in directing what had become a very large organization. In 1904, with rising public questions about the agency's tangled finances, and in the face of an impending congressional investigation, Barton resigned. She died eight years later, at the age of 91. The Red Cross surmounted its difficulties, and during the years that followed it expanded its disaster relief work, while also establishing nationwide programs for teaching first aid, home nursing, and water safety. Thus, by the time the United States entered World War I, the organization was well positioned to assume new responsibilities, including recruiting military nurses, supporting U.S. military hospitals in Europe, and organizing a vast network of volunteers on the home front.

communities surrounding the nation's 39 military camps. Leaders of the Public Health Service chose these areas for extra assistance because they wanted to control any infectious diseases that might develop there and then spread to the training camps. The primary goal, clearly, was to protect the soldiers' well-being, not the civilians'. Nevertheless, the program brought benefits such as well-baby clinics, school nursing, and sanitation improvements to many communities that needed them.[44]

Once the second wave of the influenza epidemic took off in the fall of 1918, the Red Cross intensified its attention to nursing on the home front. After a meeting of the organization's National Committee in late September, Clara Noyes wired all divisions, instructing them to "organize Home Defense nurses . . . to meet the present epidemic."[45] In Washington, a National Committee on Influenza was established, with representatives from the government and all major Red Cross divisions. Within each state, Red Cross officials were instructed to cooperate with state health officials and local staff from the U.S. Public Health Service.[46] Thus, planning was already well underway by October 1, when Rupert Blue, the head of the U.S. Public Health Service, wired the Red Cross asking it to "assume charge of supplying all the needed nursing personnel" for the emergency, and also requesting it to provide extra funds and supplies for communities that needed them.[47]

Over the next several months, the Red Cross raised more than $2 million for salaries, hospital equipment, and supplies. It also collaborated closely with local leaders to coordinate emergency services. Above all, it worked to expand its roster of Home Defense nurses. Civilian communities were already underserved, because so many of their nurses had left for the military, and once the epidemic began, the shortages became desperate. Leaning heavily on the themes of duty and service, the Red Cross published half-page ads in local newspapers, calling on "all patriotic available nurses"—or those with any training at all—to come forward.[48] The *American Journal of Nursing* sounded the same theme, stating: "Nurses must not forget that they are citizens."[49]

Even before the epidemic hit, the continual demand for more nurses had led the Red Cross to reconsider its policies regarding African-American applicants. There was nothing in the rules for the Army Nurse Corps that explicitly excluded them, but some of the admission criteria were extremely hard for them to meet. For example, the requirement that military nurses had to have trained in large hospitals was an obstacle, because the few training opportunities available to African-Americans were in segregated facilities, which tended to be small. After tireless advocacy by Adah G. Thoms, head of the predominantly black Lincoln Nursing School in New York City, the Red Cross agreed in February 1918 to remove some of the roadblocks, and five months later African-American nurses were officially invited to apply. But then a new obstacle arose: the Army Nurse Corps insisted that these women could not possibly share sleeping and eating quarters with white nurses. Constructing separate facilities took so long that no African-American nurses were accepted into the Army Nurse Corps until December 1918, a month after the war ended.[50]

Even so, some African-American nurses did get a chance to care for soldiers, because when influenza decimated the ranks of military nurses, half a dozen training camps hired civilian Red Cross nurses—including some African-Americans—to fill the gap. In fact, camp superintendents sometimes sought out black nurses when there were black soldiers to be cared for—as there often were, since they constituted about 10 percent of U.S. troops. In addition, African-American nurses served in a number of civilian communities. One of them left a lively account of caring for a black family in Greenwood, Mississippi. Having seen immediately that this devastated household needed much more than medical attention, she said, "I rolled up my sleeves and killed chickens and began to cook. I forgot I was not a cook, but I only thought of saving lives. I milked the cow, gave medicine, and did everything I could to help."[51]

Military or civilian, black or white, one threat hung over all nurses during the epidemic: the possibility of catching influenza themselves. These young women were especially vulnerable, since they belonged to the most susceptible age group, spent their days surrounded by infectious patients, and often sapped their resistance with overwork. "The flu is back again," wrote one nurse, "and everybody has it, including me. I've run a temperature of 102 for three days, can hardly breathe."[52] And so it was throughout the ranks of nurses. Overseas, it was even easier to get sick, thanks to the crowded quarters and the endless chilly rain. One nurse wrote home from France: "There isn't any way to take care of yourself here. The beds are about two feet apart and it's as cold as Greenland."[53]

No one knows precisely how many American nurses caught the flu, or how many died of it, but the numbers from individual locations suggest the scale of the problem. For instance, at just one base hospital in France, 12 nurses died in a single month.[54] In one San Francisco hospital, three out of every four nurses caught the disease.[55] The proportion was the same at Camp Cody in New Mexico, where 75 out of the camp's 100 nurses came down with influenza, and five of them died.[56] Toward the end of 1918, a nursing leader commented: "In no previous epidemic has the mortality and morbidity of nurses been so great."[57]

Doctors, too, were hit hard by influenza. For those who survived, the loss of so many colleagues was simply the final blow in a sequence of events that had shaken their certainty and undermined their professional pride. After a medical conference in December 1918, one of the participants summed up the sense of the meeting:

> It was freely confessed by all that we are at sea as to the proper methods of treatment, cure and prevention; that we do not know as yet how to prevent and control the spread of the disease, and that most of the methods employed in fighting it, though pronounced efficacious by some of their adherents, have been held of little value by others.[58]

Earlier in the century, many physicians had personally identified with the grand possibilities of scientific medicine. Now in 1918, they felt personally defeated by their inability to control influenza. "The saddest part of my life," wrote one military doctor, "was when I witnessed the hundreds of deaths of the soldiers in the army camps and did not know what to do."[59] Perhaps it is no wonder that in later years, when these same doctors sat down to write memoirs and histories of the 1918 period, they scarcely mentioned the topic that had monopolized so much of their attention at the time: the influenza epidemic. After all, what was there to commemorate in such an unsatisfying experience? Why linger over a health crisis about which, as one doctor observed, "There was just nothing you could do."[60]

Now here is the puzzle. American nurses dealt with the same epidemic, the same staff shortages, the same terrible scenes of suffering, and the same incapacity to cure. Yet as a group, nurses had far more positive memories of the experience than doctors did. The explanation seems to be that in line with their training, these women placed their primary emphasis not on curing every patient, but on caring for them. And because that was their focus, then indeed there *was* something they could do for influenza. [See an account of community nursing in Chicago, Document 7.]

Some nurses remembered the whole epidemic as a nightmare, but more typical was the woman who described it as "a most horrible and yet most beautiful experience." The beauty, as the nurses perceived it, lay in the fact that they had been able to help their fellow citizens get through a terrible time. "Can you imagine what it meant to those people," wrote one nurse, "to have a capable, willing woman appear suddenly in their midst, and without any preliminaries set to work and make them comfortable?"[61] Another struck the same note: "As we look back over the past five weeks, which we would not like to live over again, we are thankful for good health, so that we could help these people in their time of need."[62] Thus, while physicians agonized over their failure to achieve their own professional goals, nurses were able to take satisfaction in having fulfilled theirs.

As historian Nancy Tomes has pointed out, the standards that doctors and nurses set for themselves were reinforced by what the public expected of them. In terms of the doctors' performance, a *New York Times* editorial in late 1918 observed: "When the history of this influenza epidemic comes to be written, it will not reflect much glory on medical science, or . . . on the doctors in whom medical science is embodied."[63] Most Americans seemed to be more forgiving of the profession than the *New York Times* was. In general, people appreciated the personal dedication that doctors had shown during the epidemic, and offered little criticism of them as individuals. Nevertheless, the impression did linger that modern medicine had not lived up to its promises.

Nurses, on the other hand, were not expected to accomplish scientific miracles, so what they did contribute was hugely appreciated. The Philadelphia Commissioner of Health said it all, when he explained that to get through the epidemic, a city needed just three things: "Nurses, more nurses, and yet more nurses."[64] Influenced partly by Florence Nightingale's compelling vision of the profession, and partly by even older ideas about women's function in the world, the public looked to nurses for nurture, not mastery. And measured on that scale, their performance during the epidemic had not only met, but surpassed public expectations.

★   ★   ★

As we can see in the contrasting experiences of doctors and nurses, the 1918 epidemic had different meanings for different people. Depending on who you were and how you encountered the epidemic, it could represent a professional challenge or an opportunity to serve, a short bout of illness or a death-dealing blow, a scientific puzzle or a punishment from God, a source of fear and suspicion or a spur to cooperation. We have already discussed the epidemic's impact on American soldiers, and this chapter has explored what it meant to doctors and nurses. Next, we will examine how the epidemic affected community life on the home front.

NOTES

1. Cited in John M. Barry, *The Great Influenza: The Story of the Deadliest Pandemic in History* (New York, NY: Penguin Books, 2004, 2005), 403.
2. This five-paragraph section is based on: Dorothy Deming, "Influenza—1918: Reliving the Great Epidemic," *American Journal of Nursing* 57 no. 10 (October 1957). 1308–1309.
3. Katherine Anne Porter, *Pale Horse, Pale Rider* (New York, NY: Harcourt Brace, 1939), 148, 158, 159.
4. Bristow, *American Pandemic*, 45–46.
5. Nancy K. Bristow, *American Pandemic: The Lost Worlds of the 1918 Influenza Epidemic* (New York, NY: Oxford University Press, 2012), 180; David A. Davis, "Forgotten Apocalypse: Katherine Anne Porter's 'Pale Horse, Pale Rider,' Traumatic Memory, and the Influenza Pandemic of 1918," *Southern Literary Journal* 43 no. 2 (Spring 2011), 57.
6. Edward M. Coffman, *The War to End All Wars: The American Military Experience in World War I* (New York, NY: Oxford University Press, 1968), 81.
7. Paul Buelow, "Chicago," in Fred R. van Hartesveldt, Ed., *The 1918–1919 Pandemic of Influenza: The Urban Impact in the Western World* (Lewiston, NY: Edwin Mellen Press, 1992), 127; Col. Deane C. Howard, "Influenza—U.S. Army," *Military Surgeon* 46 (1920), 525.
8. Cited in Dorothy A. Pettit and Janice Bailie, *A Cruel Wind: Pandemic Flu in America 1918–1920* (Murfreesboro, TN: Timberlane Books, 2008), 145.
9. Bristow, *American Pandemic*, 47; Lynette Iezzoni, *Influenza 1918: The Worst Epidemic in American History* (New York, NY: TV Books, 1999), 100.
10. Porter, *Pale Horse, Pale Rider*, 142–143, 182–183, 197–200.
11. Carol Byerly, *Fever of War: The Influenza Epidemic in the U.S. Army During World War I* (New York, NY: New York University Press, 2005), 78.
12. Iezzoni, *Influenza 1918*, 89.
13. Iezzoni, *Influenza 1918*, 51.
14. Stuart Galishoff, "Newark and the Great Influenza Pandemic," *Bulletin of the History of Medicine* 43 no. 3 (May/June 1969), 247.
15. See, for instance, Barry, *Great Influenza*, 246–251.
16. Nancy K. Bristow, "'You Can't Do Anything for Influenza': Doctors, Nurses and the Power of Gender During the Influenza Pandemic in the United States," in Howard Phillips and David Killingray, Eds., *The Spanish Influenza Pandemic of 1918–1919: New Perspectives* (New York, NY: Routledge, 2003), 60.
17. Carol R. Byerly, "The U.S. Military and the Influenza Pandemic of 1918–1919," *Public Health Reports* 125, supp. 3 (2010), 86.
18. Gina Kolata, *Flu: The Story of the Great Influenza Pandemic of 1918 and the Search for the Virus That Caused It* (New York, NY: Simon & Schuster, 1999, 2005), 55–60. See also Myla Goldberg, *Wickett's Remedy: A Novel* (New York, NY: Anchor Books, 2006), which is based on these experiments.
19. "The Influenza Outbreak" (Editorial), *Journal of the American Medical Association* 71 no. 14 (October 5, 1918), 1138.
20. Barry, *Great Influenza*, 358.
21. Bristow, *American Pandemic*, 97.

22. Ibid. 98, 99.
23. "Vaccines Against Influenza," *Public Health Reports* 33 no. 44 (November 1, 1918), 1866.
24. Matthias Nicoll, Jr., "What We Really Know About the Epidemic," *American Journal of Public Health* 19 no. 1 (January 1919), 43–44.
25. Barry, *Great Influenza*, 139–141, 143.
26. Iezzoni, *Influenza 1918*, 88.
27. Ibid. 73–74, 119; Rebecca Bailey, "Matewan Before the Massacre: Politics, Coal, and the Roots of Conflict in Mingo County, 1793–1920," (Ph.D. dissertation, West Virginia University, 2001), 370; Quinn, *Social History of Influenza*, 141–142.
28. Barry, *Great Influenza*, 226.
29. "Beware of 'Sure Cures'," *New York Times* (October 27, 1918).
30. Teri Shors and Susan H. McFadden, "1918 Influenza: A Winnebago County, Wisconsin Perspective," *Clinical Medicine & Research* 7 no. 4 (December 1, 2009), 154.
31. Galishoff, "Newark and the Great Influenza Pandemic," 252.
32. Bristow, "'You Can't Do Anything for Influenza'," in Phillips and Killngray, *Spanish Influenza Pandemic*, 61.
33. Iezzoni, *Influenza 1918*, 114.
34. Oscar Dowling, "The Present Status of Public Health Administration," *American Journal of Public Health* 9 no. 4 (April 1919), 255.
35. Crosby, *America's Forgotten Pandemic*, 51.
36. Mark Bostridge, *Florence Nightingale: The Making of an Icon* (New York, NY: Farrar, Straus, & Giroux, 2008).
37. Much of the material in this and the following two paragraphs appeared in slightly different form in Sandra Opdycke, *No One Was Turned Away: The Role of Public Hospitals in New York City Since 1900* (New York, NY: Oxford University Press, 1999), 38–39.
38. Barbara Melosh, *The Physician's Hand: World, Culture and Conflict in American Nursing* (Philadelphia, PA: Temple University Press, 1982), 66.
39. Arlene W. Keeling, "'Alert to the Necessities of Emergency': U.S. Nursing During the 1918 Influenza Pandemic," *Public Health Reports* 125, supp. 3 (2010), 107; Barry, *Great Influenza*, 142–143.
40. Barry, *Great Influenza*, 320; Marian Jones, "The American Red Cross and Local Response to the 1918 Influenza Pandemic: A Four-City Case Study," *Public Health Reports* 125, supp. 3 (2010), 95.
41. Josephine Gillis to Carrie Brink (October 19, 1918), Folder: Base Hospital #1, Bellevue Hospital Archives, New York, NY.
42. Cited in "Editorial Comment: The Epidemic of Influenza," *American Journal of Nursing* 19 no. 2 (November 1918), 85.
43. American Red Cross, "A Brief History of the American Red Cross," available at www.redcross.org/about-us/history (accessed August 19, 2013); International Committee of the Red Cross, "The ICRC: Founding and Early Years," available at www.icrc.org/eng/who-we-are/history/founding/index.jsp (accessed August 19, 2013). See also: Elizabeth Brown Pryor, *Clara Barton: Professional Angel* (Philadelphia, PA: University of Pennsylvania Press, 1987).

44. Mary E. Lent, "Public Health Nursing in the Extra-Cantonment Zone," *American Journal of Public Health* 9 no. 3 (March 1919), 193–195.

45. Keeling, "'Alert to the Necessities'," 108.

46. Crosby, *America's Forgotten Pandemic*, 51.

47. Jones, "American Red Cross and Local Response," 93.

48. Barry, *Great Influenza*, 339.

49. "Red Cross Membership," *American Journal of Nursing* 19 no. 2 (November 1918), 86.

50. Mary Elizabeth Carnegie, *The Path We Trod: Black Nursing, 1854–1984* (Philadelphia, PA: Lippincott, 1986), 163–164.

51. Keeling, "'Alert to the Necessities'," 111.

52. Pettit and Bailie, *Cruel Wind*, 70.

53. Anne Frances Hardon, *43 bis* (privately printed, 1927), 313.

54. Mary T. Sarnecky, *A History of the U.S. Army Nurse Corps* (Philadelphia, PA: University of Pennsylvania Press, 1999), 121.

55. Rosemary Stevens, *In Sickness and in Wealth: American Hospitals in the Twentieth Century* (New York, NY: 1989), 102.

56. Keeling, "'Alert to the Necessities'," 108.

57. Edna L. Foley, "Department of Public Health Nursing: Illinois, "*American Journal of Nursing* 19 no. 3 (December 1918), 191. See full report in Document 7.

58. Cited by Bristow in "'You Can't Do Anything for Influenza'," in Phillips and Killingray, *Spanish Epidemic*, 61.

59. Janice Hume, "The 'Forgotten' 1918 Influenza Epidemic and Press Portrayal of Public Anxiety," *Journalism and Mass Communication Quarterly* 77 no. 4 (Winter 2000), 905.

60. Bristow, "'You Can't Do Anything for Influenza'," in Phillips and Killingray, *Spanish Epidemic*, 61.

61. Ibid. 63, 64.

62. Elizabeth J. Davies, "The Influenza Epidemic and How We Tried to Control It." *Public Health Nurse* 11 no. 1 (1919), 47.

63. Bristow "'You Can't Do Anything for Influenza'," in Phillips and Killingray, *Spanish Epidemic*, 66.

64. Keeling, "'Alert to the Necessities'," 110.

CHAPTER 5

Communities on Their Own

The Civilian Experience

No amount of forethought . . . could have prepared us for the
tidal wave of disease and death that all but overwhelmed the city.
Public official, Richmond, Virginia[1]

"Shall I tell you about how we took care of the influenza in a logging camp in the deep woods of northern Michigan?" This is how Anne Colon, a public health nurse, begins a description of her experience battling influenza in 1918. Originally, she admits, she and her neighbors in the town of Newberry, in Michigan's Upper Peninsula, assumed that they were safely beyond the epidemic's reach. "We read about the big cities, the suffering, and the many deaths, but still sat back, so fearless were we, and so sure of our wonderful healthy climate." They soon realized, however, that even their own pristine region was vulnerable to the epidemic. So when word came that a logging camp deep in the forest had been struck by influenza, Colon and her boss, the county Health Officer, set out in his "Ford machine" to see if they could help.[2]

"I shall never forget the conditions we found," Colon writes. "Influenza was traveling like wildfire through the little huts. There was confusion, suffering, and terror everywhere." In cabin after cabin, the sick and the well could be seen huddled listlessly together in the family's only bed, a roaring fire in the stove, the windows nailed shut, and everyone breathing the same germ-laden air. What could Colon do to help? As we know from Chapter 4, medical science had relatively little to offer. But anyone could see these families needed basic nursing care, and that she could provide. In addition, in hopes of slowing the spread of infection, Colon persuaded the loggers to improve the ventilation in their cabins by unsealing the windows, and she made extra mattresses out of rough cloth and straw, so the sick and the well could sleep in different beds.

Beyond the specific tasks she performed, Colon tried to give the families a psychological boost, simply by showing that there was someone ready and willing to help them in this desperate time. Throughout the weeks that followed, she made regular trips to the camp, and she trained several of the loggers' wives to do the nursing between her visits. After the epidemic was over, she was proud to note that although the camp had had nearly 50 cases of flu, only one person had died. She could not be sure—and neither can we—whether her presence had helped to save lives. But it is clear that she contributed everything she could.

In the fall of 1918, Americans everywhere were facing the same epidemic that hit this Michigan logging camp. Some were suffering from influenza themselves. Others were caring for those who had been stricken. Still others were trying to resolve staffing shortages and funding problems and public policy issues. But whatever their roles, certain aspects of Colon's experience at the logging camp resonated with their own—the ferocity of the disease, the inability of medical science to cure it, and the challenges involved in trying to get through the epidemic with the means at hand.

For decades after 1918, these local struggles were nearly forgotten. In fact, even when interest in the overall subject of the epidemic revived during the late twentieth century, the story of the community response was often overshadowed by horror tales about the effects of the disease and dramatic accounts of physicians' efforts to combat it. Yet the story of how American communities organized themselves in the midst of a war to deal with the flu epidemic has a drama of its own, and is well worth remembering.

LIFE AND DEATH ON THE HOME FRONT

In the United States, the first major outbreak of the epidemic's virulent fall wave occurred in Boston in early September 1918. By the end of the month, influenza had swept through New England and the Mid-Atlantic states. From there, it raced across the country, and by early October, hardly a corner of the United States was left untouched.

Within individual regions, the epidemic tended to spread outward from the cities into more rural areas. As for what brought flu to each region in the first place, troop movements were, as we have noted, a major factor. An Illinois resident observed: "My first intimation about the epidemic was that it was something happening to the troops . . . And yet in a gradual remorseless way it kept moving closer and closer."[3] We have already discussed how sailors from Boston brought the virus to training stations near Philadelphia, Chicago, and Seattle. This pattern continued throughout the fall. Again and again, when you study how the epidemic began in a particular city, you find that it reached a nearby military base first.

Here is one example. Richmond, Virginia, was still free of influenza on September 14, when the first case of flu appeared 25 miles away, among the 60,000 soldiers at Camp Lee. Although thousands of these soldiers came down with the disease and large numbers of them died, military officials chose not to put the camp under quarantine. Municipal authorities in Richmond debated establishing a quarantine of their own to keep the soldiers out of town, but they decided against it. So men from the base continued to move in and out of the city, and on September 29, Richmond had its first civilian case of flu. Within the next few months, more than 1,000 city residents would die of influenza and pneumonia.[4]

Richmond's leaders were not alone in their reluctance to take prompt action against the epidemic; large numbers of American officials chose the same path. Besides the usual desire to keep the local economy going, many of these leaders were convinced that acknowledging the seriousness of the danger might undermine public morale, which in turn could weaken the war effort. This conviction, as we have seen, went all the way up the line to President Woodrow Wilson, who discouraged any public discussion of the epidemic at all.

And so, motivated in part by military priorities, in part by community pride, in part by economic considerations, and perhaps in part by simple self-delusion, local officials tended to work their way through three consecutive stages of explaining away the danger facing their communities: (1) the epidemic will not reach our city; (2) the epidemic has reached our city, but it is not serious; and (3) the epidemic was serious, but we have turned the corner and things are now getting better. [*See interview with a Nashville health official, Document 5.*] Obviously, the credibility of these statements was weakened by the continual shifting of ground. When, as the *New York Times* observed, "the guardians of our ports at first told us that there was no danger of an epidemic here, and a little later admitted that there was not a danger but a certainty of it,"[5] it necessarily made the officials' efforts to reassure the public less convincing.

The media played their own role in the chorus of mixed messages. To understand the context, we need to remember how few sources there were in 1918 for daily national news—no Internet, no TV, no commercial radio, no *USA Today*. And although the *New York Times* and the *Wall Street Journal* both existed, neither one had yet developed much of a presence on the national scene. There were many popular weekly and monthly magazines, but they provided only minimal coverage of the epidemic. So to learn what was happening, Americans were almost entirely dependent on their local newspapers.

And what did they learn from them? On the one hand, these papers dutifully published—and often echoed in their editorials and medical advice columns—the reassuring statements of local officials. But they also printed a considerable amount of material that made it clear the disease was more serious than these reassurances suggested. Most papers published at least some brief news items about the frightening progress of the epidemic around the country, and nearly all reprinted the U.S. Public Health Service's detailed instructions on how to avoid influenza and what to do if you caught it. In addition, there was a blizzard of ads from patent-medicine manufacturers about pills and potions designed to keep the disease at bay, plus a lengthy list of obituaries that documented the local death toll.

Of course, for most Americans, the clearest proof that the epidemic was more serious than they were being told was the evidence of their own eyes. In Joliet, Illinois, a local nurse observed that the whole town had been "plunged suddenly into an acute and fearful influenza epidemic."[6] From Berlin, New Hampshire, another reported: "It is hardly possible for me to describe the conditions in this community . . . Saturday I cared for forty patients, from four to nine sick in one family."[7] A Public Health Service staffer described El Paso, Texas, as a "whole city in a panic."[8] With this kind of upheaval throughout the country, no amount of official reassurance was likely to convince people that the epidemic they were facing was just "old-fashioned grippe."

Urban immigrant neighborhoods suffered greatly during the epidemic, and Native American communities were hit particularly hard. On the other hand, for reasons that historians are still trying to understand, African-Americans seem to have had relatively low rates of infection. One letter writer to the *Chicago Defender* put it this way: "As far as the 'Flu' is concerned, the whites have the whole big show to themselves." Many thousands of African-Americans did contract influenza, but medical historians, both black and white, generally agree that their case rates as well as their death rates tended to be lower than whites. It is true that most African-Americans at that time lived in rural areas, which generally had lower rates. But that could not be the whole ex-planation, since black soldiers also seemed to be less affected by the epidemic. Some have argued

The whole world seems up-side down. So many people around here have died, and so many are sick.

Letter to a soldier, October 20, 1918[9]

that since African-Americans were usually *more* vulnerable to respiratory disease than whites, perhaps more of them had caught flu in the spring and were thus protected against the more serious fall wave. Or could it be that for once, racial segregation worked to their advantage? All of these are possibilities, but none has been confirmed.[10]

Whatever the state of people's individual health, all Americans were affected by the devastating effect that the epidemic had on public services. In Baltimore, for instance, at least a quarter of the policemen, postal workers, garbagemen, and firemen were unable to work.[11] In Memphis, the streetcar company had to cut back on service when 124 out of its 400 employees fell sick.[12] In one section of Denver, the fire department was hit so hard that when there was a fire, the only man still functioning would go by himself to the scene and then get the bystanders to help him lay out the hose.[13] And in Mingo County, West Virginia, five women had to go down into the mines with the men to keep the coal coming.[14]

However the epidemic disrupted Americans' day-to-day activities, what they remembered most vividly was the pervasive presence of death— the funeral wreaths on door after door, the playmates who disappeared from the street, the hearses waiting in line to get into the cemetery. Even modest-sized cities lost hundreds of people to flu, and in the biggest cities, the deaths ran into the thousands. An Atlanta woman observed, "They were dying just like leaves off of them trees."[15] In Philadelphia, an 8-year-old boy became obsessed with the funeral bells that kept ringing night and day. He recalled later: "I was sure I was going to die . . . I was sure those horrible bells were going to ring for me."[16] Another childhood memory comes from a woman who lost four of her six brothers and sisters to the epidemic. She says that as each of her siblings approached death, her mother would take the child in her arms and rock back and forth while she sang to them. You could hear the steady creak of the rocking chair, the woman remembers, and when the creaking stopped, you knew another child was dead.[17]

Exactly how many Americans died in the epidemic will probably never be known, because of the complications of diagnosis and statistical reporting. Indeed, even in Table 3, which covers only the country's largest cities, the Ohio city of Akron is missing because it had not yet begun submitting mortality data to the national government. Nevertheless, most of the larger American cities did report regularly, and their statistics make certain points clear. To begin with, we can see that location played at least some role in the mortality patterns. Western cities generally had lower death rates, presumably because they had more warning of the epidemic. Nevertheless, when we observe the dramatic difference between the death rates in two cities right on the East Coast—New York City

(6.4) and Philadelphia (9.1)—it is clear that there were other variables at work as well, including demography, proximity to military installations, and local leaders' own policy choices.

Table 3 also helps to clarify the timing of the cities' experience. We see that although every city was still losing significant numbers of people to influenza in 1919, most of the flu deaths occurred in the fall of 1918. Indeed, we know from other data that most cities experienced the majority of their deaths—often thousands of them—within an even shorter time frame, often just a few weeks.[18]

Thousands of deaths meant thousands of dead bodies. Early in the fall of 1918, one unusually well-organized Midwestern city sent a group of citizens east to confer with a city that had already gone through the epidemic. The officials they consulted wasted no time discussing prevention or treatment. Instead, they said:

> When you get back home, hunt up your wood-workers and
> cabinet-makers and set them to making coffins. Then take your
> street laborers and set them to digging graves. If you do this you
> will not have your dead accumulating faster than you can dispose
> of them.[19]

Unfortunately, many communities were hit too hard and too fast to prepare for the epidemic so carefully. Philadelphia was in a particularly difficult situation, being one of the very first U.S. cities to experience the fall wave, and having a health commissioner who, although well meaning, owed his job more to his political connections than to his qualifications. In the last four months of 1918, Philadelphia lost more than 13,000 people to flu. As the death toll mounted, the city morgue ran out of space, so families were instructed to keep their dead bodies at home. There they piled up, decomposing, in hallways and upstairs rooms. Finally, the city sent out wagons that went from house to house collecting the bodies. One man, whose whole family was down with flu, and whose brother died of it, recalls:

> My aunt saw the horse-drawn wagon coming down the street.
> The strongest person in our family carried Daniel's body to the
> sidewalk. There were no coffins in the wagon, just bodies
> piled on top of each other. Daniel was two; he was just a
> little boy. They put his body on the wagon and took him away.[20]
> [For more firsthand accounts of the situation in Philadelphia,
> see Document 8.]

Table 3 Deaths from influenza and pneumonia in largest cities, United States, 1918–1919

City	1920 population	Number of deaths			Excess death rate per 1,000 population
		September–December 1918	January–June 1919	Total	
Atlanta, GA	200,616	575	479	1,054	5.3
Baltimore, MD	733,826	4,033	1,284	5,317	7.2
Birmingham, AL	178,806	987	427	1,414	7.9
Boston, MA	748,060	4,959	1,549	6,508	8.7
Buffalo, NY	506,775	2,474	857	3,331	6.6
Chicago, IL	2,701,705	10,755	4,021	14,776	5.5
Cincinnati, OH	401,247	1,867	849	2,716	6.8
Cleveland, OH	796,841	3,576	1,733	5,309	6.7
Columbus, OH	237,031	781	408	1,189	5.0
Denver, CO	256,491	1,400	449	1,849	7.2
Detroit, MI	993,078	2,586	1,899	4,485	4.5
Indianapolis, IN	314,194	990	642	1,632	5.2
Jersey City, NJ	298,103	1,695	769	2,464	8.3
Kansas City, MO	324,410	1,724	772	2,496	7.7
Los Angeles, CA	576,673	2,299	908	3,207	5.6
Louisville, KY	234,891	1,894	731	2,625	11.2
Memphis, TN	162,351	724	399	1,123	6.9
Milwaukee, WI	457,147	1,562	641	2,203	4.8
Minneapolis, MN	380,582	1,058	500	1,558	4.1
New Haven, CT	162,537	948	265	1,213	7.5
New Orleans, LA	387,219	2,363	1,089	3,452	8.9
New York, NY	5,620,048	23,265	12,437	35,702	6.4
Newark, NJ	414,524	2,105	735	2,840	6.9
Oakland, CA	216,261	845	426	1,271	5.9
Omaha, NB	191,601	1,030	278	1,308	6.8

continued . . .

Table 3 Continued

City	1920 population	Number of deaths			Excess death rate per 1,000 population
		September–December 1918	January–June 1919	Total	
Philadelphia, PA	1,823,779	13,426	3,237	16,663	9.1
Pittsburgh, OH	588,343	5,340	2,028	7,368	12.5
Portland, OR	258,288	920	544	1,464	5.7
Providence, RI	237,595	1,343	504	1,847	7.8
Richmond, VA	171,667	886	354	1,240	7.2
Rochester, NY	295,750	1,125	333	1,458	4.9
Saint Louis, MO	772,897	2,883	1,199	4,082	5.3
Saint Paul, MN	234,698	908	272	1,180	5.0
San Francisco, CA	506,676	2,675	1,218	3,893	7.7
Seattle, WA	315,312	1,071	460	1,531	4.9
Syracuse, NY	171,717	943	203	1,146	6.7
Toledo, OH	243,164	716	375	1,091	4.5
Washington, DC	437,571	2,469	768	3,237	7.4
Worcester, MA	179,754	994	355	1,349	7.5

Source: U.S. Census Bureau[21]

Most cities managed better than Philadelphia, but in town after town there were accounts of crowded morgues, not enough coffins, and special drafts of labor to keep up with the grave-digging. In Washington, DC, a man whose father ran a funeral parlor remembers taking grieving relatives among the coffins stacked in his family's own apartment, conducting them to the coffin in "the third row in the living room" or "the fourth row in the dining room." Another man recalls that, as a boy in Dorchester, Massachusetts, he watched grave-diggers taking the dead bodies out of their coffins before they were buried, so the coffins could be reused.[22] In some towns, the corpses were all dumped together into common graves, while in others the family members dug the graves themselves.

When you review the record—the empty assurances with which local officials initially greeted the epidemic, the havoc the disease caused as it raced across the country, and the grim problems that arose with laying the dead to rest—you might think there was not a single positive note to be found anywhere in the American experience with the epidemic of 1918. But that would not be true. As it turned out, public officials' actions were often more constructive than their words. And American communities turned out to be more resourceful than they had thought.

ORGANIZING FOR A CALAMITY

In town after town, the local pushback against the epidemic began with a meeting. Sometimes it was the mayor who convened the first gathering; in other places it was the health commissioner, or the director of the local Red Cross, or the head of an influential volunteer organization. But whoever got the process going, the meetings nearly always evolved into coalitions that mobilized the energies of many different community organizations to fight the epidemic.

It might seem strange that local leaders could move so quickly from denying the danger of influenza to taking it very seriously indeed. But that is what happened, and sometimes with dizzying speed. For instance, the residents of Los Angeles must have rubbed their eyes when the director of public health assured the press one day that influenza would present no problem at all, so long as "ordinary precautions are observed," and then 48 hours later shut down every public gathering place in the city.[23] The most alert officials did not even wait for local cases to develop, but went into action as soon as the epidemic appeared in a nearby military camp. Other leaders were fatally slow in their responses. But whatever the timing, the great majority of American communities did pull together some kind of collaborative response to the crisis.

As they did so, their efforts showed the clear imprint of the Progressive Era years during which most of these people had come to adulthood. First of all, there was still a touch of prewar optimism in the way they joined forces to tackle this terrible challenge. They were appalled at what was happening, and yet their mobilization revealed their continuing faith in

Reflecting local leaders' hunger for ideas about how to deal with the epidemic, volunteers in Chicago were assigned to comb through the newspapers of six other cities every day, clipping stories that described how these communities were responding to the crisis. The nurse who oversaw the project later recalled: "We borrowed shamelessly, without taking time to say 'Thank you,' but we helped our patients, and after all, that was our chief concern."[24]

the power of organized action, clear thinking, and good will to conquer the problems they faced. A second progressive legacy was the importance of state and especially local governments in the community response. Some public officials performed very well, while others were quite ineffective, but they were always significant participants.

The third great legacy from the Progressive Era was the active participation of women. The myriad women's groups that had been formed during the years before the war were absolutely indispensable in the planning of each community's response and in organizing the thousands of volunteers who put those plans into effect. As for providing healthcare during the epidemic, nurses were widely viewed as the heroines of the day. (Nursing was, as we have noted, an almost entirely female occupation at this time; many nursing schools refused to accept male applicants, and men were explicitly excluded from military nursing.)

The story of the epidemic on the home front is primarily the story of communities mobilizing their own resources. As far as outside sources of assistance went, the record was quite variable. On the positive side, state leaders were sometimes ahead of local officials in recognizing the urgency of the situation. This was the case in Illinois, for instance, where the energetic actions of the state Flu Commission led Chicago residents to complain to the papers about the sluggish reaction in their own city, whereupon Chicago officials began responding more aggressively.[25] On the negative side, some state leaders offered little direction. In addition, there was frequent state/local tension over specific flu measures, particularly over the pros and cons of closing public gathering spaces.

At the federal level of government, most officials were too preoccupied with the war to devote much attention to the epidemic on the home front. The U.S. Public Health Service did make an effort to assist local communities, particularly through its Voluntary Service Medical Corps. But as we have noted, the great majority of the 70,000 doctors on the VMSC rolls turned out to be needed in their own hometowns, so fewer than 1,000 of them responded to the agency's call. The Public Health Service did appoint a Flu Director for each state, and at least some (if not all) of these individuals proved to be quite helpful. Finally, the Public Health Service sent out large amounts of informational material for the general public about how to avoid influenza, and how to keep from giving it to others.

Despite these efforts by the Public Health Service, the American Red Cross was a more important source of assistance to local communities. Its national and state leaders played a major role in recruiting nurses and raising emergency funds, while its local staff often helped plan the response in individual communities. The organization's role in recruiting nurses was especially important. Back in 1917, as we noted in Chapter 4, the Red Cross had been quite choosy about whom it accepted for service in the military, rejecting even professional nurses if they were married or over the age of 35, or if they had not trained in large hospitals. The "rejects" were assigned to the Red Cross Home Defense program. But once the epidemic struck in the fall of 1918, the demand for civilian nurses skyrocketed, and the Home Defense nurses swung into action.

Among the nurses who responded was a North Dakota woman who managed to establish an emergency hospital in the small town where she lived, and to serve dozens of farm families in the outlying territory, before she herself came down with the flu. She later admitted that she had been disappointed when she was assigned to the Home Defense Corps instead of being sent overseas. But, she said, "My experience of the last two weeks, ending in my own case of influenza, helps me to become reconciled to my stay-at-home lot. I want our nurses across to know that we at home are trying to do our part, even though it is not being talked about."[26]

Recognizing that there were not enough Home Defense nurses to meet the need, the Red Cross launched an intensive campaign to recruit more women. Trained nurses who were willing to serve in other parts of the country were referred to the Public Health Service for allocation. But the Red Cross' main contribution lay in the way it helped communities to find and put to work all the people among their own residents who could help with nursing. And this time, the Red Cross was not nearly as selective as it had been in 1917. A typical ad sought assistance from "*all* women, regardless of their lack of professional training, who are willing to give time and service in the stricken homes."[27]

As part of this recruitment effort, the Red Cross called upon the many volunteers who already belonged to its local chapters. In 1916, the organization had had only about 100 chapters nationwide, but it had expanded dramatically once America entered the war, and by 1918, there were Red Cross chapters in more than 3,500 communities. As part of this network, 8 million Red Cross volunteers (mostly women) devoted themselves throughout 1917 and early 1918 to meeting quotas for tasks such as rolling bandages and knitting socks for soldiers. Indeed, when the call went out to collect fruit pits (a source of carbon for gas masks), the volunteers went at the task so energetically that the inundated War Department had to beg them to stop. Once influenza hit, these women were put to a new set of flu-related jobs, including making gauze face masks and sewing hospital gowns and pajamas.[28]

The Red Cross had another source of volunteers as well: the many small-town homemakers who had taken the organization's short course in Elementary Hygiene and Home Care of the Sick. Once the epidemic began, many of these women came forward to help the stricken families with tasks such as cooking, cleaning, laundering, and child care. Not content with these numbers, however, local Red Cross chapters kept on canvassing for more volunteers. In New York City, for example, they ran ads in the Sunday papers, distributed 15,000 handbills on street corners and in stores, visited women's clubs, wrote a letter to be read in all the churches, and placed 5,000 placards in theater lobbies. Rather than minimizing the work ahead, these appeals invited volunteers to participate in "A STERN TASK FOR STERN WOMEN."[29]

The communities that got extra doctors or nurses from the Public Health Service were among the neediest, and the assistance they received played an important role in helping them get through the epidemic. But they represented only a small minority of all the communities in the country. In most places, the challenge for local leaders was to make the most effective use they could of the skills of their own residents. The Red Cross recruitment campaigns helped to ensure that almost all local women with nurses' training came forward, and its army of volunteers helped to fill out the local workforce further. But these individuals represented only a part of the community-wide mobilization that took place in the face of the epidemic. In Chicago, for instance, 45 civic and business groups collaborated with city and state health officials, contributing staff, office support, and fundraising.[30] Ethnic associations frequently lent a hand in their own neighborhoods, and when the local political machine in Philadelphia proved to be incapable of doing what was necessary, a group of society women took the job on themselves, mobilizing the city's charitable organizations to carry on the fight.[31]

Nearly every community started out by trying to provide better accommodations for the sick. Since the hospitals were swamped, many localities set up extra "emergency hospitals" wherever they could find space—in armories, warehouses, vacant schools, big private houses, and even in tents erected in an open field. Here is the way the process went in Joliet, Illinois, according to Florence Baldwin, the town's principal "community nurse." One morning in early October, city officials told Baldwin that because of "the fearful amount of illness and the fatalities" in town, the local country club would have to be converted into an emergency flu hospital. Baldwin started making the arrangements right away, and by one o'clock that afternoon she was admitting her first three patients. She kept the facility going for the next several weeks, operating with donated supplies, a few nurses borrowed from the main hospital, and scores of volunteers, male and female, "from all walks of life." By the time the epidemic was over, the facility had served almost 200 patients, of whom about 20 percent had died—a distressing statistic, but not unusually high for acute flu cases that fall. Reviewing what had been accomplished, Baldwin praised the "intelligent teamwork" that had made the project possible, and concluded that despite the dark moments, it had been "a truly wonderful experience."[32]

The many emergency hospitals that were established in the fall of 1918 did increase the number of available beds. But no amount of expansion could accommodate all the people who were sick, nor did all these people even need hospital care. Accordingly, the great majority of patients were cared for at home—and most of them probably preferred it that way, given the overloaded state of the hospitals. These homebound patients were mostly cared for by their families, but they did need at least periodic visits from doctors or nurses. So the second great challenge the community groups took up was organizing the delivery of care to such widely scattered locations.

For the most part, doctors continued to schedule their own time. But many communities streamlined the delivery of nursing care by establishing a single pool of nurses—contributed by city health departments, school districts, private agencies, and the Red Cross Home Defense Corps—with one central office to handle all requests. Then, so as to minimize the distance that the nurses had to travel between patients, communities were divided into districts, with a separate team of nurses assigned to each area. In the years before the war, "districting" had often been used to organize nursing services in poor neighborhoods, whereas more prosperous people hired their own full-time "private-duty" nurses. But now, under the pressure of the epidemic, even wealthier families sometimes had to wait their turn and accept brief visits from whichever nurses were assigned to them.[33]

Despite every effort to use nursing resources efficiently, the workloads were extraordinary. In Chicago, said one observer, a nurse would start out the day with a list of 15 people to see, and end up having seen 50.[34] Nor was this kind of demand limited to the cities. A nurse working in a Kentucky coal town reported: "If I did not find the number I was looking for, it really didn't matter, for there was some one sick in nearly every house." As for the length of the workdays, she explained: "Our hours are supposed to be from 10 a.m. until 4 p.m., but naturally we can't stand anything so foolish."[35]

As communities formalized their arrangements for providing medical care, they identified many ways in which volunteers could lend a hand. In Newark, New Jersey, the local Automobile Club helped drive doctors and nurses on their rounds.[36] In Roanoke, Virginia, local Boy Scouts ran errands and helped deliver meals to homebound families.[37] In Cleveland, school teachers did the chauffeuring, and they also helped the nurses with their record-keeping.[38] And in Philadelphia, a group of nuns proved to be so useful as nurse's aides at local hospitals (including Jewish ones) that they were given unprecedented permission to break their vows of silence and to spend their nights away from the convent.[39]

Volunteers also provided valuable help in patients' homes. Young fathers and mothers belonged to the same vulnerable age group as the soldiers, and hundreds of thousands of them fell prey to influenza. Moreover, even when mothers did not get sick themselves, they were often so busy caring for sick family members that they could not keep up with their other household tasks. So, besides assisting doctors and nurses in various ways, volunteers often pitched in to help these families (see Figure 5.1). In Chicago, an association of club women set up 25 canteens around the city, providing hot food for hundreds of people.[40] In Alamance County, North Carolina, volunteers made and delivered hot meals to sick patients.[41] In Wilkes-Barre, Pennsylvania, the women working in the kitchen of the local emergency hospital started making 150 extra meals every day for needy families.[42]

Figure 5.1 Volunteers in Cincinnati, Ohio, feed children from local flu-stricken families. Note that although the servers wear masks, the children do not. © Bettmann/CORBIS.

Not all community residents were so helpful. A nurse in Perry County, Kentucky, reported that she found stricken families actually starving to death, "not because there is a shortage of food but because the well are panic stricken and will not approach houses where the influenza exists." Similarly, a nurse in Michigan found that when a local woman collapsed after weeks of caring for her family, not one of her neighbors would lend a hand. When the visiting nurse telephoned the woman's sister, "she came and tapped on the window but refused to talk to me until she had gotten a safe distance away."[43] Yet if these incidents were troubling, they were certainly not the most common response. Innumerable local accounts make clear that hundreds of thousands of Americans did rise to the occasion and contribute whatever they could to help their fellow citizens through the crisis.

So did this massive communal effort actually save lives? We really cannot be sure. Given the medical limitations of the time, we have to assume that many cases of flu would have run their course in pretty much the same way, with or without the help mobilized by their communities. But it is safe to say that the outpouring of assistance did at least make many patients more comfortable, and that it helped to sustain their families through a terrible time. As for the participants themselves, it must have meant a great deal to thousands of people—both professionals and volunteers—to know that they had a role to play in this community crisis. A woman in Kentucky summed it up this way: "The work was hard and depressing, but well worth while . . . And after the worst was over, we were glad to have had our share in it."[44]

STOPPING THE SPREAD OF INFECTION

There are two main ways to fight a disease: treatment and prevention. So far, we have been discussing the treatment side of the equation. It is time now to consider what American communities did, or tried to do, about the second task, that of prevention.

Ideally, of course, there would have been a vaccine to protect the population against influenza, as our flu shots do today. But, as we have discussed, no effective vaccine had yet been developed. Nor could flu be cured, once it began. This meant that communities hoping to bring the epidemic under control had to rely primarily on the same disease-prevention measures that had been used for years: public education, sanitation, and social distancing (so as to separate sick people from healthy ones).

Community authorities had one major asset as they approached this challenge: the growing respect for—and understanding of—public health that had developed during the Progressive Era. Consider the issue of public education, through which members of the public were taught to take personal responsibility for controlling infection. This approach had flowered during the years before the war, especially in connection with the campaign against tuberculosis. Now in 1918, American civilians were besieged with information about how to recognize influenza, how to avoid catching it, and how to prevent transmitting it to others. The Surgeon General of the U.S. Public Health Service sent out a great deal of material, and many state and local health departments added their own, including posters and placards, circulars to be distributed door to door, slides to be shown before movie shows, and press releases in both English and foreign-language papers (see Figure 2.1, p. 32).

In these educational materials, the authorities placed a heavy emphasis on Americans' patriotic obligation to stay healthy themselves, and to protect the well-being of the community. In the same tone of voice in which people were urged to join the military or buy Liberty Bonds, they were reminded: "You owe it to yourself and to your fellow man to do everything you can to stay the progress of this crippling and all too swiftly fatal disease." After all, as a Public Health Service representative in Texas remarked, "The more cases of influenza we have in this country, so much more will the German Kaiser be pleased."[45]

The public information that was circulated during this period urged people to stay away from crowds, but even more, it stressed the importance of "respiratory etiquette." As one circular explained: "Cover up each cough and sneeze. If you don't, you'll spread disease."[46] Above all, people were instructed not to spit. Anti-spitting campaigns, reinforced with fines and arrests, had been developed during the anti-TB campaigns before the war, and they were vigorously revived in 1918. Philadelphia even reissued its old placards, which sternly announced: "Spitting Equals Death."[47]

Spitting is certainly an offensive habit, but the intensity with which it was pursued in 1918 owed at least as much to the sanitarian concerns of the nineteenth century as to modern theories about how flu was transmitted. In fact, the campaign against spitting was part of a larger obsession with cleanliness that pervaded the American response to the influenza epidemic. Carrying on the centuries-old association between dirt and disease—and perhaps focusing on what they *could* control, since there was so much that they could not—public authorities incorporated a ferocious war on dirt into their campaign against the epidemic. Nurses and volunteers spent hours scouring their patients' homes. Streets were swept and hosed down. Telephones were disinfected; so were drinking fountains, library books, and even store clerks' fingers between trans-actions.[48] Private citizens waged their own wars against germs; an Ohio man remembers that whenever someone passing his house would spit on the sidewalk, his mother would rush out with a tea kettle and pour boiling water on the spot.[49] All this public sanitation must have improved local environments, but it probably did not contribute a great deal to stopping the epidemic.

Even those who were strongly committed to civic cleanups recognized that most people caught flu not from environmental contamination, but directly from the air exhaled by someone who already had the disease. And that is where face masks came in. Made of several layers of gauze, the masks were produced in the hundreds of thousands by Red Cross volunteers and other women's groups. Doctors and nurses were generally expected to use them, many civilians wore them by choice, and some communities (including San Francisco) mandated their use by everyone. Newspaper ads proclaimed: "Wear a mask and save your life!"[50] Indeed, some of the most memorable photographs of the 1918 epidemic feature masked policemen marching down the street, masked soldiers on parade, and masked baseball players in the middle of a game.

The face masks were hardly user-friendly. They fit poorly, they made conversation difficult, and they had to be boiled and dried between uses. The mayor of Denver exclaimed: "Why, it would take half the population of our city to make the other half wear masks."[51] And, as if to prove his point, in the very city that was most insistent about the universal use of masks—San Francisco—the mayor was spotted at a parade with his mask dangling from one ear, and the health commissioner was fined for not wearing his mask at a boxing match. Of course, if the face masks had been effective, they would have been worth any inconvenience. But many people had their doubts about them, including the health commissioner of Detroit, who insisted that germs could easily slip through the gauze mesh.[52] Public health experts today believe the commissioner was right, particularly since the flu virus is even smaller than the bacterial germs he had in mind.

Although face masks failed to protect people as intended, we can appreciate their purpose better if we think of them in relation to the classic form of social distancing, which is to quarantine everyone who has an infectious disease or has been exposed to it. When it came to legally confining flu patients to their homes, the problem was even to know who they were. Although by the fall of 1918 most localities required doctors to report flu cases, many patients never even saw a doctor, and if they did, doctors were often too swamped to keep up with their reporting. So it is likely that most of the flu patients who stayed in isolation were there not because of some formal public policy, but simply because they were too sick to go out.

If it was hard to find everyone who was suffering from flu, it was virtually impossible to find everyone who had been exposed to the disease, let alone to place them all under quarantine. That was why face masks were adopted. The idea was that they would keep people who might be carrying the virus from transmitting it to others. It was not a realistic hope, but it represented an effort to control the spread of infection in a situation where standard quarantine measures could not possibly do the whole job.

There were, in fact, a handful of "escape communities" in 1918 that managed to institute the opposite of a quarantine, by putting the healthy people behind the fence instead of those suspected of carrying the disease. They included Princeton University, a couple of military installations, two residential institutions, and a handful of very small isolated towns. These communities did manage to keep influenza almost entirely at bay, but their success required an unusual level of control over their own boundaries. For instance, in one of the escape communities—Gunnison, Colorado— community residents were not allowed to leave town during the period of "protective sequestration," and the few visitors who were let in were confined until it was clear that they were free of disease. In addition, the highways that passed through town were blocked off, the railroad companies were told that anyone getting off a train would be arrested, and some people who tried to pass through by car were detained.[53] It is impressive that any communities at all were able to carry this off, but it was hardly a viable model for an urbanized nation of 100 million people.

Recognizing the impossibility of stopping the epidemic with methods such as quarantines and face masks, most communities turned to another time-honored form of social distancing: closing public gathering places. This approach—which had been used against plague as far back as the Middle Ages—was recommended by Surgeon General Blue in early October, and it was widely adopted by state and city health departments around the country.

Theaters were often the first facilities to be closed and the last to reopen; in mid-October, the trade paper *Variety* estimated that 90 percent of all theaters in the country were dark.[54] So drastic was the impact that the National Association of the Motion Picture Industry closed down production for a whole month, recognizing that there was no market for its output.[55] Among the other places that were typically shut down were lodge halls, restaurants, saloons, skating rinks, and dance halls. Churches, too, were often closed, which in some cities led to the unusual sight of preachers and dance hall owners making common cause to protest the regulations.

The protesters' principal grievance was the fact that workplaces and stores and public transportation were generally allowed to stay open. In fact, when the Illinois health board suggested that workplaces too might be closed, the Chicago health commissioner flatly refused, on the grounds that it would be devastating for public morale. As for closing the New York City subway, health commissioner Royal Copeland exclaimed: "You might as well try to cut off the main artery of the body as to close the subway."[56] The people protesting the closing of their own facilities were not necessarily saying that workplaces and streetcars and stores *should* be closed. But they insisted that as long as these places remained open, influenza was going to keep circulating, no matter what other facilities were shut down.

Besides churches and places of entertainment, most communities closed their schools. But in this regard, there were some notable exceptions, including the two largest cities in the country—New York and Chicago. Their rationale for keeping the doors open grew directly from the ambitious "medical inspection" programs that had been developed in the schools during the Progressive Era. When the question of closing the schools came up in New York City, Dr. Josephine Baker, director of the Division of Child Hygiene, asked the health commissioner: "If you could have a system where you could examine one-fifth of the population of this city every morning and controlled every person who showed any symptom of influenza, what would it be worth to you?" The commissioner took her point and kept the schools open, convinced that they offered the best available system for identifying new cases of flu, and that with regular monitoring and systematic home follow-up, the children themselves would do better in school than out of it. The same line of thinking influenced his counterparts in Chicago, New Haven, and a number of other cities. They were in the minority, however; most communities saw the schools as a source of contagion, just like any other public gathering place.[57]

In truth, hardly any community was entirely consistent in its closings. For instance, throughout the first weeks of October—while local hospitals overflowed with sick and dying patients, while theaters and churches remained shut tight—Americans all over the country threw themselves into the Fourth Liberty Loan campaign (goal: $6 billion) with rallies, door-to-door solicitations, public meetings, and huge parades that drew hundreds of thousands of people into the streets.

Despite these exceptions, the public closings cast a real shadow over American life. The acute phase of the epidemic generally lasted no more than six to eight weeks in any given locality, but the isolating effect of the closing laws added to the woes of the epidemic. Socially minded people missed their theaters and restaurants, parents wanted their children back in school, business proprietors were distraught over their lost income, and everyone was depressed by the dark, empty streets. A Texas woman wrote to her husband overseas: "It is terrible, even worse than it was

Fighting Over Closing Laws in Newark, New Jersey[58]

The closing of public gathering spaces nearly always sparked some controversy, especially when, as in New Jersey, the regulations were passed at the state rather than the local level. On October 10, 1918, with the total number of flu cases in New Jersey approaching 100,000, state health officials issued an order closing down all schools, churches, theaters, movies, dance halls, saloons, and arenas. Other states were adopting similar measures, but the mayor of Newark, Charles P. Gillen, was convinced that the new law was too rigid and that it would cause unnecessary panic among city residents.

The first dispute arose over the subject of alcohol. Initially, the mayor went beyond state requirements and decreed that, in addition to the other closings, local restaurants should stop serving liquor. But on the very night the new regulations went into effect, the mayor and a group of friends were reportedly prevented by police from ordering drinks at a local restaurant. The next day, the mayor personally suspended that particular rule.

The issue of alcohol sparked another dispute as well. Acting on the belief— shared by many doctors of the time—that liquor was a useful treatment for flu, the mayor let it be known that although saloons could not serve customers at the bar, they could sell packaged liquor out their side doors to people with a doctor's prescription. Within days, the *Newark News* reported that bars were open in every saloon they had checked (the city had 1,200 of them), and that bottles of liquor were being sold by the dozens to people without prescriptions. The mayor's response was to bar all *Newark News* reporters from his office.

On October 21, Mayor Gillen announced that the local epidemic had now passed its peak, so he was unilaterally ending the ban on public gatherings. When state officials demanded that it be reinstated, Gillen insisted that closing spaces such as theaters and saloons was pointless, since workplaces remained open. Moreover, he said, the closings had brought a number of local businesses close to bankruptcy, and "scared people who were slightly afflicted into a serious illness." He also maintained that half the towns in New Jersey were defying the ban, which had only been imposed because the State Board of Health was dominated by uninformed rural doctors. "No country doctors are going to close this city," he proclaimed.

The Newark City Council could have overridden the mayor and closed the city down again, but they were just as reluctant as he was to push a highly unpopular law. Luckily for everyone, the epidemic actually did begin to abate shortly thereafter, and on October 26, the state lifted the ban in all 200 New Jersey communities. Newark's epidemic was officially declared over on November 12.

> We were afraid to kiss each other, to eat with each other, to have contact of any kind. We had no family life, no school life, no church life, no community life. Fear tore people apart.
>
> Bill Sardo, Washington, DC[60]

at first. I hate to go to San Antonio as everything there is closed and people wear masks on the street."[59]

Given the psychological and economic costs of the closing laws, everyone was eager to see them end as soon as possible. By late October, the cities that had been hit first were starting to return to normal, which increased the impatience of people living in places where the epidemic was still going. To hurry things along, optimists insisted that the local danger must have passed by now, so restrictions were no longer needed, while pessimists maintained that the restrictions had never done any good, so they might as well be abandoned. Especially toward the end, even people who were fully engaged in combating the epidemic had moments of doubt and despair. But then, on November 11, 1918, like a ray of sunlight, came the end of the other war that the United States had been fighting.

THE LAST ACT

The eleventh hour of the eleventh day of the eleventh month—November 11, 1918—that was the precise moment when World War I officially came to an end. The war was over, the Allies had won, and the soldiers would soon be coming home. All over the United States, people poured into the streets, tooting horns, clanging bells, and hugging perfect strangers, as if every grim warning against public gathering had just flown out the window. Even in places where the epidemic was still going strong, jubilation over the end of the war dispelled much of the gloom (and much of the caution) that had hung over the country throughout the fall. In response, many communities rushed to lift their bans on public gatherings. One man recalls: "It was like you'd flipped a switch. Businesses and theaters opened up again. We went back to school."[61]

Within a week or two, a good number of these same communities saw their death rates starting to climb again. This final surge of influenza, which lasted in some places through the winter of 1919, is considered the third wave of the flu epidemic. Even though it was less devastating than the fall wave, it still brought serious levels of disease, leading Surgeon General Blue to remind the public that the epidemic was "by no means ended."[62] But in spite of what he said, influenza had lost its death grip on public attention—partly because the third wave hit fewer communities, and partly because having both the war *and* the worst months of the fall wave of the epidemic come to an end about the same time had taken much of the urgency out of the atmosphere. [*For Denver's problems in maintaining closing regulations during the third wave of the epidemic, see Document 9.*]

By spring 1919, the third wave of the epidemic had also come to an end, and the crisis really was over. Influenza and pneumonia levels were higher than usual during the next few winters, but the desperate conditions seen in the fall of 1918 did not return. So it is those critical months from September through December that offer the best opportunity for assessing how effectively American communities responded to the great influenza epidemic.

To begin with, it is probably unfortunate that face masks were one of the most noticeable (and most photographed) community responses, since the wearing of flimsy gauze masks may have been the least useful of all the local initiatives. As for the frenetic cleanup of streets and public buildings, this effort no doubt helped to improve community environments, but it probably did relatively little to control the epidemic. On the other hand, the ambitious mobilization of local doctors, nurses, and volunteers to expand hospital services and provide care for patients at home surely did make a significant contribution. Even though there were no really effective medical treatments available, few would deny the humanitarian importance of providing flu patients and their families with medical monitoring, basic nursing care, housekeeping assistance, and emotional support.

Then there is the question of whether Americans derived any benefit from what today are called "non-pharmaceutical interventions" (to use the World Health Organization's term)—in other words, efforts to combat disease not through medicine, but through social distancing methods such as closing public places. Over the years, many historians have questioned whether the public closings did any good. In 1920, for instance, one writer commented: "There is no evidence that variations in administrative procedure, such as the closing of schools, exerted any influence on the spread or the severity of the disease."[63] A number of modern scholars have echoed this view, pointing to communities such as Philadelphia, which shut everything down and still had unusually high death rates.

In recent years, however, several historians have taken a new look at the data and concluded that social distancing may have made more difference than was previously recognized. Rather than categorizing all communities simply as "did" or "did not" close public places, these scholars have analyzed exactly how the closings were carried out in each community. Their conclusion—at least for the cities where there is enough information to do the analysis—is that timing seems to have made a major difference. To take an extreme comparison, Philadelphia and St. Louis both engaged in widespread closings. But Philadelphia waited two long weeks after its first flu cases before it began to limit public gatherings, whereas St. Louis had its first case on October 5 and began social distancing measures on October 7. The outcome was that St. Louis' excess death rate was barely half that of Philadelphia (see Table 3, p. 92).[64] Of course, any two communities can have different outcomes for a variety of reasons, but the link between early intervention and lower death rates has now been documented in studies covering a good number of American cities.[65]

The other critical aspect of timing is how long each city's public closings were kept in place. As we noted above, many historians believe that the third wave of the epidemic in the United States was triggered by cities that rushed to reopen their public facilities before the local epidemic was really over. The record is not entirely consistent—some cities lifted their bans early and seemed to suffer no ill consequences. But this fact remains: no city was hit by the third wave while its closing laws were still in place.[66] Taken together, all these findings suggest that the public closings did help to soften the impact of the epidemic, in the places where they were begun promptly and sustained until death rates were definitely on the decline.

Given this evidence about the potential value of public closings, along with the importance of the services that were provided to flu patients and their families, it seems fair to say that American communities may have achieved more in their struggles with the epidemic than they were aware of at the time. With death all around them, some people became deeply disheartened, while others took comfort simply in providing help. But their reactions, good or bad, were based primarily on their own immediate experiences, since during the hectic weeks of the crisis, they had very little solid information about whether their efforts were actually having an impact, and how their performance compared to that of other cities.

Local records were being maintained, however, even if they were not widely published or closely analyzed at the time. And using those records, recent historians have been able to document what was not clear at the time—that in the fall of 1918 many American communities managed, through their own cooperative efforts, to exert at least some control over the worst health crisis the country had ever seen.

NOTES

1. David Rosner, "Spanish Flu, or Whatever it Is . . .," *Public Health Reports* 125, supp. 3 (2010), 45.

2. This four-paragraph section is based on Anne L. Colon, "Influenza at Cedar Branch Camp," in "Experiences During the Epidemic," *American Journal of Nursing* 19 no. 8 (May 1919), 605–606.

3. John M. Barry, *The Great Influenza: The Story of the Deadliest Pandemic in History* (New York, NY: Penguin Books, 2004, 2005), 340–341.

4. Marian Jones, "The American Red Cross and Local Response to the 1918 Influenza Pandemic: A Four-City Case Study," *Public Health Reports* 125, supp. 3 (2010), 100.

5. Cited in Debra E. Blakely, *Mass Mediated Disease: A Case Study Analysis of Three Flu Pandemics and Public Health Policy* (New York, NY: Lexington Books, 2006), 31.

6. Florence C. Baldwin, "The Epidemic in Joliet, Ill.," *Public Health Nurse* 11 no. 1 (1919), 49.

7. Lynette Iezzoni, *Influenza 1918: The Worst Epidemic in American History* (New York, NY: TV Books, 1999), 125.

8. Barry, *Great Influenza*, 345.

9. Nancy K. Bristow, *American Pandemic: The Lost Worlds of the 1918 Influenza Epidemic* (New York, NY: Oxford University Press, 2012), 75.

10. Vanessa Northington Gamble, "'There Wasn't a Lot of Comforts in Those Days': African Americans, Public Health, and the 1918 Influenza Epidemic," *Public Health Reports* 125, supp. 3 (2010), 119–120; Alfred W. Crosby, *America's Forgotten Pandemic: The Influenza of 1918*, 2nd ed. (New York, NY: Cambridge University Press, 2003), 228–229; U.S. Bureau of the Census, *Mortality Statistics 1918* (Washington, DC: Government Printing Office, 1920), 11.

11. Monica Schoch-Spana, "'Hospital's Full-Up'; The 1918 Influenza Pandemic," *Public Health Reports* 116, supp. 2 (2001), 32.

12. Thomas A. Garrett, "Pandemic Economics: The 1918 Influenza and its Modern-Day Implications," *Federal Reserve Bank of St. Louis Review* (March/April 2008), 88.

13. Judith Navarro, "Influenza in 1918: An Epidemic in Images," *Public Health Reports* 125, supp. 3 (2010), 12.

14. Rebecca Bailey,"Matewan Before the Massacre: Politics, Coal, and the Roots of Conflict in Mingo County, 1793–1920," (Ph.D. dissertation, West Virginia University, 2001), 366.

15. Francine King, "Atlanta," in Fred R. van Hartesveldt, Ed., *The 1918–1919 Pandemic of Influenza: The Urban Impact in the Western World*, (Lewiston, NY: Edwin Mellen Press, 1992) 108.

16. Iezzoni, *Influenza 1918*, 152.

17. Gloria Gambale, "Nicola and Constance Maffeo," *Pandemic Influenza Storybook*, available at www.flu.gov/pandemic/history/storybook/stories/courage/maffeo (accessed August 18, 2013).

18. Barry, *Great Influenza*, 5.

19. Richard Hobday and John W. Carson, "Open-Air Treatment of Pandemic Influenza," *American Journal of Public Health* 99 no. 52, supp. 2 (2009), S 237.

20. Iezzoni, *Influenza 1918*, 135.
21. "Population: U.S. Census Bureau, Table 15, Population of the 100 Largest Urban Places, 1920," available at www.census.gov/population/www/documentation/twps0027/tab15.txt (accessed August 18, 2013). Deaths: U.S. Bureau of the Census, *Mortality Statistics 1919* (Washington, DC: Government Printing Office, 1920), 31. Death rate calculations by the author.
22. Ibid. 80, 105.
23. Crosby, *America's Forgotten Pandemic*, 92.
24. Edna L. Foley, "Department of Public Health Nursing: Illinois," *American Journal of Nursing*, 19 no. 3 (December 1918), 192. For full article, see Document 7.
25. Paul Buelow, "Chicago," in van Hartesveldt, *1918–1919 Pandemic*, 129–130.
26. G.R., "Experiences During the Influenza Epidemic," *American Journal of Nursing* 19 no. 3 (December 1918), 204.
27. Buelow, "Chicago," in van Hartesveldt, *1918–1919 Pandemic*, 132.
28. Barry, *Great Influenza*, 130; Jones, "American Red Cross and Local Response," 93–95.
29. Permelia Murnan Doty, "A Retrospect of the Influenza Epidemic," *Public Health Nurse* 11 no. 12 (1919), 951. "A Stern Task for Stern Women" (poster), New York Academy of Medicine Archives, Public Health Committee Collection, Folder: Influenza, 1918–1919.
30. "Report of an Epidemic in Chicago Occurring During the Fall of 1918," in *Octennial Report of the Department of Health, City of Chicago, 1911–1918* (Chicago Department of Health, 1919), 115–116.
31. Barry, *Great Influenza*, 323–325.
32. Baldwin, "Epidemic in Joliet," 49–50.
33. See, for instance, Jane A. Delano, "Meeting the Spanish Influenza Situation," *American Journal of Nursing* 19 no. 2 (November 1918), 109–110.
34. Mary E. Westphal, "Influenza Vignettes," *Public Health Nurse* 11 no. 2 (1919), 129.
35. Foley, "Department of Public Health Nursing: Kentucky," (December 1918), 194.
36. Stuart Galishoff, "Newark and the Great Influenza Pandemic," *Bulletin of the History of Medicine* 43 no. 3 (May/June 1969), 254.
37. Bristow, *American Pandemic*, 54.
38. Foley, "Department of Public Health Nursing: Cleveland," 194.
39. Barry, *Great Influenza*, 329.
40. Foley, "Department of Public Health Nursing," 191, 194.
41. Robert Mason, "Surviving the Blue Killer, 1918," *Virginia Quarterly Review* 24 no. 2 (Spring 1998), 350.
42. Iezzoni, *Influenza 1918*, 124.
43. Bristow, *American Pandemic*, 56.
44. Beulah Gribble, "Experiences During the Epidemic, III: Influenza in a Kentucky Coal-Mining Camp," *American Journal of Nursing*, 19 no. 8 (May 1919), 611.
45. Bristow, *American Pandemic*, 102–103,
46. Ibid. 93.
47. Barry, *Great Influenza*, 221.
48. Iezzoni, *Influenza 1918*, 128.
49. Richard Krause, "The Swine Flu Episode and the Fog of Epidemics," *Emerging Infectious Diseases* 12 no. 1 (January 2006), 40.

50. Iezzoni, *Influenza 1918*, 129.

51. Ibid. 161.

52. Nancy Tomes, "'Destroyer and Teacher': Managing the Masses During the 1918–1919 Influenza Pandemic," *Public Health Reports* 125, supp. 3 (2010), 57, 59.

53. Barry, *Great Influenza*, 345–346; Monica Schoch-Spana, "The 1918–1920 Influenza Pandemic Escape Communities Digital Document Archive," *Bulletin of the History of Medicine* 81 no. 4 (Winter 2007), 863–865. See also Thomas Mullen's novel, *Last Town on Earth* (New York, NY: Random House, 2006).

54. Tomes, "'Destroyer and Teacher'," 54.

55. Richard Koszarski, "Flu Season: Moving Picture World Reports on Pandemic Influenza, 1918–1919," *Film History* 17 no. 4 (2005), 468.

56. Chicago: Barry, *Great Influenza*, 337. NYC: Tomes, 'Destroyer and Teacher'," 55.

57. Alan M. Kraut, "Immigration, Ethnicity, and the Pandemic," *Public Health Reports* 125, supp. 3 (2010), 129–130; Alexandra Stern, et al. "'Better Off in School': School Medical Inspection as a Public Health Strategy During the 1918–1919 Influenza Pandemic in the United States," *Public Health Reports* 125, supp. 3 (2010)," 67–69.

58. Galishoff, "Newark and the Great Influenza Pandemic," 251, 254–257.

59. Paul Spellman, "'A Million Kisses': Love Letters from a Doughboy in France," *Southwestern Historical Quarterly* 114 no. 1 (July 2010), 53.

60. Iezzoni, *Influenza 1918*, 154.

61. Ibid. 182.

62. Blakely, *Mass-Mediated Disease*, 37.

63. Charles–Edward Amory Winslow and J. F. Rogers, "Statistics of the 1918 Epidemic of Influenza in Connecticut: With a Consideration of the Factors Which Influenced the Prevalence of This Disease in Various Communities," *Journal of Infectious Diseases* 26 no. 3 (March 1920), 215.

64. Richard Hatchett, et al., "Public Health Interventions and Epidemic Intensity During the 1918 Influenza Pandemic," *Proceedings of the National Academy of Sciences of the United States* 104 no. 18 (May 1, 2007), 7582.

65. Ibid. 7582–7587; Martin C. J. Bootsma and Neil M. Ferguson, "The Effect of Public Health Measures on the 1918 Influenza Pandemic in U.S. Cities," *Proceedings of the National Academy of Sciences of the United States* 104 no. 18 (May 1, 2007), 7588–7593; Howard Markel, et al., "Nonpharmaceutical Interventions Implemented by US Cities During the 1918–1919 Influenza Pandemic," *Journal of the American Medical Association* 298, no. 6 (August 8, 2007), 644–654. See also: John M. Barry, et al. "Nonpharmaceutical Interventions Implemented During the 1918–1919 Influenza Pandemic" (Letter to Editor and Reply), *Journal of the American Medical Assn.* 298 no. 19 (November 17, 2008), 2260–2261.

66. Hatchett, "Public Health Interventions and Epidemic Intensity," 7585.

CHAPTER 6

After the Storm

The Legacy of 1918

After the flu I was a pretty lonely kid. All my friends had
died . . . The neighborhood changed. People changed.
Everything changed.

John Deleno, New Haven resident[1]

All through the winter of 1919, the delegates at the Paris Peace Conference kept coming down with the "Paris cold." This rash of "colds" was, in fact, the third and last wave of the influenza epidemic, which reached the city just as thousands of diplomats and their advisers were convening for the great conference that would officially end World War I. In Paris alone, the deaths from influenza and pneumonia climbed from about 1,400 in December to 1,500 in January to 2,600 in February.[2] Meanwhile, as the delegates orated and socialized and negotiated, the flu virus circulated among them as busily as the gossip and the rumors.

The American participants at the conference seemed to be particularly susceptible. The U.S. ambassador, who had flu himself, observed that if the disease kept on spreading through the delegation like this, "we won't have anyone left to do the work." One staffer wrote in his diary: "It is the most depressing atmosphere I have ever been in. Everyone around seems to have something the matter with them."[3] Historians have commented on the disorganization among the Americans at the peace conference—especially the lack of solid staff work.[4] One contributing factor may well have been the number of people in the delegation who were weakened by flu and its aftereffects.

American energy and focus had never been more needed. Back in January 1918, President Wilson had won international praise with his call for just peace terms and a League of Nations to prevent future wars. And a year later, when he arrived in Europe for the peace conference, he was hailed as a hero. But however much the Europeans applauded the president's idealism, their bitterness over the war spoke louder. Since August 1914, 15 million people had died, and huge swaths of territory had been ravaged by war. Someone had to pay. So when it came to drawing up peace terms, popular sentiment within the allied countries focused almost entirely on punishing the losers.

Wilson was convinced that vengeful peace terms would only make war more likely in the future, and despite the public mood, he believed he could win over to his view the other two dominant figures at the conference: Prime Minister David Lloyd George of Great Britain and Premier Georges Clemenceau of France. However, it was not at all clear that Wilson could get his own country to ratify the peace treaty, once it was completed, since the U.S. Senate was dominated by his political opponents. So after attending the opening sessions of the conference in January 1919, he went back to the United States for a month, to shore up his political support. Meanwhile, his representatives soldiered on at the conference, though many of them were either suffering from flu or trying to recover from it.

On Wilson's return to Paris in early March, he entered the final weeks of intensive negotiations with Lloyd George and Clemenceau. During Wilson's absence, Clemenceau had survived an assassination attack that left him badly shaken. Over the weeks that followed, he developed a series of "colds" that were almost certainly influenza. In March, Lloyd George too was stricken by flu. Wilson himself was tense and exhausted, but he held up until April 3, when in the course of a single day, he developed laryngitis, spasms of coughing, a sky-high fever, and severe diarrhea. The onset was so sudden, his doctor initially thought the president had been poisoned, but he soon concluded that it was just a severe case of flu. (Because Wilson had a series of strokes later in the year, some historians have speculated that his problems in April might have been stroke-related, but the consensus today is that flu was the right diagnosis.)[5]

When Wilson returned to the conference table after several days in bed, his debilitated condition struck everyone who saw him. Colleagues commented on his weakness, fogginess of mind, and moments of paranoia. Lloyd George referred later to Wilson's "nervous and mental breakdown" at this time.[6] The negotiations among the Big Three proceeded, however, with Wilson now accepting almost every punishing measure he had opposed in the past. So, for instance, the final treaty required only the defeated nations to disarm, forced the losers to hand over sizable chunks of territory, and held them responsible for paying huge reparations to cover the cost of all civilian damage during the war.

Wilson did come out of the negotiations with the victory he valued most—the inclusion of the League of Nations in the treaty. But in the end, that victory too was diminished, since the U.S. Senate refused to ratify the treaty, or to join the League. Wilson's desperate efforts to stave off this defeat brought on a series of strokes in the fall of 1919 that reduced him to a helpless invalid and effectively ended his presidency. For the remaining 18 months of his term, the president stayed in seclusion, while his wife took over as his spokesperson. He left office in 1921 a broken man, and died in 1924.

Wilson's losses in 1919 had big consequences. The harsh terms imposed on Germany fed national resentment and undermined the German economy, thus discrediting the country's postwar leaders and helping to pave the way for the rise of Adolf Hitler. As for the League of Nations, the loss of the United States as a member was hardly fatal, but it did serve to weaken the organization, which in turn made it harder still for the League to present a united front against fascism in the years ahead. And so, in different ways, each of Wilson's defeats after World War I helped to make World War II at least somewhat more likely.

How large a role did influenza play in these events? Certainly, the controlling majority in the U.S. Senate was going to oppose joining the treaty and the League of Nations, no matter what the state of Wilson's health. If he had been in better mental and physical shape, he might have lobbied the American public more effectively, and might conceivably have been more willing to accept certain compromises that his supporters endorsed but that he refused to consider. Nevertheless, influenza was probably not a decisive factor in this sad story.

On the other hand, influenza may indeed have played a role in the way the peace terms were actually determined. However eager the British and French public were for revenge, one can imagine that with a healthier staff and with Wilson himself in sharper condition, it might have been possible to avoid the almost total collapse of the American negotiating position that occurred in the final weeks of the conference. We need to remember, too, that Clemenceau and Lloyd George were also weakened by influenza. There are indications that Lloyd George, at least, understood that a more generous peace might actually be a better solution.[7] Unfortunately, in his case and Clemenceau's, the course requiring the least energy was to stick to the harsh peace terms that their constituents were demanding. So, while Wilson's physical condition diminished his will to push for more generous terms, theirs probably made them cling more tightly than ever to the political safety of the punitive approach.

It is strange to think that the fate of millions of people could be affected by the decisions of a handful of men sitting around a conference table.

And it would be stranger still if it turned out that the behavior of those men was determined, at least in part, by a microscopic virus masquerading as "the Paris cold."

COUNTING THE COST

As the Paris Peace Conference came to an end in the spring of 1919, so did the influenza epidemic that had so terrorized the world. At one point in the fall of 1918, when the number of flu cases was spiraling upward by the day, physician Victor Vaughan had warned: "If the epidemic continues its mathematical rate of acceleration, civilization could easily disappear from the face of the earth within a matter of a few more weeks."[8] Fortunately, not every human being in the world was susceptible to the disease. And so, after racing three times around the globe, assaulting every susceptible person in its path, there came a time—a little over a year after the initial flare-up in Haskell County, Kansas—when the epidemic simply ran out of new people to infect.

Efforts to calculate how many people had died began almost as soon as the epidemic ended. The earliest estimates set the global death toll at 6 to 10 million,[9] but the obstacles to getting accurate statistics were monumental, given the large number of countries involved, the inadequate record-keeping in many localities, and the challenges of compiling, analyzing, and transmitting data in that pre-computer era. Nevertheless, scholars persevered in the effort, and in 1927 Edwin O. Jordan increased the estimate to about 22 million.[10] The number has been climbing ever since.

One of the most important factors in the continual raising of the global mortality estimates has been the growing availability of information about how the epidemic affected non-industrial societies. For instance, current calculations indicate that deaths in India alone totaled nearly 20 million—as many as Jordan's initial estimate for the whole world. The figures for China's losses are lower, but scholars are not certain whether this represents a true lower death toll or simply less complete reporting.[11]

Similarly, in Table 4, Germany's mortality rates are lower than one would expect, given the terrible reports of conditions in that country during the epidemic. Perhaps the chaotic wartime conditions there contributed to underreporting. This is a reminder that even though many gaps in the record have been filled in, the estimated totals are still a work in progress. So the figures in Table 4, compiled by demographers Niall Johnson and Juergen Mueller in 2002, should not be taken as final data, but simply as another step in the continuing struggle to calculate the full impact of the 1918 epidemic.

Table 4 World mortality estimates, selected countries, influenza epidemic, 1918–1920

	Population 1918	Approximate deaths	Rate per 1,000
AFRICA			
Egypt	12,936,000	138,600	10.7
Ghana (the Gold Coast)	2,298,000	88,000–100,000	43.5
Nigeria	18,631,000	455,000	24.4
South Africa	6,769,000	300,000	44.3
AMERICAS			
Brazil	26,277,000	180,000	6.8
Canada	8,148,000	50,000	6.1
Mexico	14,556,000	300,000	20.6
USA	103,208,000	675,000	6.5
ASIA			
China	472,000,000	4,000,000–9,500,000	8.4–20.1
India	305,693,000	18,500,000	6.1
Indonesia	49,350,000	1,500,000	30.4
Japan	55,033,000	388,000	7.0
EUROPE			
England and Wales	34,020,000	200,000	5.8
France	32,830,000	240,000	7.3
Germany	58,450,000	225,000	3.8
Hungary	7,880,000	100,000	12.7
Italy	36,280,000	390,000	10.7
Spain	20,880,000	257,000	12.3
Sweden	5,810,000	34,000	5.9
OCEANIA			
Australia	5,304,000	14,000	2.7
GLOBAL MORTALITY TOTAL	**Estimated rate:** 2.5–5.0		
	Estimated deaths: 49,000,000–100,000,000		

Source: Johnson and Mueller[12]

As Table 4 indicates, scholars now believe that at least 50 million people died in the 1918 epidemic, and the total may well have been as high as 100 million. No war in history—and no epidemic—has ever killed so many people in such a short time. For example, World War I killed about 15 million soldiers and civilians. Even using the most conservative estimates of the epidemic death toll, these war deaths—which took place over the course of more than four years—represent less than a third of the people killed by flu in about 14 months. The worldwide mortality from the Black Death during the Middle Ages probably came closer to the flu epidemic's death toll, but that took decades to accomplish.

Overall, the 1918 flu epidemic is thought to have killed about 2.5 percent of its victims. This rate is many times higher than that of ordinary seasonal flu, but it barely compares to a disease such as cholera, which without treatment has a mortality rate of 50 to 60 percent, or untreated plague with a mortality rate of 66 percent. Even so, because the 1918 strain of influenza infected such a big share of the world's population so quickly, it was able to kill more people in a single year than many more lethal diseases.

No corner of the world—no continent except Antarctica—escaped in 1918. The epidemic generally hit cities harder than rural areas, but some of the most calamitous experiences occurred in very isolated areas, where the residents had had little previous exposure to contagious diseases. A number of Pacific islands, for instance, suffered death rates of from 15 to 20 percent, while certain Inuit villages in the Arctic were all but annihilated.[13]

When it came to gathering statistics about the epidemic in the United States, the task was certainly not as difficult as in some parts of the world, but it did present challenges. The country had no system for tracking national disease patterns, and nearly a third of the population lived in areas that did not even regularly report births and deaths to Washington. During the worst months of the epidemic, the Public Health Service arranged for state and municipal health departments to send in weekly and sometimes daily reports; these data were then compiled and published in the weekly *Public Health Reports*. This was a valuable emergency measure, but given the burden on local officials at the time, the information they provided was necessarily sketchy.

To flesh out this picture, as early as December 1918 the Public Health Service launched a series of door-to-door surveys in 10 cities and towns around the country, asking people about their experiences during the epidemic.[14] Other investigations were started as well, including a massive analysis of state and local data carried out by the Census Bureau, in collaboration with the military and the Public Health Service.[15] Then in 1927, public health scientist Edwin O. Jordan produced a 600-page book, *Epidemic Influenza*, which pulled together vast amounts of material about the disease and its impact in the United States.

As with the rest of the world, estimates of the American death toll have risen over time. At the end of 1919, scholars were putting the number at between 450,000 and 550,000.[16] Building on their work and extrapolating further to cover obvious gaps in the data, historians today estimate that about 675,000 Americans died in the influenza epidemic. We can understand the scale of this disaster better when we remember that about half of these fatalities occurred in just six weeks—from mid-September to early December 1918.[17]

Overall, the number of American deaths in the flu epidemic surpasses the death toll from any war in U.S. history except the Civil War (now estimated at 750,000). Indeed, it exceeds the *combined* American fatalities in World War I, World War II, Korea, Vietnam, Iraq, and Afghanistan. As for epidemics, in the 30-plus years since AIDS was first identified, that disease has killed about 620,000 Americans—fewer people than the flu epidemic killed in just 14 months.[18]

To analyze the impact of epidemics more precisely, public health experts sometimes calculate mortality patterns in terms of "excess deaths"— that is, the number of people who die of a particular disease in a given year *beyond* the number who usually die of that disease each year. Looking at the 1918 epidemic in that way still produces a huge number: 546,000 *excess* American deaths.[19] This means that even in an era when flu and pneumonia were typically killing at least 100,000 Americans a year, the epidemic took more than half a million additional lives.

When it comes to counting *cases* of flu in the United States, as opposed to deaths, the true total will probably never be known. For one thing, many patients never got sick enough to call a doctor, especially during the mild first wave of the epidemic. Furthermore, by the time that mandatory reporting of influenza began in the fall, doctors were so busy that their reporting was undoubtedly somewhat hit or miss. With those data limitations in mind, the best available estimates suggest that about 25 million Americans contracted flu at some point during the epidemic— roughly one person out of every four.[20] To imagine the equivalent today— since the current U.S. population is three times larger—we would need to picture how it would feel if, in just over a year, 75 million Americans suddenly fell ill with the same disease.

In the nearly 100 years since the epidemic ended, researchers have pored over the data, looking for patterns. As we have noted, the most obvious pattern was by age. Older people proved to be *less* susceptible than expected (perhaps because of their previous exposure to the epidemic of the 1890s), and children were hit somewhat harder than usual. But the excess deaths among young adults were extraordinarily high. This helps to explain why the epidemic affected the armed forces so severely, and why young mothers and fathers died in such numbers. In this strange epidemic, as historians Dorothy Pettit and Janice Bailie have observed, children were more likely to lose their parents than their grandparents.[21] Young women who were pregnant were especially vulnerable; their flu was more likely to turn into pneumonia, and when it did, they were more likely to die. A nurse in St. Louis summed up the pattern bleakly: "If women were pregnant, it just seemed like they were doomed."[22]

Everyone agreed about which age groups were hit the hardest in 1918, but there was more contention about the pattern of vulnerability by income. Commentators at the time frequently observed that this epidemic was "no respecter of persons," that it was attacking rich and poor alike. Since there were plenty of flu victims in every income group, this interpretation had a certain plausibility; indeed, some historians continue to repeat it to this day. But in 1927, when Edwin O. Jordan reviewed firsthand accounts from the epidemic, he found "almost universal agreement" that the flu had been worse in poor urban neighborhoods.[23] A few years later, Edgar Sydenstricker came to the same conclusion. After analyzing the Public Health Service survey data, he concluded not only that poor urban neighborhoods had had more influenza cases per capita, but also that when poor people caught flu, they were more likely to die.[24] This would help to explain the high rates of death and disease among immigrant groups such as Italians and Russian Jews, the majority of whom in 1918 were both city dwellers and poor.

What made the urban poor more vulnerable? Contributing factors probably included being in worse health to start with, lacking access to care, and having to keep working even when they became sick. Another factor was crowding, which was an almost universal feature of poor urban neighborhoods in 1918. We have already discussed how congestion in the military camps helped to spread influenza among the soldiers, and it is likely that congestion in urban slums helped to spread the disease among poor civilians.

However disproportionally the epidemic chose its victims, no group of Americans emerged unscathed. And although the impact in the United States was less deadly than in some of the world's poorer countries, the epidemic was still a punishing experience for everyone who lived through it, with aftereffects that simmered below the surface for many years.

SCARS AND LEGACIES

Running for president in 1920, Senator Warren G. Harding promised the American people "a return to normalcy." Nothing could have pleased his audience more. Over the past two years, they had experienced the final year of the war, the devastating flu epidemic, the collapse of Woodrow Wilson's presidency, a wave of postwar strikes, a Red Scare involving mass arrests and deportations, and a recession. Carrying his reassuring message like a banner, Harding won the election in a landslide, and when he was sworn into office in March 1921, he used the words "normal" and "normalcy" five times in his inaugural address.[25]

Once Harding actually took office, his term was marred by scandal and it ended abruptly when he died in office of a heart attack. But American life did indeed become more "normal" than it had been during the traumatic period between 1918 and 1920. The war was over, and so were the difficult years just after the war. As for the flu, local hospitals no longer had beds in the halls, the downtown streets were busy again, people could gather at parties without worrying about what they might catch, and hearses no longer waited in line at the cemetery gates. The great 1918 epidemic was a thing of the past.

Or was it? In fact, a country cannot snap back immediately from so devastating an experience as the 1918 epidemic. Consider, for example, the fact that in the course of a single year, the Unites States had lost to influenza hundreds of thousands of young men and women who were just reaching the most productive period of their working lives. The famous surgeon Harvey Cushing, who barely survived the epidemic himself at that age, called these flu victims "doubly dead in that they died so young."[26] We can only imagine what all those un-lived years might have contributed to the American economy and American society.

The loss of so many bread-winners left thousands of families in desperate financial straits. In response, some widows turned for help to relatives or public charity, while others took jobs themselves, or put their children to work.

During the 1918 epidemic, life insurance companies had to pay out such huge sums in death benefits that many of them came close to bankruptcy. But the industry profited in the long run, because the fact that so many breadwinners had died so suddenly made even young families afraid to be without coverage. Targeting that vulnerability, one insurance ad in the early 1920s read: "Can You Afford Sudden Death? If Not, Protect Your Family and Business By Life Insurance."[27] It is not hard to understand the combination of memories and fears that made this ad so effective.

Recognizing that all these changes had social as well as economic implications, a Chicago settlement report observed: "The after effects of the influenza will be felt in family life for some time. Motherless children, heavy debts incurred, impaired general health—these problems will last over many a year."[28]

One striking indicator of the epidemic's long-term effects was the number of orphans; in New York City alone, about 21,000 children lost both their parents.[29] Even losing one parent could turn your life upside down. Caroline Wernecke was just 4 weeks old when her father, a Wisconsin doctor, died of flu. Decades later, she said: "I've been told what a wonderful man he was, but couldn't he have lived a little longer? Why did he die at the age of 39? Here I am, almost 90, and I still think of 'what might have been'." Dr. Wernecke's death was an economic blow to his family, as well as an emotional one. His widow supported the children as best she could, but funds were always tight, and when Caroline and her brother finished high school, neither one of them could afford to attend college as they had hoped.[30]

Given women's limited earning capacity in 1918, it is not surprising that the death of a father could plunge a family into financial trouble. But in an era when it was widely assumed that men could not raise children on their own, the death of a mother could also destroy a family. For instance, Michael Wind lost his mother to flu when he was 5 years old. The day after she died, Wind's father took all six children to the subway and bought them each a candy bar. "I knew then that something was wrong," says Wind. "My father couldn't afford such treats. Sure enough, we were on our way to an orphanage." Looking back on these events many years later, he describes a lifetime shadowed by that early loss.[31]

Novelist Mary McCarthy, who lost both parents to the epidemic, highlights another long-term effect of this kind of early loss, when she describes how she and her brother have struggled over the years to reconstruct the facts of their own childhood. She writes: "My brother Kevin and I have a burning interest in our past, which we try to reconstruct together, like two amateur archaeologists, falling on any new scrap of evidence, trying to fit it in, questioning our relations, belaboring our own memories." With no parents to pass on the family lore and no relatives who remember much about the children's early years, says McCarthy, "the chain of recollection—the collective memory of a family—has been broken."[32]

The emotional burdens of the epidemic were nearly as heavy when the situation was reversed, and parents lost their children. An Atlanta woman describes the blow her grandmother suffered when both her husband and her youngest daughter died of influenza. She carried on, raising her remaining children on her own. But, says her granddaughter, "I don't think she was ever really happy again."[33] A Syracuse man tells an even darker story about his mother, recalling how losing a son to the disease, plus having a severe case of flu herself, changed his mother from a buoyant, active woman into a gloomy spectator of life who throughout the rest of his childhood rarely left her chair. Her sorrow pervaded the household, and when she died at 60, her husband said sadly that his only comfort in looking at her in the coffin was to see once more the untroubled face of the woman he had loved when he was young.[34]

People who had had influenza themselves also found the effects hard to shake, even long after they had supposedly recovered. Katherine Anne Porter wrote:

> The experience simply divided my life, cut across it like that . . . It was, I think, the fact that I really had participated in death, that I knew what death was, and had almost experienced it . . . Now if you have had that, and survived it, come back from it, you are no longer like other people, and there's no use deceiving yourself that you are.[35]

Porter felt alone in her alienation, but in fact there were millions of other Americans who, like her, were deeply affected by having come face to face with death.

Besides the people who carried emotional scars, there were others whom the epidemic left physically disabled. Disability was not the typical outcome of influenza. Usually the disease sapped patients' energies for a month or perhaps two, after which they fully regained their health. But some people experienced a puzzling array of aftereffects, including loss of smell and taste, hair turned white, cardiac trouble, kidney problems, and vascular damage. Not all these conditions were scientifically proved to be a result of influenza, but there was enough evidence to suggest a strong connection.[36]

There were also indications that influenza could leave patients vulnerable to disorders of the brain and nervous system. As we have noted, a good number of flu patients suffered from delusions or hallucinations while they were sick. Furthermore, some autopsies suggested that in fighting off flu, the patients' immune systems had attacked their brain cells. All this made it seem reasonable to look for an association when, in later years, some former flu patients developed neuropsychiatric problems such as twitching, dementia, paralysis, meningitis, and even a rare form of schizophrenia.[37]

The Puzzle of Flu and Encephalitis Lethargica[38]

One of the lingering medical mysteries from 1918 is whether the flu epidemic had anything to do with the epidemic of encephalitis lethargica (EL) that swept Europe and North America during the 1920s. First identified by an Austrian neurologist, Constantin von Economo, during World War I, this disease—which is sometimes called "sleepy" (not sleeping) sickness—can produce muscle pains, slowness of motion, tremors, stiffness, and even psychosis. But its most dramatic effect is a coma that can last for years. It is estimated that between 1917 and 1928, more than 5 million people died from this disease.

The best-known book for general readers about EL is *Awakenings* (1973) by British neurologist Oliver Sacks—an account of the author's own experience with a group of EL patients. While working at a chronic-care hospital in New York City in the mid-1960s, Sacks learned that a number of the hospital's comatose patients had had EL in the past. He was struck by the similarity between their symptoms and those of Parkinson's disease, and he wondered whether a new treatment for Parkinson's—dopamine replacement—could also be helpful to them. Using the drug L Dopa, Sacks managed to revive all the EL patients, some of whom had been asleep for decades. Unfortunately, the effects were short-lived, and every one of the patients soon fell back into the same deep sleep as before. In 1990, this story was retold in a film, also entitled *Awakenings*, with Robin Williams portraying the character based on Dr. Sacks, and Robert DeNiro playing one of the patients.

Because the timing of the EL epidemic was so close to that of the influenza epidemic, scientists have long debated whether having had flu made people more likely to develop EL. After years of research, the possibility has still not been totally ruled out, but most authorities today believe the two epidemics were unrelated.

All the physical aftereffects we have discussed so far involved flu patients themselves. But there is also distressing evidence of medical problems among the babies that pregnant women were carrying when they got influenza in 1918. Several localities noticed an increase in the number of stillbirths during and immediately after the epidemic—in Philadelphia, which was hit particularly hard, the increase was more than 100 percent.[39] Subsequent studies confirmed that pregnant women who had flu during the epidemic—especially those who got sick early in their pregnancies—were disproportionately likely to lose their babies.[40] Nor did the troubles stop there. A study of census data from 1960–1980 showed that people born in 1919 to women who had flu while they were pregnant paid the price of that pre-birth exposure for the rest of their lives. Compared to people born in all the other years between 1911 and 1925, these individuals had poorer school records, lower wages, higher poverty rates, more disabilities, and worse health.[41] Thus, the epidemic that circled the globe in 1918 was still exacting a cost more than five decades later.

Despite these dramatic effects on individual Americans' lives, the epidemic had less long-term impact on the fields of health and medicine than one might expect. For instance, in the early 1920s, American reformers hoped that the lack of federal leadership during the epidemic might galvanize support for establishing a national health department. This is what happened in Great Britain, where memories of 1918 sparked the creation of a new Ministry of Health. But in the United States, the only change was a modest increase in funding for the very limited mission of the U.S. Public Health Service. More than three decades would pass before the federal Health, Education, and Welfare Department (the forerunner of today's Health and Human Services Department) was established in 1953.

And what about the medical profession? Of all America's caregivers, physicians had had the worst time during the epidemic, because they felt responsible for finding a way to prevent or cure influenza, and they had not been able to do either. It was not for want of trying. As Edwin Jordan observed, "Rarely if ever before in the annals of medicine has a manifestation of epidemic disease been studied by numerous observers with so much ardor and reported with so much fullness as was the epidemic."[42] But nothing had come of their efforts, and the more deeply physicians believed in scientific medicine, the more the defeat rankled. As one medical leader observed in October 1918: "There has never been anything which compares with this in importance . . . in which we were so helpless."[43]

Once the epidemic was over, most physicians dealt with their defeat by obliterating all reference to it and going on with their careers. There were some research-minded doctors, both in the United States and abroad, who did continue with their investigations. But no breakthrough was achieved, the flu did not return in any massive form, and gradually the sense of urgency diminished. By the late 1920s, only a handful of scientists were still continuing the work.

> In the face of the almost certain recurrence some day of another worldwide pandemic, we remain nearly as helpless to institute effective measures of control as we were before 1918.
> Edwin O. Jordan (1927)[44]

★   ★   ★

The influenza epidemic of 1918 left a grim trail of aftereffects. Did its presence at the Paris Peace Conference in 1919 help pave the way to World War II? That question can probably never be answered definitively. But the epidemic's other results are undeniable. Worldwide, it constituted the worst loss of life since the Black Death—far greater than the death toll of World War I. Every part of the globe was affected, and in some remote communities, the population was almost wiped out.

In the United States, hundreds of thousands of people died. And when we look more closely at the impact on American society, we can see a host of other effects, including orphaned children, bereaved husbands and wives, broken homes, financial hardships, and lingering physical and mental disabilities.

One would think that the story of such an overwhelming event in our country's history would have been told and retold for years thereafter. Certainly, the epidemic produced enough deaths to justify a monument in every town, and enough drama to inspire dozens of histories and memoirs, novels and movies. But, as we will see in the next chapter, that is not what happened. Instead, for decades after 1918, the way the American people dealt with their memories of the epidemic can be summarized in one word—silence.

NOTES

1. Lynette Iezzoni, *Influenza 1918: The Worst Epidemic in American History* (New York, NY: TV Books, 1999), 184–185.
2. Alfred W. Crosby, *America's Forgotten Pandemic: The Influenza of 1918*, 2nd ed. (New York, NY: Cambridge University Press, 2003), 181.
3. Dorothy A. Pettit and Janice Bailie, *A Cruel Wind: Pandemic Flu in America 1918–1920* (Murfreesboro, TN: Timberlane Books, 2008), 160, 161.
4. Crosby, *America's Forgotten Pandemic*, 177.
5. Pettit and Bailie, *Cruel Wind*, 171–172, Crosby, *America's Forgotten Pandemic*, 194.
6. Crosby, *America's Forgotten Pandemic*, 192–194.
7. Ibid. 186.
8. Richard Collier, *The Plague of the Spanish Lady* (London, UK: Allen & Busby, 1974), 266.
9. Cited in Col. Deane C. Howard, "Influenza—U.S. Army," *Military Surgeon* 46 (1920), 522.
10. Edwin O. Jordan, *Epidemic Influenza: A Survey* (Chicago, IL: American Medical Association, 1927), 228–229.
11. Niall P. A. S. Johnson and Juergen Mueller, "Updating the Accounts: Global Mortality of the 1918–1920 'Spanish' Influenza Pandemic," *Bulletin of the History of Medicine* 76 (2002), 112, 115.
12. Ibid. 105–115.

13. John M. Barry, *The Great Influenza: The Story of the Deadliest Pandemic in History* (New York, NY: Penguin Books, 2004, 2005), 360–361, 364.

14. Gary Gernhart, "Forgotten Enemy: PHS' Fight Against the 1918 Influenza Pandemic," *Public Health Reports* 114 no. 6 (November 1999), 560.

15. Pettit and Bailie, *Cruel Wind*, 198–199; John Eyler, "The State of Science, Microbiology, and Vaccines Circa 1918," *Public Health Reports* 125, supp. 3 (2010), 34.

16. Wade Hampton Frost, "Epidemiology of Influenza," *Public Health Reports* 34 no. 33 (August 15, 1919), 1832; Raymond Pearl, "On Certain General Statistical Aspects of the 1918 Epidemic in American Cities," *Public Health Reports* 34 no. 32 (August 8, 1919), 1743.

17. Barry, *Great Influenza*, 5.

18. "U.S. Statistics: HIV in the United States," AIDS.gov, available at http://aids.gov/hiv-aids-basics/hiv-aids-101/statistics/ (accessed August 18, 2013).

19. Jeffery K. Taubenberger and David M. Morens, "Influenza: The Once and Future Pandemic," *Public Health Reports* 125, supp. 3 (2010), 17.

20. Crosby, *America's Forgotten Pandemic*, 205.

21. Pettit and Bailie, *Cruel Wind*, 29.

22. Margaret Boehm, Interview and memoir. Interview by Karen Gregg, 1972. Norris L. Brookens Library, Archives/Special Collections, University of Illinois at Springfield, available at http://library.uis.edu/archives/collections/oral/pdf/BOEHMMARG.pdf (accessed August 19, 2013).

23. Jordan, *Epidemic Influenza*, 476.

24. Edgar Sydenstricker, "The Incidence of Influenza among Persons of Different Economic Status During the Epidemic of 1918," *Public Health Reports* 46 no. 4 (January 23, 1931), 154–169. See also: Patricia J. Fanning, *Influenza and Inequality: One Town's Tragic Response to the Great Epidemic of 1918* (Amherst, MA: University of Massachusetts Press, 2010), esp. 1–12.

25. Warren G. Harding, Inaugural Address (March 4, 1921), available at www.presidency.ucsb.edu/ws/?pid=25833 (accessed August 18, 2013).

26. Barry, *Great Influenza*, 4.

27. Allison Bell, "1918 Flu Pandemic Hit Insurers Hard," *National Underwriter, Life & Health* (March 31, 1997), 46–47.

28. Paul Buelow, "Chicago," in Fred R. van Hartesveldt, Ed., *The 1918–1919 Pandemic of Influenza: The Urban Impact in the Western World* (Lewiston, NY: Edwin Mellen Press, 1992), 143.

29. Barry, *Great Influenza*, 391.

30. Caroline Wernecke Pharis, "Otto Wernecke," *Pandemic Influenza Storybook*, available at www.flu.gov/pandemic/history/storybook/stories/courage/wernecke/index.html (accessed August 19, 2013).

31. Iezzoni, *Influenza 1918*, 159, 217.

32. Mary McCarthy, *Memories of a Catholic Girlhood* (New York, NY: Harcourt, 1957), 5.

33. Pete Davies, *The Devil's Flu: The World's Deadliest Influenza Epidemic and the Scientific Hunt for the Virus That Caused It* (New York, NY: Henry Holt, 2000), 99.

34. Ellen Rhodes Haberer, personal email communication, March 27, 2012.

35. David A. Davis, "Forgotten Apocalypse: Katherine Anne Porter's 'Pale Horse, Pale Rider,' Traumatic Memory, and the Influenza Pandemic of 1918," *Southern Literary Journal* 43 mp/2 (Spring 2011), 57–58.

36. Pettit and Bailie, *Cruel Wind*, 30.

37. Barry, *Great Influenza*, 378–381.

38. Sherman McCall, et al. "The Relationship Between Encephalitis Lethargica and Influenza: a Critical Analysis," *Journal of Neurovirology* 14 no. 3 (May 2008), 177–185; Paul Bernard Foley, "Encephalitis Lethargica and Influenza: I, II, and III." *Journal of Neural Transmission* 116 (2009), 143–150, 1295–1321.

39. U.S. Bureau of the Census, Special Tables of Mortality from Influenza and Pneumonia in Indiana, Kansas, and Philadelphia, PA, (Washington, DC: Government Printing Office, 1920), 9.

40. Kimberly Bloom-Feshbach, et al., "Natality Decline and Miscarriages Associated with the 1918 Influenza Pandemic: The Scandinavian and United States Experiences," *Journal of Infectious Diseases* 204 (October 15, 2011), 1157–1164.

41. Douglas Almond, "Is the 1918 Influenza Pandemic Over? Long-term Effects of In Utero Influenza Exposure in the Post-1940 U.S. Population," *Journal of Political Economy* 114 no. 4 (August 2006), 672–712. See also: Douglas Almond and Bhashkar Mazumder, "The 1918 Influenza Pandemic and Subsequent Health Outcomes: An Analysis of SIPP Data," *American Economic Review* 95 no. 2 (May 2005), 258–262.

42. Cited in Nancy Tomes, "'Destroyer and Teacher': Managing the Masses During the 1918–1919 Influenza Pandemic," *Public Health Reports* 125, supp. 3 (2010), 51.

43. Barry, *Great Influenza*, 403.

44. Cited in George E. Dehner, *Influenza: A Century of Science and Public Health Response* (Pittsburgh, PA: University of Pittsburgh Press, 2012), 50.

CHAPTER 7

The Long Silence

Suppressing the Memory

*The public is quickly forgetting that there ever was such a
thing as an epidemic of influenza.*

                            Moving Picture World (1919)[1]

Miranda, the central character in Katherine Anne Porter's *Pale Horse,
Pale Rider*, is lying in bed, delirious with influenza and floating
blissfully through a dream landscape. Suddenly, a "vague tremor of
apprehension" runs through her, and a thought comes to her mind "as
clearly as a voice in her ear." It says: "*Where are the dead? We have forgotten
the dead, oh, the dead, where are they?*"[2] Was the voice referring to the people
who had died in World War I? Or in the epidemic? Probably both. But
in terms of the epidemic, this much is clear: in the decades after 1918,
forgetting the dead is exactly what happened—at least in the public sphere
of American life.

THE EPIDEMIC VANISHES

There is a reason that hundreds of American towns have a statue of a
Civil War soldier in the courthouse square. There is a reason that there
are monuments to the two world wars all over the United States, and
that the opening of the Vietnam Memorial in Washington, DC, was taken
by many veterans of that war as a sign that they were finally being
welcomed home. There is a reason that crowds of people gather whenever
the AIDS Memorial Quilt is put on display. Monuments and memorials
play a vital role in our society—they pay tribute to those who have died,
they acknowledge the experience of the survivors, and they keep all of us
in touch with important moments in our shared past.

So it matters that in the years after 1918, Americans created hardly any visual reminders of the influenza epidemic. In Raleigh, North Carolina, there is a monument to caregivers who were struck down by the disease. In Ligonier, Pennsylvania, there is a memorial to the local children who died of flu. And if you search Hillside Cemetery in Silverton, Colorado, you will find a plaque marking the place where more than 100 of the town's flu victims were buried in a mass grave. But that is about it.

Beyond these local memorials, and a handful more like them, the only visual evidence of the great epidemic is the hundreds and thousands of individual graves scattered through military and civilian cemeteries, both in the United States and overseas. Some of them specifically mention influenza as the cause of death. More often, you have to make your own guess, guided only (in the civilian cemeteries) by the relatively young age of the victims and the fact that most of them died in the fall of 1918. Nowhere in the 50 states is there a monument that speaks to the whole epidemic experience, or conveys the scale of the calamity that assaulted American society in 1918.

Read the popular press during the years just after the epidemic, and you can almost see the experience starting to sink out of sight. As early as the winter of 1919, while influenza was still going strong in many parts of the country, magazines and newspapers had already begun to refer to the epidemic in the past tense. Over the next year the press occasionally published retrospective articles about it, or offered predictions about when the next outbreak might occur. And there was a brief increase in media attention during the winter of 1920, when flu deaths started climbing again. But the danger passed, and after that the subject virtually disappeared.

American novelists paid hardly more attention to influenza than the journalists. To take four notable examples, Ernest Hemingway, F. Scott Fitzgerald, William Faulkner, and John Dos Passos all made their names during the 1920s writing compelling novels about their own times. Yet not one of them included in his work more than a passing mention of the epidemic, despite the fact that all four of them lived through it and Dos Passos nearly died of it.

A handful of literary works did deal with the subject, including Thomas Wolfe's *Look Homeward, Angel*, Willa Cather's *One of Ours*, William Maxwell's *They Came Like Swallows*, Mary McCarthy's *Memories of a Catholic Girlhood*, and—most memorably—Katherine Anne Porter's *Pale Horse, Pale Rider*. These authors aside, the generation of American writers who directly experienced the epidemic remained virtually silent on the subject. And that silence has continued almost unbroken into our own time. With the exception of a very few recent novels, such as Myla Goldberg's *Wickett's Remedy* and Thomas Mullen's *The Last Town on Earth*, it is fair to say that the 1918 epidemic remains unexplored territory in American fiction. As for drama, Horton Foote's *1918* (made into a movie in 1985) is about the only notable play dealing with the epidemic.

Nor have American poets had much to say on the subject. Even the great poet William Carlos Williams left the topic of influenza untouched, despite the fact that as a full-time physician, he was intensely involved in combating the disease. In fact, about the only well-known American poem that emerged from the epidemic was the rhyme that children used to chant as they skipped rope in 1918. It went as follows:

> I had a little bird. Its name was Enza.
> I opened the window, and in-flu-Enza.

Historians might have filled the gap left by the novelists and the poets, but for the most part they did not. From the 1920s right up to the present day, histories and biographies dealing with the years around 1918 have had remarkably little to say about the epidemic, rarely giving it more than a few paragraphs and sometimes disposing of it in a footnote.[3] As for full-length treatments, nearly 60 years would pass before Alfred Crosby became the first professional historian to devote an entire book to the subject. (His 1976 book, *Epidemic and Peace: 1918*, was later republished under the title *America's Forgotten Pandemic*.) Within the past decade, more historians have written on the subject, but the total number remains fairly small.

One might expect that American medical leaders would have taken the lead in retelling the story of the epidemic, but for years they barely touched it. The perfect example is Vincent Vaughan, a leading physician of the World War I era, who had the opportunity to visit Camp Devens during the terrifying first weeks of the fall wave. In his 464-page auto-biography, Vaughan devoted exactly two paragraphs to the epidemic —the first describing the terrible scene at Devens, and the second, 50 pages later, noting briefly that the disease swept the world and saying flatly, "I am not going into the history of the influenza epidemic."[4] As science writer Gina Kolata observes: "If men like Vaughan did not want to remember the flu, who did?"[5]

> Many Americans know more about medieval plague than about the greatest mass death in their grandparents' lives.
> Arno Karlen, medical scholar[6]

Certainly not America's other military doctors, or medical historians, or the biographers of great men of medicine. Instead, if they discussed the epidemic at all, they generally presented it as a minor exception to the dominant trend of medical progress. Here are some examples, with my own italics added. From a physician at Camp Devens: "Taken as a whole, the incidence of disease, *except during the epidemic of influenza and pneumonia*, was what may be called normal."[7] A statistician reviewing hospital records from 1918 observes that admission rates were unusually low, "*if the epidemic influenza months September and October are excluded*."[8] And finally, a medical historian describing twentieth-century disease trends writes: "*If deaths from the influenza pandemic of 1918–1919 (a worldwide pandemic that killed millions) are omitted*, the declining role of infectious diseases as a cause of mortality becomes readily apparent."[9]

These writers are correct that on the whole, medical science did become increasingly effective during the first half of the twentieth century, that infectious disease rates declined significantly, and that the proportion of soldiers who died from disease during World War I was the lowest on record. So it is true that the medical setbacks experienced during the epidemic of 1918 were an exception to the overall trend. But what an exception! Given the fact that this particular exception infected perhaps a quarter of the world's population and killed at least 50 million people, it surely merited greater attention than the parenthetical references it typically received from historians throughout the 1920s and for many years thereafter.

WHY THE SILENCE?

When we study the epidemic today, one of the hardest things to understand is how such an epic event could have sunk so completely out of sight for so many years. We can understand physicians' reluctance to dwell on an experience that represented one of the great medical failures of the twentieth century. But what about everyone else?

In fact, many other Americans, too, had been shaken by their powerlessness in the face of the epidemic. As long as the crisis lasted, they could lose themselves in the day-to-day demands of responding to it— putting to full use the systematic problem-solving, the organizational experience, the public health capacities, and the networks of volunteers that the country had developed during the years before the war. No matter how desperate the situation might be, there was at least some satisfaction in mobilizing the resources to meet it.

But once the emergency was over, the memory of those efforts seemed dwarfed by the scale of the losses. For instance, how could the commander of Camp Sherman in Ohio balance the value of his struggle to control the disease against the fact that it had still managed to kill more than 1,100 of his men?[10] How could the residents of Pittsburgh take pride in their fight against influenza when, despite all their efforts, the city had lost more than 7,000 people? To put the question more broadly: how could the American people as a whole live with the memory of an experience that seemed to negate the very optimism and self-confidence that had defined them as a society?

In the face of such a defeat, perhaps it is not surprising that many Americans simply chose to push the memory aside and move on. The truth is, none of us likes to remember painful experiences. War veterans, in particular, have often expressed such feelings. For instance, a young private writing home from France during World War I must have spoken for many of his fellow soldiers when he said he had stopped keeping a diary because he did not want to remember what he had seen. He and his comrades, he said, "only long for the time when these memories will be drowned out by the love of our dear ones and the pursuit of peaceful duties."[11]

Flu survivors, too, were eager to put the epidemic behind them. Thomas Mullen discovered this fact while doing research for his novel, *The Last Town on Earth*. Mullen says that when he talks with people whose parents survived the flu, "their stories always end with some variation of the line: '. . . but she never talked about it.'"[12] Just like battle veterans, many of the people who survived the epidemic must have felt that the best way to put the terrible experience behind them was to bury it deep inside.

The parallel with battle veterans is especially relevant, because the war and the epidemic were so closely intertwined. We have seen how influenza raced through America's troops, and how war priorities helped to keep the flu virus circulating through civilian society as well. There was also the matter of timing—the fact that the first two waves of the epidemic coincided almost exactly with the period of the United States' most intense involvement in World War I—both of them started early in 1918 and ended in the late fall. And because of limited troop transports, most U.S. soldiers did not actually make it home from Europe until about the time the third wave of the epidemic was ending, in the spring of 1919. Given these circumstances, it was inevitable that the war and the epidemic should have been associated in Americans' minds.

Not everyone wanted to banish entirely their memories of

> Dorothy Langan was born a few years after the epidemic ended. As a child, she discovered that in 1918 her father had lost all three of his brothers to influenza in just four days. Yet however huge this event had been in her father's life, within the Langan household it was almost never mentioned.[13]

recent events, but even when they allowed these memories to surface, they tended to be selective. And again and again, it was the war, not the epidemic, that people chose to focus on. Compare the epidemic to World War I, and you can see why the epidemic may have been harder to shape into a satisfactorily "memorable" event. It had no official beginning, no definable enemy, it was only sporadically covered in the press, and above all, it did not end in victory—in fact, it had no clear end at all; it simply melted away over time. Nor did the epidemic produce any popular heroes—certainly no one as picturesque as flying ace Eddie Rickenbacker, who brought down more than 20 German planes, or Sergeant Alvin York, who single-handedly knocked out 32 German machine guns.

The epidemic must have seemed especially anticlimactic—and unheroic—to America's soldiers. Whatever their dreams of valor at the battlefront, half of them never even left the United States, while another quarter of them remained stuck behind the lines in Europe. And in these mundane settings, hundreds of thousands of them came down with influenza, and tens of thousands died. What did it mean to die in this way? What exactly were they dying *for*? Nothing, it seemed. As literary critic David A. Davis observes, "The soldiers died heroically, but the sick just died."[14] No wonder that most American histories of World War I, and most of the country's memorials to that war, have little to say about the disease that accounted for so many of the war dead.

Even in civilian circles, the war offered a much more compelling narrative to hold onto than the epidemic. After all, from the time the United States entered the conflict in April 1917 until the Armistice in November 1918, the American people were bombarded with daily reminders that supporting "the war to end all wars" was a noble, patriotic, and historically significant endeavor, requiring the dedicated effort of every person in the country. This message was reinforced through the draft (and the prosecution of those who opposed it), as well as through speeches, books, advertisements, celebrity appearances, songs, newspaper stories, magazine articles, food conservation drives, and the huge nationwide Liberty Bond campaigns.

By contrast, given the federal government's lack of involvement in combating the epidemic and the spotty coverage in the media, most Americans experienced influenza primarily as a local event. Having only a limited sense of the epidemic's global significance, local residents worked together to combat the disease during the eight or 10 weeks that it threatened their own communities, but they did so more or less in isolation. And when the epidemic was gone, it left them with little to take pride in, other than the memory of their own struggles to hold death at bay. By contrast, the war offered something much more impressive: the

> We arouse and arrange our memories to suit our psychic needs.
>
> Michael Kammen (1991)[15]

memory of having participated in a sustained national crusade against a visible—and, in the end, decisively vanquished—enemy.

Under these circumstances, perhaps it is not surprising that as Americans' public memory of 1918 began to take formal shape during the 1920s—expressed in histories, memoirs, novels, songs, movies, biographies, and monuments—the epidemic virtually disappeared from sight. And, naturally enough, this censored version of the past helped to define what would be remembered—and *not* remembered—by subsequent generations.

Medical historians could have recovered the story; certainly the epidemic was one of the most dramatic medical events in American history. But they were caught up in chronicling medicine's victorious campaign against infectious disease. And in that grand narrative, studded with achievements such as the germ theory revolution and the introduction of antibiotics in the 1940s, there was simply no place for the dismal failure of medicine against influenza in 1918.

And so, from a reluctance to dwell on past suffering, plus a tendency to subordinate memories of the epidemic to memories of the war, as well as physicians' eagerness to focus on their victories rather than their biggest defeat, for many years the 1918 epidemic sank from public view.

AIN'T WE GOT FUN?

As the 1910s gave way to the 1920s, the country entered the "Jazz Age"—an era now romantically associated with carefree flappers, raccoon coats, and bootleg liquor. "Night and daytime, always playtime," went the 1921 song, "ain't we got fun?" Of course, most Americans did not spend all their time dancing the Charleston and drinking bathtub gin. But with the reform-minded Progressive Era and the death-haunted war years behind them, Americans did seem to devote more of their energies than ever before to simply enjoying life.

People's inclination to concentrate on their own immediate well-being was reinforced by the country's prosperity. After a brief depression in 1920–1921, the economy rebounded quickly, spurred on by mass-produced cars, a burgeoning advertising industry, and expanding distribution networks for everything from groceries to electrical appliances. The stock market kept climbing, car ownership soared, the production of cosmetics tripled, and by 1929 weekly attendance at the movies was close to 80 million. In the past, Americans had tended to think of themselves primarily as producers, but in the new economy their role as consumers became just as important.

Besides the booming economy, most historians agree that during the decade after 1918, a kind of backlash developed against the patriotic fervor of the war years, and that this played a part in Americans' increasing tendency to concentrate on their own pleasures. More than 115,000 U.S. soldiers had died in the war. Had all that slaughter really helped to "make the world safe for democracy," as President Wilson had promised? Many people were unconvinced. If recent experience taught any lesson at all, it was that no matter how grand the initial speeches, most wars ultimately came down to the same thing: rain and mud and death. And what had all that aspiration and self-sacrifice produced? An unsettled peace in Europe, handsome profits for the bankers who had made the war loans, and no gain at all for ordinary citizens. Surveying the outcome, many Americans seem to have concluded that it made more sense to take pleasure in the moment and stop worrying so much about saving the world.

What scholars have *not* generally linked to the pleasure-seeking inclination of the 1920s is the emotional aftereffect of the influenza epidemic. But if Americans' encounter with mass death in World War I contributed to their change of mood in the 1920s, then surely it is significant that far more Americans died, and infinitely more of them came face to face with death, during the epidemic than during the war. So it would not be surprising if these survivors—like battle veterans—emerged from their experience determined to enjoy the time they had left.

Americans were certainly not the first to respond to an epidemic in this way. As early as 430 BC, the Greek historian Thucydides noted a similar reaction after the Plague of Athens. He wrote that, having been reminded how fragile and unpredictable life could be, the Athenians who survived the epidemic "resolved to spend quickly and enjoy themselves, regarding their lives and riches as alike things of a day."[16] This is exactly how a great many Americans must have felt after the 1918 epidemic. Hundreds of thousands of them had barely survived, and nearly everyone had watched people dear to them sicken and die. So it is not hard to understand why, in the years that followed, they might have concluded that in an unpredictable world, getting the most out of today was the one thing they could count on.

★   ★   ★

And so, within a few years after 1918 flu epidemic ended, it more or less vanished from public view, subordinated to commemoration of the war, and praise of medical science, and the pleasures of peacetime prosperity.

Indeed, not until the late twentieth century, when infectious disease began once again to loom as a major threat, did the epidemic begin to be recognized as a significant event in American history.

But out of sight does not mean out of mind. Below the surface, that searing encounter with influenza lived on in the minds and hearts of those who had gone through it. Time passed, and people went on with their lives. But, as Thomas Wolfe wrote after his brother died of flu, "It was not, could never be, all right."[17]

NOTES

1. Richard Koszarski, "Flu Season: *Moving Picture World* Reports on Pandemic Influenza, 1918–1919," *Film History* 17 no. 4 (October 2005), 466.
2. Katherine Anne Porter, *Pale Horse, Pale Rider* (New York, NY: Harcourt Brace, 1939), 200–201. Italics added.
3. See, for instance, David M. Kennedy, *Over Here: The First World War and American Society* (New York, NY: Oxford University Press, 1980), which devotes one sentence and a footnote to the epidemic; John Duffy, *The Sanitarians: A History of American Public Health* (Champaign, IL: University of Illinois Press, 1990), which in three chapters about the period 1900–1930, devotes less than two pages to the epidemic; John Keegan, *The First World War* (New York, NY: Knopf, 1999), which covers the epidemic in one long sentence; and Michael Neiberg, *Fighting the Great War: A Global History* (Cambridge, MA: Harvard University Press, 2005), which includes only two brief mentions of the epidemic.
4. Victor C. Vaughan, *A Doctor's Memories* (Indianapolis, IN: Bobbs-Merrill, 1926), 383–384, 432.
5. Gina Kolata, *Flu: The Story of the Great Influenza Pandemic of 1918 and the Search for the Virus That Caused It* (New York, NY: Simon & Schuster, 1999, 2005), 49.
6. Cited in Pete Davies, *The Devil's Flu: The World's Deadliest Influenza Epidemic and the Scientific Hunt for the Virus that Caused It* (New York, NY: Henry Holt, 2000), 63.
7. Cited in Carol R. Byerly, *Fever of War: The Influenza Epidemic in the U.S. Army During World War I* (New York, NY: New York University Press, 2005), 11.
8. Ibid. 186.
9. Gerald N. Grob, *The Deadly Truth: A History of Disease in America* (Cambridge, MA: Harvard University Press, 2002), 215.
10. Kolata, *Flu*, 22.
11. Ronald Schaffer, *America in the Great War: The Rise of the War Welfare State* (New York, NY: Oxford University Press, 1991), 173.
12. Catherine Belling, "Overwhelming the Medium: Fiction and the Trauma of Pandemic Influenza in 1918," *Literature and Medicine* 28 no. 1 (Spring 2009), 58.
13. Barbara Reynolds, "Thomas Langan," *Pandemic Storybook*, available at www.flu.gov/pandemic/history/storybook/stories/courage/langan/index.html (accessed Augusut 19, 2013).
14. Davis, "Forgotten Apocalypse," 61.

15. Michael Kammen, *Mystic Chords of Memory: The Transformation of Tradition in America* (New York, NY: Knopf, 1991), 9.

16. Cited in John Akritas, "Castoriadis and Thucydides and the Greek Riots," in Benjamin DeMott, Ed. *First of the Year*, v. III (Piscataway, NJ: Transaction Publishers, 2010), 288.

17. Thomas Wolfe, *Look Homeward, Angel* (New York, NY: Scribner's, 1929, 1957), 443.

CHAPTER 8

Feeling Vulnerable Again

Fears of Another 1918

They fancied themselves free, [but] no one will ever be free so long as there are pestilences.

Albert Camus, The Plague[1]

Picture a pig with a fever, a cough, and a runny nose. Now picture a barn full of them. This is the sight that greeted Richard Shope, a young research scientist, in the course of a family visit to Iowa in 1929. Shope had recently been studying hog cholera, in connection with his work at the Rockefeller Institute for Medical Research. When he began asking local farmers about this current disease—swine flu—he learned that it had been circulating in the Midwest for more than a decade. Federal veterinarians had managed to transmit the flu from one pig to another by taking nasal mucus from a sick animal and administering it to a healthy one. But they had not been able to separate out whatever it was in the mucus that was making the pigs sick.

Shope took some samples back to his lab at the Rockefeller Institute and started his own investigation. Using filters so fine that they strained out all the bacteria, he was able by 1931 to demonstrate that what was left—the "filterable virus," as it was then called—had the power to cause swine flu in healthy animals. Although the infecting organism was too small to be seen under the microscopes of the day, Shope had effectively isolated the swine flu virus.[2]

Shope had the idea that his findings might be helpful in understanding human influenza, and his hopes were soon fulfilled. In 1933, Britishers Christopher Andrewes, P. P. Laidlaw, and Wilbur Smith demonstrated that Shope's methods could be used to communicate human flu to ferrets. But even more helpful was an accident that occurred in the Britishers' lab—a sick ferret sneezed in a research assistant's face. When the assistant came down with flu, it was clear that influenza could also travel in the other direction—from ferrets to humans.[3] Then in 1937, flu outbreaks in two American mental institutions were followed by outbreaks in nearby pig farms, suggesting that, in addition, the virus could be passed from humans to pigs.[4]

As Shope explored the past history of swine flu, he learned that the disease had made its first recorded appearance at the Cedar Rapids Swine Show in October 1918, shortly after the second wave of the flu epidemic hit the United States. Millions of pigs ultimately came down with the same respiratory disorder. Scientists at the time disagreed about what was ailing them, but J. S. Koen, a veterinarian with the U.S. Bureau of Animal Husbandry, had no doubts. He wrote in 1919: "It looked like flu, it presented the identical symptoms of flu, it terminated like flu, and until proved it was not flu, I shall stand by that diagnosis."[5] Shope was convinced that Koen had been right. And he concluded that since influenza had been circulating among humans for seven or eight months in 1918 before the Swine Show, it was probably the pigs who caught the disease from humans, rather than vice versa.[6]

So here was the critical question: was the flu virus that was circulating among pigs in the 1930s the same one that had swept through both humans and pigs in 1918? The answer to that question came from testing people's immune reactions to the 1930s swine flu virus. Both in England and later in the United States, it was found that people who were old enough to have lived through the 1918 epidemic generally produced antibodies against the virus when they were exposed to current cases of swine flu. This showed that their immune systems recognized the flu strain, whereas younger people's reactions indicated that this was their first exposure. These experiments suggested that the 1918 flu virus had been circulating among pigs ever since the epidemic.[7] More importantly, they indicated that Shope had isolated not just the swine flu virus, but a descendant of the virus that had caused the 1918 epidemic among humans.

LEARNING FROM EPIDEMICS

By the late 1930s, the invention of powerful new microscopes made it possible to actually see viruses. With this new capacity and the pioneering example of Shope and his colleagues, scientists carried out hundreds of studies of influenza during the 1930s and early 1940s. They learned a good deal about the workings of the virus, and in 1941 the army developed the first successful preventive flu vaccine.

In the years that followed, researchers' experience with a succession of flu epidemics (1946, 1957, 1968) taught them that developing a vaccine tailored to one particular year's virus was not enough, because flu viruses are continually changing–either through gradual mutation (viral *drift*) or through exchanging genes to create a new subtype (viral *shift*). Given the rate of viral change, the only way to keep producing effective vaccines would be to monitor flu outbreaks all the time, and factor each year's changes into the "recipe" for the next year's vaccine. Building the necessary global surveillance system took many years, but scientists' first disconcerting encounters with viral change in the early postwar years provided a major spur to the development of this network.

One of the effects of viral *shift* is to change the surface proteins that control how a virus seizes and lets go of individual cells. These proteins are of two kinds: HA (hemagglutinin) and NA (neuraminidase), so viral subtypes are identified by their different H and N numbers. For instance, the 1918 virus, being the first that was identified, is known as H1N1, whereas a different subtype that first surfaced in 1957 is known as H2N2. Once a new subtype has established itself, the older one often sinks out of sight, and this is what happened with H1N1, which after 1957 was not seen again among humans for nearly 20 years, although a related strain continued to circulate among pigs.

By the mid-1970s, scientists had made considerable progress in understanding viral change. But whenever there were significant alterations within a single year, it still took too long to recognize the change, design the new vaccine, and produce it in quantity. In fact, between the development of flu vaccine in 1941 and the mid-1970s, there was not a single major flu epidemic for which manufacturers were able to produce the necessary vaccine in time to be useful. The lesson seemed to be that in order to respond effectively, health planners needed to start getting ready before the epidemic even began. But how could they do that?

Many scientists believed that the recent past suggested an answer to that question. Noting that since World War II there had been a global flu epidemic every 11 years—1946, 1957, and 1968—they theorized that the next one could be expected shortly. Accordingly, on February 13, 1976, Edwin D. Kilbourne, a medical advisor to President Gerald Ford, published an op-ed article in the *New York Times* with the arresting title: "Flu to the Starboard! Man the Harpoons! Fill 'em With Vaccine! Get the Captain! Hurry!" In the article, Kilbourne described the terrors of past flu epidemics, explained the 11-year cycle theory, and urged the country to undertake an immediate mass vaccination campaign.[8]

Six days after Kilbourne's piece appeared in the *New York Times*, the U.S. Centers for Disease Control announced that swine flu (H1N1) had broken out among the soldiers at Fort Dix in New Jersey. Over the next several weeks, many more soldiers came down with the disease and one died. This presented federal officials with a fundamental question: was the Fort Dix outbreak a solitary event, or was it the first stage of the next global epidemic? A number of considerations pushed them toward taking the more serious view: (1) the conviction that a major epidemic was about due; (2) the knowledge that H1N1 was a direct descendant of the 1918 virus; and (3) a recognition of the potential for disaster if they took a "wait and see" approach and then turned out to be wrong.

Throughout the spring and summer of 1976, high-level officials debated what should be done. On the one hand, the disease did not seem to be spreading beyond Fort Dix. On the other hand, true flu season would not begin until fall; perhaps the virus would come surging out again once cold weather arrived. So the debate proceeded, but so did the preparations for the vaccination campaign. When the vaccine was ready, President Ford made the decision to go ahead, and starting in October, it was administered to 45 million Americans.[9]

In some respects, the National Immunization Program of 1976 was an impressive achievement. Despite numerous glitches along the way, the country did manage to identify a specific flu virus subtype, develop the appropriate vaccine, produce it in bulk, and administer it to a quarter of the U.S. population—and all in less than nine months. But to the American public, the program's successes counted for nothing compared to its two overwhelming problems. First, the promised epidemic never developed. And second, about 500 of the people who were immunized developed a rare side effect—a paralyzing neurological disorder called Guillain-Barré Syndrome—and 17 of them died. In December 1976, with the epidemic still nowhere in sight and public outrage over the side effects rising, the National Immunization Program was closed down.[10]

Years later, a virologist at the U.S. Centers for Disease Control observed that he and his fellow flu researchers still carried two powerful and contradictory images in their minds. The first was the devastation of the 1918 epidemic, and the second was the fiasco of the 1976 swine flu outbreak. The first showed how terrible uncontrolled influenza could be, while the second showed the danger of moving too quickly. Each experience, said the virologist, revealed the terrible cost of guessing wrong. He added: "These things have haunted people."[11]

In the fall of 1977, a year after the swine flu episode, there really was a global flu epidemic. (Because it was first seen in Russia, it was called "Russian flu," although it is now thought to have started in China.) It was quite mild, affecting mostly young people. Strangely enough, this new epidemic involved a strain of H1N1 that had not been seen in general circulation since the 1950s. Why had it reappeared? That question has never been fully answered, but many scientists suspect that it escaped from a laboratory, perhaps in connection with work on germ warfare. Thus, the legacy of this particular epidemic was the ugly reminder that influenza, besides being a feared disease, could also be a weapon.

As if to make a mockery of the 11-year cycle theory, there were no more worldwide human flu epidemics for more than 25 years. But, starting in the 1990s, there was a series of bird flu epidemics that aroused grave concern, because birds, like pigs, serve as "hosts" for the influenza virus—that is, they provide it with a permanent home between outbreaks of human flu. Unlike flu in mammals, which affects the respiratory system, bird (or avian) flu settles in the host's digestive tract. It is spread through the droppings of migratory birds, and it can also establish itself in flocks of domesticated poultry, such as ducks and chickens. Indeed, wild birds often transmit the virus to domestic flocks, and vice versa. The role of domestic birds as hosts helps to explain why southeastern China has been the source of so many flu outbreaks, because nowhere else in the world do so many millions of people and domesticated birds live in such close proximity. Chinese farmers and market workers generally catch avian flu through contact with poultry that are carrying the virus.

There have probably been poultry epidemics in Southeast Asia for many generations, with periodic infection of humans. But it took the epidemics of the 1990s to highlight for modern scientists the fact that humans could catch flu from birds. When the first human victims of avian flu were identified—during a poultry epidemic in Hong Kong in 1997—once again, no one could be sure whether these few cases were the whole story, or the start of a global human epidemic. Moreover, out of the 18 people who caught avian flu that year, six died—a frightening mortality rate.[12] To keep the numbers of human victims from climbing higher, Chinese authorities engaged in an unprecedented kill-off of 1.2 million infected birds—more than half of them slaughtered in the course of a single day.[13]

The first lesson that scientists learned from the poultry epidemics of the 1990s was the fact that humans can catch flu from birds, and that if they do, many of them will die. But the second, more comforting lesson was that a scattering of human cases does not necessarily lead to an epidemic. In order to get an epidemic going, it is not enough for the virus to

Watching the extraordinarily high death rate among humans infected with avian flu in 1997, a scientist at the University of Hong Kong remembers asking himself if this was going to be 1918 all over again. "Everybody was frightened," he says. "You could feel the weight of the world pressing down on you."[14]

infect a single individual. It must also adapt sufficiently to human biology so that the virus copies that the infected person exhales are contagious to other people. Luckily for humanity, the avian flu subtype that has caused most of the recent poultry epidemics—H5N1—has so far proved unable to master the second of these tasks. So, although more than 600 people have acquired the H5N1 virus from birds since 1997, and more than half of those people have died, there are no confirmed cases of sustained human transmission.[15] And without large-scale human-to-human transmission, there can be no flu epidemic among humans.

While scientists were absorbing these facts, and working to establish more comprehensive surveillance systems to monitor avian flu trends around the world, another group of researchers was pursuing an entirely different line of inquiry. And in doing so, they would demonstrate that there were lessons to be learned not only from current flu outbreaks, but also from the great epidemic of 1918—the one that virologist Jeffery Taubenberger calls "the mother of all pandemics," because so many subsequent outbreaks have been caused by descendants of that same virus.

During the 1990s, Taubenberger was working at the Armed Forces Institute of Pathology in Washington, DC, which maintains a repository of minute tissue samples taken from dead American soldiers, all the way back to the Civil War. One day in 1995, when Taubenberger was casting about for a historical puzzle that he could explore using the institute's holdings, a colleague pointed out how little scientists knew about the virus that caused the 1918 epidemic. They had worked with the virus' drifted descendants, but no one had seen it in its original form. Could Taubenberger possibly retrieve the original virus from tissues taken from soldiers who died of flu in 1918? "That's it," exclaimed Taubenberger. "That's the project!"[16]

Taubenberger and his colleagues combed the institute's files until they found a tissue sample—preserved in a small block of waxy paraffin—from a 1918 flu victim. Taubenberger's colleague Ann Reid then began the painstaking process of separating out the tiny gene fragments—too small to be seen under a microscope—from the surrounding wax and tissue, and then amplifying and sequencing them. The work went slowly, with many setbacks, but in the early summer of 1996, Reid identified the first gene linked to the 1918 epidemic. A chill went through her. "Very few in science," she says, "are given that kind of moment."[17]

Over the next several months, working with the same specimen plus another from a second dead soldier, Taubenberger, Reid, and their colleague Amy Krafft identified fragments from four of the 1918 virus' eight genes. Because they had so little material to work with, they could not produce the full genetic sequence. Nevertheless, to have found this evidence of the 1918 virus represented a giant step forward. Taubenberger and his colleagues announced their findings in the journal *Science* in March 1997.

With the help of a retired pathologist named Johan Hultin, Taubenberger's team obtained additional samples of the 1918 virus from the still-frozen lungs of an Inuit woman who had been buried in Alaska. Pooling these samples with the ones they had been working on before, Taubenberger and his colleagues were able to announce in 2005 that they had achieved two historic goals: they had worked out the entire genetic sequence of the 1918 flu virus, and they had actually recreated the original virus in a secure lab at the U.S. Centers for Disease Control.[18]

Johan Hultin's Search for the 1918 Virus[19]

Among the people who read the 1997 *Science* article about Taubenberger's research on the 1918 flu virus was a retired pathologist named Johan Hultin. Many years earlier, as a graduate student in Iowa, Hultin had been struck by a visiting scientist's casual comment that the best place to look for well-preserved specimens of the 1918 flu virus would be in the bodies of flu victims buried in the permanently frozen ground (permafrost) of Alaska. The young Hultin determined to follow up on that possibility.

Knowing how brutally the epidemic had hit Alaska's Inuit villages, Hultin spent months poring over local maps and records to identify villages that were built on permafrost and had nearby missions with good medical records. Then in 1951, he selected the three most promising locations and traveled to Alaska to investigate them. The ground beneath two of the villages had thawed, but there was still permafrost under the village of Brevig, where 72 of the 80 inhabitants had died of flu in 1918. Exploring the frozen ground, Hultin found the bodies of five flu victims. He dug them up and extracted tissue samples from their lungs. But when he took the samples home and tried to use them to grow more of the virus, he got nothing. So he put the project aside and went on with his life.

Forty-six years later, in 1997, the news of Tauenberger's research reawakened Hultin's interest. He immediately contacted Tauenberger and arranged to go back to Brevig for another try. In August 1997, after unearthing a number of badly decomposed corpses, he had the luck to come upon the body of an obese woman whose layers of fat had helped to keep her organs intact. He cut out her two still-frozen lungs, sliced them into tissue samples, placed them in preservative, and shipped them to Taubenberger, who confirmed that they did contain genes from the 1918 virus. The genes were even more degraded than the ones Taubenberger's team had been working with, but because Hultin's samples contained 100 times more gene fragments than those samples, they made an invaluable contribution to the work.

One of the most striking of Taubenberger's findings was the discovery that none of the eight genes in the 1918 virus was human in origin; all appeared to be avian.[20] Scientists had formerly thought that a flu virus could not achieve mass circulation among humans unless it included at least some human flu genes. The idea that the 1918 epidemic was caused by a virus in which all the genes came directly from birds—no human genes at all—forced a reassessment of that theory. Many questions still remained unanswered, including when and where the 1918 virus first began to circulate among humans, how that adaptation took place, why the disease hit young adults so hard, and why the epidemic's second wave was so lethal. But by unlocking the virus' genetic code, Taubenberger's team had opened promising new pathways for exploring all those questions.

Overall, from the 1940s on, medical researchers' experience with a succession of flu epidemics helped them to burrow ever deeper into the mysteries of influenza. They learned about viral change, confronted the possibility of avian flu in humans, worked to build a global surveillance network, and struggled with the challenge of producing effective vaccines. And in 2005, with Taubenberger's findings, they made dramatic progress toward understanding the most frightening flu virus in history: the one that caused the 1918 epidemic.

WAKE-UP CALLS

Throughout the latter part of the twentieth century, as scientists were trying to learn as much as possible from each new flu epidemic, the social context within which they were doing this work was changing. That is because, over the course of these same decades, the resurgence of infectious disease was shaking people's long-held assumptions about historical trends in world health.

In 1958, medical historian George Rosen optimistically asserted that modern medicine had achieved "the virtual eradication . . . of communicable diseases."[21] Rosen's grand claim reflected a widespread conviction that during the first half of the twentieth century, mankind had gone through an epoch-making "health transition." For most of recorded history, the theory went, infectious disease had represented the dominant threat to human life. But with the rise of scientific medicine— as well as improvements in the standard of living and advances in public health—the diseases that had once terrorized humanity had gradually receded. So instead of dying young of infectious disease, people were surviving into adulthood and old age. There was a price: they were now living long enough to die of chronic and "man-made" ailments such as heart disease and cancer. But in exchange, they were getting many more years of healthy life. This was what the "health transition" had produced: the growing prevalence of chronic disease, but also the longer life spans that came with the conquest of infectious disease.

Similar predictions about the disappearance of infectious disease had been circulating for years, starting almost as soon as the first successes of the bacteriological revolution became known in the late nineteenth century. And it is true that as early as 1910, the microbial causes of many epidemic diseases had been identified, and a number of these diseases had been brought under control—either, like cholera, through improved public health measures, or, like typhoid and rabies, through vaccines. Yet despite these gains, as late as the 1940s many infectious diseases remained unconquered, including tuberculosis, measles, whooping cough, and polio—and, of course, influenza. Indeed, the helplessness of the medical profession in the face of the 1918 flu epidemic had provided the most painful reminder possible that infectious disease was still a potent threat.

But then came antibiotics. And as these "miracle drugs" showed their power over a host of infectious diseases, they seemed to make all the promises of the past come true. First explored in the 1930s, and developed during World War II to treat Allied soldiers, these drugs reached a broad civilian market during the postwar years. They functioned superbly against bacterial infections, and it was widely assumed that viral infections would soon be conquered as well. Sure enough, in the 1950s and 1960s, Jonas Salk and then Alfred Sabin developed vaccines against one of the most feared viruses of all—polio. Within a decade, the number of new polio cases in the United States plummeted from tens of thousands every year to less than 100. Medical researchers made little further progress against viruses, but the power of antibiotics to control bacterial infection was so dramatic that in 1967 the U.S. Surgeon General announced to Congress: "The time has come to close the book on infectious diseases. We have basically wiped out infection in the United States."[22]

As we have noted, influenza epidemics continued to appear about every 10 years throughout this period, but perhaps because of the regular recurrence of seasonal flu in the years between epidemics, people tended to take the disease less seriously. In a way, that was strange, since influenza remained a leading cause of death worldwide and still killed between 30,000 and 50,000 Americans every year. Nevertheless, the public tended to focus on the conquest of more dramatic diseases, such as cholera and plague, and there were many such conquests to celebrate.

It was true that, at least so far, the benefits of the health transition were being enjoyed mainly by people in industrial societies. But transition theorists were convinced that the developing nations of the world were already showing signs of moving in the same direction, and that with Western medical and financial support, they could be helped to move faster. A compelling example of the kind of progress they had in mind was the World Health Organization's successful 11-year campaign against smallpox. When, in 1980, WHO leaders announced that there was not a single case of smallpox left in the entire world, the idea that the health transition represented a better future for all seemed wonderfully confirmed.[23]

But even while people were celebrating the imminent disappearance of infectious disease, the tide was starting to turn. In 1961, for instance, the first case of a drug-resistant bacterial infection—staphylococcus—appeared in a British hospital. Known as MRSA (multidrug-resistant staphylococcus areus), this strain reached Boston in 1968, and ultimately spread throughout the world. And as it spread, the list of antibiotics that MRSA was able to withstand kept growing longer. More problems followed, including the emergence of Lyme disease (1975), Ebola fever and legionnaires' disease (1976), HIV/AIDS (1981), hepatitis C (1988), the human variant of "mad cow disease" (mid-1990s), and West Nile virus (1999).

Of all these new infections, the one that shook the world most profoundly was HIV/AIDS, because of its relentless spread, its devastating symptoms, and—in those years—its rapid progress to death. Until the mid-1990s, there was not even an effective form of treatment for HIV/AIDS. By 2011, it had infected almost 70 million people around the world, and 35 million had died.[24]

On top of the many new infections that emerged in the late twentieth century, there was also a resurgence of many familiar diseases that had supposedly been vanquished long ago, including TB, malaria, diphtheria, whooping cough, and cholera. Observing this onslaught, many scholars concluded that the world had now entered a third health transition, during which infectious disease would once again become a major threat to human life, just as it had been in ages past.[25]

Why this resurgence of infectious diseases? Public health experts have identified dozens of contributing factors. For instance, in poorer parts of the world, climate change and population pressures have led farmers and settlers to push deeper into forests and jungles, unleashing an army of unfamiliar germs carried by the birds and animals that live there. Climate change has also led to more extreme weather events, which have often wrecked local arrangements for sanitation and healthcare. At the same time, the exponential growth of urban slums, especially in developing countries, has exposed more and more people to crowding, poverty, poor healthcare, and contaminated food and water. Moreover, the global spread of the HIV

HIV/AIDS and Influenza: Comparing Two Epidemics

There are two epidemics that frighten nearly everyone: the *ongoing* HIV/AIDS epidemic, and the *potential* for a new global influenza epidemic like the one in 1918. Both diseases are contagious, and both have the power to kill millions of people. But in most other respects, they are quite different.

Identification: One of the dangers with both HIV/AIDS and influenza is the fact that infected people begin spreading the disease before they show any signs of being ill. With HIV, the virus may exist in someone's body—and be transmitted to others—for as long as five to seven years before the patient shows any symptoms. With influenza, the infectious period is much shorter—usually just a week or so. Nevertheless, because influenza spreads so quickly, considerable damage can be done even in that short period.

Prevention and control: There is currently no HIV vaccine. However, because infection is only transmitted via bodily fluids (usually blood, semen, or breast milk), the spread of infection can be effectively controlled by measures such as the use of condoms, sterile needles, treatment of expectant and nursing mothers, and careful monitoring of blood supplies.

In the case of influenza, the fact that there is a vaccine is an obvious advantage, but the current production method takes many months to complete. In the interim, it is extremely difficult to limit the spread of the disease, because flu patients continually exhale the virus into the air (especially when they sneeze or cough).

Medication: If HIV infection goes untreated, people generally survive only a few years—the virus rapidly destroys their immune systems, increasing their vulnerability to disease. And once they enter the final stage, called AIDS (acquired immune deficiency syndrome), they fall prey to a host of fatal infections.

The introduction of anti-retroviral therapy (ART) in the 1990s made medical history, changing HIV infection from a death sentence to a chronic but manageable disease. If HIV-positive people follow their prescribed regimen—daily medication and a healthy lifestyle—their life expectancy can be virtually the same as anyone else's, and their infectiousness to others can be greatly reduced.[26]

With influenza, medications are less important, although antivirals can be of some help in controlling the symptoms. However, antibiotics do play a major role in treating the secondary infections that pose the greatest threat to patients with either HIV/AIDS or influenza.

Duration: At present, HIV infection is considered a permanent condition, although there have been a few cases—not yet thoroughly studied—that suggest possible paths to a cure. Influenza, by contrast, is temporary. It may take some time for patients to recover their strength, but the actual viral infection is gone in a matter of weeks.

Case numbers: About 34 million people in the world today are living with HIV/AIDS, and approximately 2.5 million people were newly diagnosed in 2011.[27]

It is difficult to compare these statistics to the potential scale of a new influenza pandemic, but if the disease were to affect even *half* the proportion of the world's population that it did in 1918, then the number of cases in a global flu epidemic could be as high as 850 million (12.5 percent of 6.9 billion people). As for fatalities, about 35 million people in the world have died of AIDS since it was first identified in the early 1980s. This is far below the number of deaths that could be expected in just one year of a global flu epidemic—current estimates range from about 60 million to as high as 100 million.[28]

Impact: Many parts of the world are still suffering terribly from HIV/AIDS, and even areas where the rates are improving bear scars from the years when the epidemic swept the globe with no treatment available (1980s through mid-1990s). Nevertheless, in recent years both the number of new cases and the number of deaths per year have finally begun to inch down. There is a long road ahead, but after more than 30 hard-fought years, it does appear that the campaign against HIV/AIDS is starting to gain ground.

A global influenza epidemic would behave quite differently. In any specific locality, the crucial period would probably last only a couple of months. But during that period, infection rates could resemble those rarely seen with HIV/AIDS except in the hardest-hit countries of Africa. Moreover, societies around the world would probably be affected within a few weeks of each other, leaving no untouched region that could render assistance to the others. Thus, although HIV/AIDS represents a heavier long-term burden on society, it is probably accurate to say that a worldwide influenza epidemic would, *while it lasted*, constitute an even greater crisis.

virus has left millions of people with compromised immune systems, which in turn make them more susceptible to other diseases.

Ironically, the provision of healthcare has sometimes made the situation worse instead of better. For instance, the overuse and misuse of antibiotics has speeded the mutation process in bacteria and viruses, helping them to develop drug-resistant strains. Hospitals, too, have facilitated the spread of infection through the use of non-sterile needles and instruments, the circulation of contaminated air, and—most commonly—through the caregivers' own unwashed hands. The anti-vaccine movement has also played a role. As rising numbers of parents have chosen not to immunize their children, a number of diseases—including whooping cough, measles, and mumps—have reappeared after having been controlled for many years by vaccines.[30]

As scientists have watched the steady increase of infectious disease in recent years, they have started passing around this grim little summary of medical history: "The nineteenth century was followed by the twentieth century, which was followed by the nineteenth century."[29]

If all these changes had occurred 60 years earlier, they would not have had the same impact, because in earlier times the different parts of the world were less interconnected. But in our own time, with extensive global travel, streams of refugees, and the continual shipping of food and other products around the globe, the transmission of germs from one region to another has become virtually unavoidable.

For many people, it was the global reach of the HIV/AIDS epidemic that first hammered this message home. As Susan Sontag observes: "The AIDS crisis is evidence of a world in which nothing important is regional, local, limited; in which everything that can circulate does, and every problem is, or is destined to become, worldwide."[31] AIDS offers the darkest kind of proof, says Sontag, that we do indeed live in a global village.

Many of these trends could be seen at work in the first international disease scare of the twenty-first century—an outbreak in 2003 of SARS ("severe acute respiratory disease"), a type of viral pneumonia caused by a coronavirus (as opposed to an influenza virus). Within weeks of its emergence in China, SARS had infected more than 5,000 people there and was being carried by travelers to countries all over the world. In the six months after the first patient was diagnosed, more than 8,000 people on several continents became sick with SARS, and 774 died. (There were 27 cases in the United States, none of them fatal.)[32]

The initial response to SARS was delayed because of the Chinese government's reluctance to publicize its problems, but international health agencies heard about the outbreak through their own sources and reacted quickly. In the end, thanks to decisive action by many countries including China, and continuous information-sharing among an international network of health experts, SARS did not turn into the global catastrophe that some had feared. But everyone who was involved understood that they had had one huge advantage: patients who develop SARS do not become contagious until they are also visibly ill. This is infinitely more manageable than influenza, where the victims can infect other people for several days before they show any symptoms themselves. So in some respects, the SARS outbreak offered useful lessons for the future; in others, it was simply a reminder of how much more difficult it would be to control a flu epidemic.

Flu itself appeared in multiple forms in 2003. There was an avian flu (H5N1) outbreak in China, and a huge second one (H7N7) in northern Europe.[33] In addition, Europe, Australia, and the United States were hit hard by human flu that year. The particular subtype, H3N2, had been circulating since the "Hong Kong flu" epidemic of 1968, but this outbreak involved a strain ("Fujian flu") that was new to people's immune systems, and by bad luck it emerged too late to be included in the formula for that year's vaccine.

Six years later, in 2009, a new strain of H1N1 human flu emerged in Mexico and southern California. It spread so widely that by the end of the year it had reached all 50 states and more than 200 other countries. Most cases were extremely mild, which was fortunate, since once again it took nearly six months to produce an effective vaccine. In fact, the mildness of the outbreak led to an international debate over the fact that the World Health Organization had declared it a pandemic—that is, a global epidemic. Some suggested that this term should be reserved for epidemics that are both widespread (which 2009 was) and unusually severe (which it was not). However, the WHO's definition continues to be based solely on how widely an outbreak spreads.[34]

Today, many scientists are convinced that we will not always be as fortunate as we were in 2009. They believe that within the foreseeable future there will be a worldwide attack of influenza that, like the one in 1918, will be both widespread *and* severe—a pandemic by anyone's definition.[35]

ARE WE READY FOR A FLU PANDEMIC?

Suppose there is a great influenza pandemic in our future. One of the first things that would be helpful to know is: how soon might it happen? In 1931, the editors of the *Journal of the American Medical Association* observed: "It does not seem possible, with our present knowledge, to make any prediction as to whether or not an epidemic might be expected in the near future."[36] More than 80 years later, we are in about the same position. The theory that flu epidemics happen every 11 years has been demolished, and nothing better has taken its place. We do know that epidemics are most likely to develop when a new viral strain or subtype emerges. We can describe the type of mutational or reassortment process that is likely to be involved, and we have learned how to recognize it once it occurs. But we are no better at predicting when it might happen than our great-grandparents were in 1918.

Besides being uncertain about the timing of the next pandemic, we are also in the dark about which virus is most likely to cause it. It will probably not be one of the two subtypes (H1N1 and H3N2) that have been circulating over the past few decades, because so many people in the world have already been exposed to them. Could it be the much-feared avian flu virus H5N1, or perhaps the new avian virus that emerged in the Shanghai region in 2013—H7N9?

Given the terrible mortality rates that have occurred when humans have acquired these viruses from birds, it is clear that if either one of them

Richard Krause, former director of the National Institute for Allergy and Infectious Disease, points out that in Elizabethan times the popular name for influenza was "the Newe Acquayantance." We should bear in mind, he says, that no matter how carefully we track the viruses we already know about, the next one that sweeps us off our feet may well be an entirely "new acquaintance."[37]

could adapt sufficiently to start a human epidemic, it would be devastating. But neither has done so thus far—not even H5N1, which has now been circulating among domesticated birds, with periodic human cases, for more than 15 years. Will this trend continue? Or have we just been lucky? No one is certain. Thanks to Jeffery Taubenberger and his team, we know that in 1918 a virus consisting entirely of bird flu genes was able to cause a pandemic among humans. And if this could happen once, then presumably it can happen again.

In recent years, scientists in several countries started manipulating the H5N1 influenza virus genetically, in order to study the process by which it might mutate into a more contagious form. When the public learned about these experiments in 2011, there was widespread fear that the manipulated virus might escape from the labs (or perhaps be stolen), and trigger a major pandemic. This led to a temporary moratorium on the experiments, but work resumed in 2013—controlled in a number of countries (including the United States) by new guidelines to ensure heightened security.[38]

One area where we have made considerable progress is in spotting new viral subtypes once they emerge, thanks largely to the research and surveillance activities of the World Health Organization, the U.S. Centers for Disease Control and Prevention, and other health agencies around the globe. The U.S. Public Health Service, too, has become a much more important participant in disease surveillance, with a force of 6,200 specialists posted in cities all over the world. With these resources at our disposal, it is extremely unlikely that we would find ourselves in the situation of 1918, when the first wave of the epidemic spread across the United States for several months without arousing any national attention, and when even at the height of the crisis in the fall, individual states and cities were left with little more than news bulletins about the progress of the disease beyond their borders. Today, with the Internet to share information, and with jet planes to speed supplies, specimens, and personnel where they are needed, we would be in a much better position to pool our knowledge and our resources.

Of course, jet planes that carry people and supplies around the world also carry germs. Indeed, the rise of global air travel is generally recognized as a significant factor in the recent re-emergence of infectious diseases, and it would certainly spread influenza germs at breakneck speed. On the other hand, the population movements associated with World War I also gave the flu virus plenty of opportunity to race from country to country—far more than would otherwise have been the case in that era. Most scholars think the virus would travel still faster today, but even if it were only slightly faster, there are other factors in the way we live now that could well make us more vulnerable—most notably the increase in the world's population since 1918.

With almost four times as many people in the world as there were in 1918, the pressure for space and resources has greatly facilitated the transmission of disease, especially in cities. In 1950, there were only two metropolitan areas in the whole world with a population over 10 million (New York and Tokyo). By 2011, there were 23 of these "megacities." Nearly all of them are in Asia or Latin America, and most of them include huge slums packed with desperately poor people.[39] Bearing in mind how easily flu spreads from person to person, especially in crowded conditions, one can only imagine the havoc that a flu pandemic could create among, say, the 14 million inhabitants of Karachi, Pakistan, or the 20 million people of Mexico City.

But if we are at a disadvantage compared to 1918 in some respects, we do have one significant advantage—the progress that has been made on the medical front. At present, there are three principal medical interventions that can be used against influenza: vaccines, antiviral medications, and antibiotics. Vaccines, if they are properly tailored to the dominant virus, can provide quite high levels of protection. Antivirals can shorten the duration of a patient's illness and reduce the likelihood of secondary complications. And while antibiotics will not touch the virus itself, they can be very effective against bacterial pneumonia, which is one of the most frequent causes of death among flu patients.

Unfortunately, these medical interventions also have their limitations. For instance, drug resistance is a growing problem with both antivirals and antibiotics. And when it comes to vaccines, the established method for producing them is still agonizingly slow. For one thing, the process involves growing the virus in fertilized chicken eggs—using roughly one egg for every dose of vaccine needed. In a pandemic situation, simply obtaining the number of eggs needed to produce, say, 300 million doses of vaccine would be a tremendous challenge. Scientists are working on an alternative cell-based method that does not require eggs. But that still does not address the other continuing problem, which is the need to redesign the vaccine and produce a whole new supply every year, so as to keep pace with the virus' mutations.

Many experts believe that the only real solution is to develop a "universal" flu vaccine that will be effective against all viral strains of the disease, and can therefore be stockpiled in advance. But no such vaccine has yet been developed. So at present, probably the most that can be hoped for is to speed up the existing production methods as much as possible, and plan ahead for how scarce supplies will be allocated and distributed— not only in the United States, but around the globe.

Another challenge we would be certain to face in the event of a pandemic would be a shortage of healthcare facilities and staff. Such shortages are a well-recognized problem in poorer parts of the world, but they could well represent a significant problem in the United States as well. In recent decades, financially pressed hospitals have balanced their budgets by cutting back dramatically on both beds and personnel. This has enabled them to avoid the expense of maintaining (and staffing) beds that often stand empty, but it has virtually eliminated the hospitals' "surge capacity" for coping with emergencies. The probable scarcity of staff and beds during a pandemic would be especially important because of the way that Americans' medical expectations have changed. Back in 1918, home care was the norm, except in cases of dire emergency. Today, if people's conditions are at all serious, they expect to be hospitalized, with a full battery of tests and medical assistance. It is hard to imagine how those expectations could be met under the conditions of a major pandemic. Nor are Americans likely to be satisfied with 1918's version of an emergency flu hospital, which often involved simply setting up cots in a high school gym, or erecting tents in an open field.

LESSONS FROM 1918

So here we are, almost 100 years after the last great influenza crisis. In some respects, we are much better equipped to face a flu pandemic today, but in other respects, we are burdened with new limitations and vulnerabilities. Given these circumstances, what we can learn from the American experience in 1918?

To begin with, we can learn from their failures. Not the medical failures—decades of scientific work have taken us far beyond the heartbreaking defeats faced by medical researchers in 1918. Nor are we likely to devote major resources to some of the less effective methods of disease control that were widely used then, such as the wholesale disinfection of public buildings and the wearing of flimsy gauze masks.

But there was one major flaw in the country's performance in 1918 that we *can* learn from—the failure of leadership, particularly at the national level. Except for Surgeon General Rupert Blue of the Public Health Service, it is hard to think of a single top federal official—civilian or military—in 1918 who devoted significant energy to dealing with the epidemic as a national catastrophe, or to supporting the American people as they dealt with it themselves.

It is true that up to that time, the federal government had had little to do with combating infectious disease, except for the Public Health Service's quarantine activities in the seaports. But the Wilson administration did not hesitate to assume sweeping new powers when it came to fighting World War I, including the imposition of strict wage regulations, the federal takeover of the railroads, and the vigorous suppression of dissent. So it worth noting that when it came to the epidemic, these leaders were remarkably passive—no national response plan, no systematic outreach to state governors, no forceful drive to ensure that the most underserved communities had medical coverage, and no move to curtail the greatest crowd-generating activity of the whole fall—the Fourth Liberty Bond campaign—which was promoted at the height of the epidemic with parades and rallies all over the country, even in cities that were otherwise enforcing strict social distancing rules.

Above all, the nation's leaders failed in their obligation to communicate honestly with the public about what was happening. From President Wilson, who does not seem to have uttered a single public word on the subject, to the many local officials who continually denied the obvious gravity of the situation, leaders of the time seemed possessed by the idea that acknowledging what was going on would undermine the war effort. The Surgeon General did offer periodic policy recommendations and disseminated a great deal of educational material about influenza. But none of his suggestions had the impact that would have been achieved by forceful and honest updates on the situation from the nation's top political leaders.

In an emerging crisis, it is always difficult to strike the right balance between saying too much and saying too little. The journal *Nature* highlighted this dilemma—specifically in relation to a possible flu pandemic—in a 2009 editorial appropriately entitled "Between a Virus and a Hard Place." As the authors pointed out, "If the agencies alert people and the pandemic fizzles out, they will be accused of hyping the threat and causing unnecessary disruption and angst." On the other hand, "if the agencies downplay the threat and an unprepared world is hit by a catastrophe on the scale of 1918, the recriminations will come as fast as you can say 'Hurricane Katrina.'"[40] The task is indeed challenging, but when the nation is facing a crisis like the 1918 epidemic, officials have an absolute obligation to provide prompt and honest information, so as to counter rumors, explain what is happening, describe the steps that are being taken, and reassure people that they are not alone in their struggle. This kind of public communication was sorely lacking in 1918.

Obviously, the fact that America's leaders were facing the double challenge of an epidemic and a world war made things more difficult for them, and one can understand that many of these men felt absolutely obligated to put the war first. On the other hand, with the advantage of hindsight, one could question whether even military priorities were best served by pursuing policies that kept the epidemic spreading—for instance, the continued draft calls, the frequent transfers from camp to camp, and the massive troop shipments. Certainly any other set of decisions that resulted in the death of 43,000 soldiers and sailors might be thought to merit review. But the tension between continuing the war and stopping the epidemic did present the nation's leaders with an unusually difficult set of choices.

Hopefully, the pandemic we face will not come in the middle of a world war. Furthermore, modern-day airplanes and computers and cell phones, as well as new organizations such as the Centers for Disease Control and the Federal Emergency Management Agency, can all help to ensure that local needs are promptly identified, and that staff and supplies are sent to the areas of greatest need. But, as we have seen in disasters such as Hurricane Katrina in 2005 and Hurricane Sandy in 2012, successful disaster management takes more than a closetful of resources—it also requires solid advance planning, good coordination, speedy responses, and excellent public communication. None of these was particularly visible in 1918; all would be needed to see us through the next pandemic.

What about what Americans did right in 1918? Two initiatives stand out particularly, both carried out at the community level: the mobilization of local professionals and volunteers to care for the sick, and the social distancing policies, such as theatre closings, that were established to control the spread of infection.

In terms of mobilizing local residents to care for the sick, we could hardly do better than what American towns and cities accomplished in 1918, with strong support from the Red Cross, local charitable agencies, and innumerable civic organizations. On the professional side, the centralized allocation of nurses (and, in some places, of doctors) made the best possible use of the resources available, and would be well worth adopting ourselves. As for volunteers, the emergence of female voluntarism as a major social force during the Progressive Era—reinforced by the strong emphasis on women's volunteer activities during World War I—meant that in 1918 millions of American women were already accustomed to doing organized work for their communities. Today, when so many more women have paying jobs, female voluntarism is far less common.

Certainly, volunteers in our own time have responded nobly to crises such as the World Trade Center disaster in 2001 and Hurricane Katrina in 2005. But in those cases, residents from outside the affected area converged to help those in trouble. The challenge would be far greater if communities all over the country were struck at more or less the same time. Under those circumstances, could we mobilize as many local volunteers as our great-grandparents did—and on such short notice? The performance in 1918 certainly sets a standard we should reach for.

When it comes to social distancing, the most direct method is to identify and confine everyone who has caught the disease, as well as those who have been exposed to it. Despite some initial delays, this was done quite effectively during the 2003 SARS outbreak. But the reason the method worked so well there is because SARS victims do not become infectious until they are visibly ill. With influenza, by the time people show any signs of being sick, they have already been spreading the disease for several days. Thus, although isolating flu patients played some part in the 1918 response, and probably would again in a future flu pandemic, it is not likely to be anywhere near as effective as it was with SARS.

The truth is that once an influenza epidemic gets going, one has to assume that any public gathering will include at least some people carrying the virus. That is why so many American communities in 1918 chose to apply the broader form of social distancing—that is, to close as many public gathering places as possible. Some historians have questioned the value of these closings, but the consensus today seems to be that they did help to limit the spread of infection, when they were started quickly and maintained until the local epidemic was really over. There is still some debate about the pros and cons of closing schools,[41] but with regards to the other kinds of closings—theaters, bars, churches, athletic contests, etc.—these are generally thought to have been useful.[42]

Public compliance with these social distancing regulations was generally quite good in 1918, although resistance did increase as the weeks went by. But in 1918 the obedience and public-spirited restraint that were required for social distancing harmonized well with the qualities that were continually being asked of Americans anyway, because of the war. How would public closing regulations fare today? On the positive side, the limitations might be somewhat easier to live with, thanks to the proliferation of social media, TV, and other sources of home entertainment. Nevertheless, in today's changed political climate, any limit on public gatherings would probably face more aggressive legal challenges than in 1918, and could also be impeded by the generalized distrust of government that has been expressed more widely in recent years.

Depending on people's point of view, then, social distancing policies may strike Americans of the twenty-first century as futile or restrictive or old-fashioned. But we need to remember that the more modern approaches we might prefer, such as vaccines and antiviral medications, are likely to take some time to prepare in sufficient quantity. Until they are ready, we are likely to find ourselves dependent on exactly the same social distancing policies that our great-grandparents used in 1918.

★   ★   ★

America's experience with the great epidemic of 1918 offers useful lessons for the future, and scholarly interest in the subject has risen in parallel with our growing concern about the possibility that we ourselves may face another flu pandemic. Indeed, historian George Dehner observes that, however much past generations may have suppressed the memory of 1918, it is now the specter that lurks continually in health planners' minds "as if it were a crazy aunt in the attic."[43] More than anything else, the mention of the 1918 epidemic has become shorthand for describing the dangers that may lie ahead of us.

But this country's encounter with influenza in 1918 constitutes more than a reference manual for the future. The epidemic was a devastating experience in its own right, and a major event in American history, notable for its unprecedented levels of death and disease, the wounded lives it left behind, the impact it had on the nation's armed forces during World War I, and the challenges it presented to individual American communities. The 1918 epidemic may well help to illuminate our own future, but it also deserves to be remembered because, for the millions of Americans who experienced it firsthand, it was truly a matter of life and death.

It is never easy to grasp the enormity of other people's experience, especially when it happened many years ago. But if we do not try, we will miss the most vital part of what history can do for us. The Latin word for "remember" is *recordari*. It comes from *cor*, which means "heart." In that sense, to remember something means to pass it once more through your heart.[44] This interpretation suggests how we should remember America's great flu epidemic—not simply by documenting the facts of a bygone catastrophe, but by passing once more through our hearts the compelling story of what the epidemic meant to the people who were there.

NOTES

1. Albert Camus, *The Plague* (New York, NY: Vintage, 1991), 37.
2. Shope collaborated with his mentor, Paul Lewis, until Lewis' death in 1929. Gina Kolata, *Flu: The Story of the Great Influenza Pandemic of 1918 and the Search for the Virus That Caused It* (New York, NY: Simon & Schuster, 1999, 2005), 66–73; Christopher Andrewes, *Richard Edwin Shope, 1901–1966: A Biographical Memoir* (Washington, DC: National Academy of Sciences, 1979), 354.
3. George E. Dehner, *Influenza: A Century of Science and Public Health Response* (Pittsburgh, PA: University of Pittsburgh Press, 2012), 62–63; Kolata, *Flu*, 73–75.
4. Andrewes, "Richard Edwin Shope," 356.
5. Alfred W. Crosby, *America's Forgotten Pandemic: The Influenza of 1918*, 2nd ed. (New York, NY: Cambridge University Press, 2003), 297.
6. Edwin D. Kilbourne, "Influenza Pandemics of the 20th Century," *Emerging Infectious Diseases* 12 no. 1 (January 2006), 9.
7. Kolata, *Flu*, 78–80.
8. Edwin D. Kilbourne, "Flu to the Starboard! Man the Harpoons! Fill 'em With Vaccine! Get the Captain! Hurry!" *New York Times* (February 13, 1976), 32.
9. Richard Krause, "The Swine Flu Episode and the Fog of Epidemics," *Emerging Infectious Diseases* 12 no. 1 (January 2006), 41–42; Kolata, *Flu*, 121–150; Pete Davies, *The Devil's Flu: The World's Deadliest Influenza Epidemic and the Scientific Hunt for the Virus that Caused It* (New York, NY: Henry Holt, 2000), 262–267.
10. Kolata, *Flu*, 151–185.
11. Ibid. 185.
12. John M. Barry, *The Great Influenza: The Story of the Deadliest Pandemic in History* (New York, NY: Penguin Books, 2004, 2005), 114.
13. Kolata, *Flu*, 219–241.
14. Ibid. 237, 238.
15. World Health Organization, "Cumulative Number of Confirmed Human Cases for Avian Influenza A(H5N1) Reported to WHO, 2003–2013" (July 5, 2013), available at www.who.int/influenza/human_animal_interface/H5N1_cumulative_table_archives/en/ (accessed August 21, 2013).
16. Kolata, *Flu*, 192.
17. Ibid. 214.
18. Jeffery K. Taubenberger, et al., "Characterization of the 1918 Influenza Virus Polymerase Genes," *Nature* 437 no. 7060 (October 6, 2005), 889–893; Terence M. Tumpey, et al., "Characterization of the Reconstructed 1918 Spanish Influenza Pandemic Virus," *Science* 310 no. 5745 (October 2005), 77–80.
19. Ibid. 85–115, 255–266, 308.
20. Jeffery K. Taubenberger and David M. Morens, "Influenza: The Once and Future Pandemic," *Public Health Reports* 125, supp. 3 (2010), 19–20.
21. Cited in David Rosner, "Spanish Flu, or Whatever it Is . . .," *Public Health Reports* 125, supp. 3 (2010), 46.
22. Cited in Ross Upshur, "Ethics and Infectious Disease," *Bulletin of the World Health Organization* 86 no. 8 (August 2008), available at www.who.int/bulletin/volumes/86/8/08-056242/en/ (accessed August 21, 2013).

23. Laurie Garrett, *The Coming Plague: Newly Emerging Diseases in a World Out of Balance* (New York, NY: Farrar, Straus, & Giroux, 1994), 40–47.

24. World Health Organization, "Global Health Observatory: HIV/AIDS," available at www.who.int/gho/hiv/en/ (accessed August 20, 2013).

25. See, for instance, Ronald Barrett, et al., "Emerging and Re-emerging Infectious Diseases: The Third Epidemiologic Transition," *Annual Review of Anthropology* 27 (1998), 256–265.

26. World Health Organization, "Consolidated Guidelines on the Use of Antiretroviral Drugs for Treating and Preventing HIV Infection: Recommendations for a Public Health Approach" (June 30, 2013).

27. UNAIDS, "Global Fact Sheet 2012," available at www.unaids.org/en/media/ unaids/contentassets/documents/epidemiology/2012/gr2012/20121120_FactSheet_ Global_en.pdf (accessed August 20, 2013).

28. See, for instance, Christopher J. L. Murray, et al., "Estimation of Potential Global Pandemic Influenza Mortality on the Basis of Vital Registry Data from the 1918–1920 Pandemic: A Quantitative Analysis," *Lancet* 368 no. 9554 (December 23, 2006), 2211–2218; and Taubenberger and Morens, "1918 Influenza," 21.

29. Crosby, *America's Forgotten Pandemic*, xiii.

30. See, for instance, Seth Mnookin, *The Panic Virus: A True Story of Medicine, Science, and Fear* (New York, NY: Simon & Schuster, 2011).

31. Susan Sontag, *AIDS and Its Metaphors* (New York, NY: Farrar, Straus, & Giroux, 1988), 180–181.

32. World Health Organization, "Global Response Alert: Summary of probable SARS cases with onset of illness from 1 November 2002 to 31 July 2003" (as of December 31, 2003), available at www.who.int/csr/sars/country/table2004_04_ 21/en/ (accessed August 20, 2013).

33. Barry, *Great Influenza*, 114.

34. Nancy K. Bristow, *American Pandemic: The Lost Worlds of the 1918 Influenza Epidemic* (New York, NY: Oxford University Press, 2012), 196; "Round Table" (contributions by Peter Doshi, Daniel J. Barnett, Luc Bonneux and Wim Van Damme, Heath Kelly, Nicholas F. Phin, and Angus Nicoll), *Bulletin of the World Health Organization* 89 no. 7 (July 2011), 532–544.

35. See, for instance, Barry, *Great Influenza*, 450–456; Michael Osterholm, "Preparing for the Next Pandemic," *New England Journal of Medicine* 352 no. 18 (May 5, 2005), 1839–1842; Kilbourne, "Influenza Pandemics of the 20th Century," 12–13; Taubenberger and Morens, "Influenza: The Once and Future Pandemic," 23–25.

36. Cited in Taubenberger and Morens, "Influenza: The Once and Future Pandemic," 22.

37. Krause, "Swine Flu Episode," 40, 43.

38. "Research to Resume on Modified, Deadlier Bird Flu," *New York Times* (January 24, 2013), A8; David Malakoff, "U.S. Announces More New Rules for Potentially Risky Research," *ScienceInsider* (February 21, 2013), available at http://news.sciencemag.org/people-events/2013/02/u.s.-announces-more-new-rules-potentially-risky-research (accessed August 20, 2013).

39. United Nations, Department of Economic and Social Affairs, Population Division, *World Urbanization Prospects: The 2011 Revision: Highlights* (United Nations, 2012), 6–7.

40. "Between a Virus and a Hard Place" (Editorial), *Nature* 459 no. 7241 (May 2009), 9.

41. Alexandra Stern, "Closing the Schools: Lessons from the 1918–1919 U.S. Influenza Pandemic," *Health Affairs* 28 no. 6 (2009), W1066–1078; Gerardo Chowell, et al., "Measuring the Benefits of School Closure to Mitigate Influenza," *Expert Reviews in Respiratory Medicine* 5 no. 5 (2011), 597–599.

42. See, for instance, Richard Hatchett, et al., "Public Health Interventions and Epidemic Intensity During the 1918 Influenza Pandemic," *Proceedings of the National Academy of Sciences of the United States* 104 no. 18 (May 1, 2007), 7582–7587; Martin C. J. Bootsma and Neil M. Ferguson, "The Effect of Public Health Measures on the 1918 Influenza Pandemic in U.S. Cities," *Proceedings of the National Academy of Sciences of the United States* 104 no. 18 (May 1, 2007), 7588–7593; Howard Markel, et al., "Nonpharmaceutical Interventions Implemented by US Cities During the 1918–1919 Influenza Pandemic," *Journal of the American Medical Association* 298 no. 6 (August 8, 2007), 644–654; Joel K. Kelso, et al., "Simulation Suggests that Rapid Activation of Social Distancing Can Arrest Epidemic Development Due to a Novel Strain of Influenza," *BMC Public Health* 9 (April 29, 2009); Stephen S. Morse, "Pandemic Influenza: Studying the Lessons of History," *Proceedings of the National Academy of Sciences* 104 no. 18 (May 1, 2007), 7313–7314; Maria Balinska and Caterina Rizzo, "Behavioral Responses to Influenza Pandemics: What Do We Know?" *PLoS Current* 1 (September 9, 2009).

43. Dehner, *Influenza*, 202.

44. This point is made by Hector Abad in *Oblivion: A Memoir* (Brecon, Wales: Old Street Publishing, 2011), 241–242.

Documents

Putting the War First

The course of the 1918 flu epidemic was profoundly influenced by the fact that it coincided with the final year of World War I. Thus, for instance, in the summer of 1918 when European ships began arriving in New York City carrying passengers stricken with the new virulent strain of flu, the port health officer, Dr. Leland Cofer, flatly ruled out the possibility of slowing down the harbor's wartime traffic by holding incoming ships in quarantine. Instead—as is explained in the newspaper interview below—he sent any obviously sick passengers to local hospitals, and released everyone else. A few days after this interview, Cofer's approach was warmly endorsed by Colonel J. M. Kennedy, the army's chief medical officer at the port, who explained, "We can't stop this war on account of Spanish or any other kind of influenza."[1]

Cofer's policy had two effects. First, it placed large numbers of contagious patients in local hospitals, where the infection inevitably spread to other patients and staff. And second, it released into the city several thousand passengers and crew who had been exposed to the disease, some of whom were bound to come down with it soon. Indeed, influenza began spreading in the city almost immediately, and within a few weeks of Dr. Cofer's interview, the city health commissioner announced that new cases were being reported in New York City at the rate of 150 a day.[2]

New York Times, August 16, 1918

HEALTH HEAD CALLS FOR INFLUENZA INQUIRY

Eleven New Cases Arrive on Another Ship, but Authorities Not Alarmed

No Fear of an Epidemic

Health Officer of the Port Says He Does Not Intend to Quarantine Against the Disease

NEW YORK.—Eleven more cases of Spanish influenza, or whatever it is, were reported at Quarantine yesterday from a ship arriving from one of the Scandinavian countries. The ship's surgeon reported that all his patients were in the convalescent stage and none had developed pneumonia. The ship was passed.

The New York Board of Health, at its meeting yesterday, took official notice of the fact that there is influenza, germinated in Europe, in this city. The board ordered that cultures be taken from each one of the patients now in the Norwegian Hospital in Brooklyn, and that these cultures be sent to the board's bacteriological laboratory for observation and analysis. This was done as a precautionary measure and not, so Health Commissioner Copeland reiterated, because he or any member of the board believes there is the slightest danger of an influenza epidemic breaking out in New York.

Dr. Cofer, Health Officer of the Port of New York, was asked yesterday if he intended to establish at this port a quarantine against foreign-bred influenza. "I am glad you asked that question since it gives me an opportunity to clear up an evident confusion in the minds of many of the people of this city," he said. "To give you first a direct answer to your question, I do not intend to establish a quarantine against Influenza, Spanish or any other kind. And right here let me digress long enough to say that Spanish influenza is altogether a misnomer. We have had epidemics of influenza in this country with symptoms very like those of the cases developed in Spain. Yet the world didn't rise up and call it American or United States influenza. Nobody knows definitely whether this European variety that we have heard of recently is Spanish or Norwegian or Swedish or what.

"Now you see, and you'd better make careful notation of these, there are just six diseases which are recognized the world over by health authorities, as proper diseases against which to declare a marine quarantine. They are smallpox, leprosy, yellow fever, plague, . . . typhus fever and cholera. Just let a ship stick her nose into this harbor with a case of any one of these diseases on board and she will find herself tied up in the stiffest kind of a quarantine.

"But there are other diseases, like diphtheria, scarlet fever, tuberculosis and typhoid fever, against which there is no need of establishing a marine quarantine. There is need of exercising common sense in quarantine as in everything else. To hold up and examine every ship reporting cases on board of diseases like the last I mentioned would require, first, an immense quarantine station, and second, an immense staff. And what is much more, it would entail an interminable tie-up of shipping and a closing of the port.

"This country is at war and, besides having on our hands the winning of the war, we have also the job of supplying our Allies with much that they need with which to enable them to fight on successfully. This port cannot be clogged for a minute longer than necessity requires. Therefore, when we find what may be called minor communicable diseases on ships entering the port, such as the ones I have spoken of, and to which must be added influenza, we simply report them to the city Board of Health, which is splendidly able and enthusiastically willing to take care of each case when or before it leaves the ship at its pier.

"There is not the slightest danger of an influenza epidemic breaking out in New York, and this port will not be quarantined against that disease."

Source: "Health Head Calls for Influenza Inquiry," New York Times (August 16, 1918).

DOCUMENT 2

Battling Flu at Camp Devens

Camp Devens was a huge army training facility located about 30 miles from Boston, Massachusetts. It was not the first U.S.-based camp to be hit by the fall wave of the epidemic—that distinction belonged to Commonwealth Naval Pier, in Boston. But Devens' flu outbreak began just a few days later, and it was extraordinarily destructive. During the first week of September 1918, the Devens base hospital admitted 300 flu patients; a couple of weeks later, patients were coming in at the rate of 1,000 a day.[3] The letter below was written by a physician at the camp.

Military surgeon's letter, September 29, 1918

Camp Devens, Mass.
Surgical Ward No. 16
(Base Hospital)

My dear Burt–

It is more than likely that you would be interested in the news of this place, for there is a possibility that you will be assigned here for duty, so having a minute between rounds I will try to tell you a little about the situation here as I have seen it in the last week . . .

Camp Devens is near Boston, and has about 50,000 men, or did have before this epidemic broke loose. It also has the Base Hospital for the Div. of the N. East. This epidemic started about four weeks ago, and has developed so rapidly that the camp is demoralized and all ordinary work is held up till it has passed. All assemblages of soldiers taboo.

These men start with what appears to be an ordinary attack of LaGrippe or Influenza, and when brought to the Hosp. they very rapidly develop the most viscous type of Pneumonia that has ever been seen. Two hours after admission they have the Mahogany spots over the cheek bones, and a few hours later you can begin to see the Cyanosis extending from their ears and spreading all over the face, until it is hard to distinguish the coloured men from the white. It is only a matter of a few hours then until death comes, and it is simply a struggle for air until they suffocate. It is horrible. One can stand it to see one, two or twenty men die, but to see these poor devils dropping like flies sort of gets on your nerves. We have been averaging about 100 deaths per day, and still keeping it up. There is no doubt in my mind that there is a new mixed infection here, but what I dont know. My total time is taken up hunting Rales [*rattling in the chest*], rales dry or moist, sibilant or crepitant or any other of the hundred things that one may find in the chest, they all mean but one thing here—Pneumonia—and that means in about all cases death.

The normal number of resident Drs. here is about 25 and that has been increased to over 250, all of whom (of course excepting me) have temporary orders—"Return to your proper Station on completion of work". Mine says "Permanent Duty", but I have been in the Army just long enough to learn that it doesnt always mean what it says. So I dont know what will happen to me at the end of this.

We have lost an outrageous number of Nurses and Drs., and the little town of Ayer is a sight. It takes Special trains to carry away the dead. For several days there were no coffins and the bodies piled up something fierce, we used to go down to the morgue (which is just back of my ward) and look at the boys laid out in long rows. It beats any sight they ever had in France after a battle. An extra long barracks has been vacated for the use of the Morgue, and it would make any man sit up and take notice to walk down the long lines of dead soldiers all dressed and laid out in double rows. We have no relief here, you get up in the morning at 5:30 and work steady till about 9:30 P.M., sleep, then go at it again. Some of the men of course have been here all the time, and they are TIRED . . .

I dont wish you any hard luck Old Man but I do wish you were here for a while at least. Its more comfortable when one has a friend about. The men here are all good fellows, but I get so damned sick of Pneumonia that when I go to eat I want to find some fellow who will not "Talk Shop" but there aint none nohow. We eat it, live it, sleep it, and dream it, to say nothing of breathing it 16 hours a day. I would be very grateful indeed if you would drop me a line or two once in a while, and I will promise you that if you ever get into a fix like this, I will do the same for you.

Each man here gets a ward with about 150 beds, (Mine has 168) and has an Asst. Chief to boss him, and you can imagine what the paper work alone is—*fierce*—and the Govt. demands all paper work be kept up in good shape. I have only four day nurses and five night nurses (female), a ward-master, and four orderlies. So you can see that we are busy. I write this in piecemeal fashion. It may be a long time before I can get another letter to you, but will try . . .

Good By old Pal,
"God be with you till we meet again"
Keep the Bouells open.

Roy

Source: Copy of original letter found among other medical papers donated to the University of Michigan. Posted at http://web.archive.org/web/20081216021541/http://web.uct.ac.za/depts/mmi/jmoodie/influen2.htm l (accessed August 21, 2013). Full text also appears in Quinn, *Flu: A Social History*, 128–130.

DOCUMENT 3

Night Train to Georgia

*O*ne *of the principal factors helping to spread influenza around the United States during the fall of 1918 was the continual movement of soldiers from one training camp to another. On September 25, 1918, for instance, several trainloads of transfers set out from Camp Grant, Illinois, even though flu was already rampant there. These transfers went ahead despite a local health official's recommendation that Camp Grant be quarantined, and despite the recommendation of Army Surgeon General William Gorgas that all transfers from infected camps be stopped.*

In the document below, Benjamin DeBoice describes his own experience with the transfers. A second lieutenant, he was assigned to escort one trainload of soldiers, who were headed to Camp Hancock, Georgia. As usual, men who were visibly sick were kept from boarding the train. Nevertheless, large numbers of other soldiers must already have been infected, because more than 200 of them came down with flu in the course of the train ride from Illinois to Georgia.

DeBoice's account makes clear how troop transfers contributed to spreading the epidemic. It also highlights the limited medical resources available for treating influenza—although DeBoice anticipated trouble with flu, the only medications that were stockpiled for the journey were laxatives and aspirin.

Oral history interview, 1978

BENJAMIN S. DEBOICE MEMOIR

The flu struck Camp Grant along in the early fall of 1918. We knew what we were up against because it had hit the Great Lakes Naval Training Station in Waukegan, Illinois, before it hit Camp Grant. And they died like flies at Great Lakes . . . It was early in the fall of 1918 as I said, just at the time when they had had six deaths at Camp Grant. I was ordered to take a troop train to Camp Hancock, Georgia, [part of] a troop movement that involved two thousand troops to Camp Hancock, Georgia, and two thousand troops to Camp McArthur, Texas. I had five hundred and some odd men on my train.

When I went up to the headquarters to get my orders, travel orders, I met for the first time the . . . captain of the medical corps who was to accompany our train, and I told him "You know if this train moves we're going to have a flu epidemic on that train." And he kind of pooh-poohed the idea that touched me off and I said "Well, if you're going to treat it that lightly I'm going to give you my first order right now" . . .

I was a lieutenant and he was a captain, but the line officer commands. Now I was in command of the train. I said, "[When] you report for duty on this train, I want you to come with three times as much compound cathartics [*a laxative*] and aspirin as you think we can use for five hundred men on this train this trip." When he showed up at the train he showed me a pint bottle about three-fourths full of compound cathartics . . . and a box about three inches square and six inches tall half full of aspirin tablets and says, "Well I followed your orders." Kind of made light of it.

Well he retired to his state room and we were loading the troops and my troops were examined. They'd been examined three times in the last twenty-four hours, and as they filed onto the train the doctors watched them and anybody with a flushed face was pulled out of the line. They pulled six men out of the line with a flushed face and put a thermometer in their mouth, and they had a temperature and they fired them back so I lost six men before I started . . . But as we progressed towards Chicago on the train they began showing up and I . . . found myself walking up and down the aisles and spotting fellows that were beginning to show fever and isolating them in the back coach. I followed that procedure until we got to Evansville, Indiana, along about midnight that night. I was just completely worn out, I had a soldier trailing me with a bucket of water and I was feeding them compound cathartics, aspirins, and water.

Well, I went to bed around midnight and the next day it continued again, but they got to the point where I couldn't isolate them. There were just too many on the train. We got down to Memphis—and incidentally I was carrying the bottle of aspirin or the bottle of compound cathartics and the box of aspirin. My doctor stayed in his state room. I had a very low opinion of him, but I won't go into that . . .

We got down to . . . Chattanooga and I telegraphed ahead to the Red Cross for another supply of compound cathartics and aspirin . . . And I telegraphed ahead to Camp Hancock that I'd be in the next morning at seven o'clock with two hundred cases of flu on board, and I had somewhere between five hundred and six hundred men on my train. Well, no commanding general ever got the reception that we got when I showed up there . . . When we got there the commanding general was down at the train to meet us and all of the ambulances that they had in the camp.

I got off and met the Major who was receiving the troops and I told him, I said, "Now they're all here because they're too darn sick to get away, no joke about them being here. Here's the roll call, you call the roll and I've got their service records up in my state room and I'll go up and get them." I started up the train to the car where my state room was . . . and a runner caught up with me and said, "General so and so wants to see you." . . . When I reported he said, "Are you in command of that train?" I said "yes sir." "Well what the blankety blankety, blankety, blank, blank, blakety, blank did you bring that outfit down here for?" Well it was so utterly ridiculous asking a second lieutenant why he moved troops around that I was just thoroughly disgusted. I moved up close and breathed all over him and I hope he got the flu.

⋆ ⋆ ⋆

Another train load that was heading from Camp MacArthur, Texas, came through my home town of Clinton [*Illinois*]. It happened on that particular day that they were having a liberty bond program to boost the sale of liberty bonds and a general town celebration. A cousin of mine, Harry McDonald, was sort of in charge of the program and he heard that this troop train was coming through Clinton, and he thought I might be on it, so he telephoned down to the depot and told them to get ahold of the commander of that troop train and invite him to parade his troops in the parade in Clinton. Well that train was just like the one I had. It had flu, I mean it had flu on it, but the damn fool who was in charge of it—I'm sorry—consented to parade his troops. They paraded the troops through Clinton and as a result my home town got the flu in a really big way, and they were still having the flu when I was discharged.

Source: Interview D352 with Judge Benjamin DeBoice by Charles Ruyge, 1978 and Cullom Davis, 1979, pp. 22–23, except the final sentence of the first paragraph in the above selection comes from p. 8, and the final paragraph comes from p. 27. Archives/Special Collections, Norris L. Brookens Library, University of Illinois at Springfield, available at http://library.uis.edu/archives/collections/oral/pdf/DEBOICE.pdf (accessed August 20, 2013).

DOCUMENT 4

Managing the Epidemic in Minneapolis

During the 1918 epidemic, nearly every American community imposed regulations of one kind or another to control the spread of infection. In some states, such as New Jersey, these regulations originated at the state level. In others, as illustrated by this document from Minneapolis, Minnesota, the rules were developed locally, by the city Health Department. (As we have noted, the federal government made no move to establish national guidelines for dealing with the epidemic, although the U.S. Public Health Service did periodically offer recommendations and consultation.)

The document below, excerpted from the department's annual report for 1918, summarizes the measures taken in Minneapolis to respond to the epidemic, and also explains the limitations of two measures that were used quite widely in other cities— gauze face masks and experimental vaccines. Regarding the closing of public gathering places—which Minneapolis did adopt—the report acknowledges the hardships this policy involved and the protests it engendered, but maintains that at the height of the epidemic, the benefits outweighed the costs.

The report's discussion of the debate in Minneapolis over closing the schools is of particular interest, because it contests the arguments made in Chicago and New York for keeping the schools open—that children would get regular "medical inspection" in school, and that they would be in greater danger of infection if they stayed at home in their crowded neighborhoods. The Minneapolis report questions the value of school medical inspections and argues that, at least in smaller cities, children were better off at home than in school. For this reason, the report says, the Minneapolis health department overrode the school board's objections and closed the city schools for several weeks.

Annual Report, 1918, Department of Health, Minneapolis, Minnesota.

INFLUENZA: METHODS OF CONTROL

Early in the epidemic the Commissioner of Health appeared before the Hennepin County Medical Association and received their co-operation and also before many other societies for explanation of measures taken.

Under indirect advice from the United States Public Health Service and after due consideration of the matter before the City Council the following procedure was entered into:

1. Campaign of Education. The newspapers daily chronicled the number of new cases and deaths and reported preventative measures with great courtesy. The Health Department ran a few advertisements in the papers and printed many pamphlets and distributed them to factories and other places. Moving picture men showed some slides prior to the closing of the theatres. Large placards and posters were obtained for windows and bill-boards. The street cars gave space for a large poster in all cars. This literature advocated walking to work, proper ventilation, keeping in physical trim, an avoidance of crowds and coughing and sneezing in public, boiling dishes after use, avoidance of common cups and common towels, avoidance of hand shaking, washing hands before eating, avoiding the sick, and going to bed when sick and calling a doctor.

2. Health Department employees removed common towels and cups throughout the town and campaigned against unsanitary drinking fountains. The City Council voted the loan of other Court House employees to aid the Health Department. Soda fountains, saloons, and restaurants were canvassed on the adequate sterilization of dishes.

3. On October 11, the City Council gave the following order:

    "Notice is hereby given that the Department of Health of the City of Minneapolis at a meeting thereof held on October 11th, 1918, adopted and passed the following resolution and made the following order, to wit:

    RESOLVED, By the Department of Health of the City of Minneapolis, that whereas the disease commonly known and de-scribed as Spanish Influenza has become and is epidemic in the City of Minneapolis and is dangerous to the health of the citizens of the City of Minneapolis; and whereas the public safety and health of the City of Minneapolis demand that for a time all gatherings of a public character be discontinued in the City of Minneapolis:

Now therefore, it is hereby ordered by the Department of Health of the City of Minneapolis that all schools, theaters, moving picture shows, moving picture theaters, dance halls, pool-rooms, billiard halls, churches, all other public gatherings in the City of Minneapolis are hereby closed and all gatherings therein are hereby prohibited until the revocation of this order by the Department of Health, and that notice hereof be forthwith posted and published by the Department of Health . . ."

This order came at this date because there were then enough deaths occurring to give reasonable cause for a mandate requiring considerable personal hardship. These orders were kept on from October 11th, the date when closing went into effect, to November 18th, a period of nearly 5 weeks, and gave rise to considerable dissension and attempts to remove the ban.

4. Streetcars. Three windows were required open on days not inclement until cold weather came, when ventilators only were used. Thirty additional cars were put into use in October and 15 more in November . . .

   Business hours of opening and closing were staggered to a mild degree. There was always too much crowding on street cars for the general good.

5. Vaccine. Rosenow's pneumonia vaccine was advocated as being worthy of a trial. There were no statistics to prove its value.

   Larson's pneumonia vaccine, made of several strains of pneumonia and streptococci . . . was used to a limited extent. The originator of this vaccine claims success for those on whom it was used, mainly University students. Further light may show vaccine to be of use.

6. Masks. The question of masks was seriously considered. Because of the problems causing inconvenience to a large populace, unsanitary masks of inadequate thickness, wearing at wrong time, and dispensing with them at the wrong time, they were not generally advocated. They were advocated in contact with the sick by nurses and doctors. Some doctors and many nurses and a few householders wore them. In the City Hospital 41 nurses wearing masks in contact with the sick came down with influenza.

7. Schools. The school board refused to close the schools claiming that under inspection the students would be more free from Influenza.

Because of the great prevalence and nature of this disease and apparent high percentage of carriers among the population it was doubtful if any amount of inspection was sufficient. In out-of-school hours there is no crowding together of children as there is in the tenement districts of many Eastern cities. We closed the schools under authority of law despite the opposition. In December the disease again increased and many school children were involved and some deaths occurred. The problem was that of their acting as carriers to the adults to and from the home. The schools were again closed . . . They remained closed until December 30th.

8. Isolation of all patients and all contacts was requested . . .

[Additional comment on the closing laws:]
Compulsory closing orders were questioned. There could be no possible figures to prove their value. The emergency was great enough to justify them. The members of a community must by necessity earn their daily bread in order to exist. When the hardship of a general closing of business exceeds the problematic value of the life saving measures caused by such closing, it becomes necessary to take the lesser of the two evils, and allow commerce to pursue its way. In the 5 weeks of closing measures we came to the point where personal hardship began to become dominant and therefore dispensed with them. The disease was then on the decline and the apparent number of carriers and non-immunes greatly decreased.

It was argued that unless all places of contact such as street cars, elevators, stores, etc., were included, closing orders were inconsistent. A total closing would undoubtedly have ameliorated the trouble, [but] . . . such a condition could not be accomplished . . . By lessening points of contact we lessen the cases and carriers that lead to an ever widening circle. To lessen these points of contact by every means that can be tolerated or will not lead to an over-balancing hardship has seemed to us to be a reasonable procedure.

Source: Minneapolis Department of Health, Annual Report of the Department of Health, Minneapolis, Minnesota For the Year Ending 1918 (1919), 9–11, posted on *American Influenza Epidemic of 1918–1919: A Digital Encyclopedia*, available at http://hdl.handle.net/2027/spo.2890flu. 0012.982 (accessed August 20, 2013).

DOCUMENT 5

Teaching the Public About Influenza

Fliers offering advice on how to deal with influenza were circulated by the thousands during the fall months of the epidemic. Many were prepared by the United States Public Health Service, and then sent to local health departments for distribution. Local health officials also developed a great many of their own educational materials, which were disseminated through handouts, posters, slides shown at movie theaters, and newspaper ads.

Besides distributing informational materials, public health officials gave frequent press interviews, during which they worked hard to alert the public to the need for proper precautions, while at the same time assuring them that they were in no serious danger. An example of these interviews—this one from Nashville, Tennessee—is shown below.

Nashville Banner, *October 1, 1918*

"OLD FRIEND GRIP," SAYS DR. HIBBETT

City Health Officer Declares New Epidemic is Grip—No Cause for Panic

Dr. W. E. Hibbett, city health officer who has just recovered from an attack of the malady now epidemic in Nashville—and everywhere else—and who, therefore, is qualified to speak from the standpoint of a victim as well as a physician, declares that the newfangled epidemic is nothing more than our old friend, the grip. The type, he finds, is rather mild, but extremely contagious.

"The name by which it is so widely advertised—Spanish influenza—is most unfortunate," said Dr. Hibbett. "It suggests something new, mysterious and terrible, and causes consternation. In truth, it is regular 'stampede stuff.' As a matter of fact, the disease is just our old friend, the grip, sailing under new colors.

"It is well to fear grip, for it is many times a serious disease, but it is very foolish to have any extreme dread because it comes labeled 'Spanish influenza.' This pandemic had its origin, as such, in Spain, it is true; but at this time we have no especial reason to fear anything that is Spanish. The use of the new term to frighten people is good German propaganda, and should be so regarded.

"It is to be hoped that people will take a sensible view of the situation," continued Dr. Hibbett, "and remember that the new-named malady is one with which they have long been familiar. There is no cause for any panic, but plenty of reason for using good common sense in seeking to minimize the spread of the disease and to treat it properly when it is contracted.

"Grip is about the most contagious disease known, except measles. Many general precautions may be taken to avoid it, such as keeping away from crowded public places and out of closed rooms or closed cars with a promiscuous assemblage. But, on the whole, the helpful measures of this character must be of a purely personal nature. Personal care is the only thing that avails in the majority of cases.

"It is the duty, in a time like this, for everyone who has a cold or who is 'feeling bad,' to stay at home, for his own good and for the good of the community, until a physician can diagnose the trouble. When you cough or sneeze, use a handkerchief to prevent the scattering of expelled germs. Expectorated matter should be burned, invariably.

"If a child is sick, keep it at home. Do not send it to school, as thereby you may scatter contagion far and wide, and on the other hand, if the child has not the grip but is ailing otherwise, its lowered vitality will make it especially susceptible to the contagion, if somebody else has brought the disease to school. Have the sick child examined by a physician.

"You cannot successfully quarantine grip. Some of the cases are extremely mild. The victim merely has a cold apparently, or sneezes a few times, and goes about his business, with nobody suspecting that he is one of the most dangerous disseminators of the germ.

"Grip manifests itself in a variety of ways. Sometimes, as just said, it appears as nothing but an ordinary cold. Again, there may be severe bronchial affections, neuralgia, chills, fever, or sometimes stomach and bowel disorders.

"So far there is no specific treatment known for grip, nor have we a vaccine for its prevention. From first to last, let me repeat, it is matter of personal care. The danger is in the complications that may develop. To prevent these go home, go to bed, keep the surface of the body warm. Have plenty of fresh air. Pneumonia is the most frequent complication, and good ventilation is the best preventive of pneumonia. But beware of drafts, or any exposure that may chill the patient.

"Grip is a disease that prostrates and weakens. Therefore keep quiet. Stay in bed; don't exert yourself and tax the weakened heart; don't get chilled; eat a light diet.

"Let me repeat again, for it is so important—keep the body warm, and keep quiet. Absolute rest is imperative.

"In spite of all precautions, practically everybody in Nashville not immune to the disease will have it before the epidemic passes. That means probably one-third of the population will take it. And remember, grip is not scattered by the wind—it is carried about by persons. It will circle the globe at the ordinary rate of human travel."

Source: *Nashville Banner*, October 1, 1918, posted on *American Influenza Epidemic of 1918–1919: A Digital Encyclopedia*, available at http://hdl. handle.net/2027/spo.2940flu.0006.492 (accessed August 20, 2013).

DOCUMENT 6

Flu in a Southern Mill Town

In the document below, an elderly couple named James and Nannie Pharis recall their experience with the 1918 epidemic in the North Carolina town of Spray (now Eden). Born on tenant farms in the countryside, both James and Nannie came to Spray as youngsters, when their fathers brought their families to town to look for work in the cotton mills. Both James and Nannie started working in the mills themselves before they were 10. After meeting at a local square dance, the two got married in 1911. Both were still working in the mill when the flu epidemic broke out in 1918.

Unlike many American communities, the town of Spray did not impose any limits on public gatherings during the epidemic. But the Pharis' account does include a number of other elements that echo Americans' experience elsewhere, including the lack of reliable medical treatments for influenza, the high mortality rate among pregnant women, the shock of seeing someone move from good health to sudden death in a matter of hours, and the heartbreak of losing a beloved family member to the epidemic.

Oral History Interview, 1978—James and Nannie Pharis

IMPACT OF THE 1918 FLU EPIDEMIC ON SPRAY, NORTH CAROLINA

Q: Do you remember this flu epidemic back in 1918?

Nannie: Oh, yes. I lost one sister.

Q: Did you get it, either of you?

Nannie: No, I didn't take it. The doctor told us to eat onions and drink whiskey. I didn't do that, though. I ate onions.

James: And wear asafetida [*dried sap of the Ferula herb*], did you ever hear of asafetida?

Nannie: I wouldn't have none in the house. That's the stinkingest stuff I ever smelled. Go to wash your shirts and smell it on the collar. They said you could avoid contagious diseases by wearing that stuff.

James: Well, we didn't have it and we done O.K.

Nannie: When I went into the house, they called me that morning. [My sister] had a little baby in the casket. I went in and it was a little girl. She already had a little girl two years old. She wasn't but twenty-two herself, married young. I walked in and the doctor . . . told me not to drink after her and not to sit in the room much. When I walked in her room, she knew everything. She said "Nannie, did you see my little baby?" Yes, I did. She says, "Oh, it would have broke my heart, just killed me if it had been a little boy." She wanted a little boy. That was the last thing she ever said. He come in and give her a shot. You had to give them a shot, they'd have spasms before they'd die. She stayed quiet until she died. Most of them had to hold them on the bed. Along towards the last they had these shots they could give. Kind of paralyzed them. That's what he said.

James: That epidemic happened in the worst part of Prohibition . . . You couldn't hardly get liquor under no circumstances right at that time. Doctor was all worried to death that people dying everywhere. He says, "We don't know what to do. The only thing I can tell you to do, if you can get any whiskey, get it and drink it. That's the only thing that we know what to do."

Nannie: That was happening in World War I. And they was hauling soldiers in trucks, by the truckload, to take them and bury them and take care of them. That's where it started, in camp, in the army.

Q: Did you lose any other relatives?

Nannie: I lost several aunts and cousins.

Q: What did people think of all that?

Nannie: Well, I'll tell you. Every woman that was pregnant died that taken that flu, that influenza. I had a sister-in-law die, and my sister died. And then I had several cousins die.

James: Another thing about it: people that die, the very stoutest of people. We had a fireman at the place I worked. I used to go out to the boiler room and smoke a cigarette. Me and him were pretty good friends. One day I went out there and they said he was sick. And I went out the next day and they said he was dead. They died just that quick with it.

Nannie: And the man across the street did the same thing with it. Died overnight. Walking around in his yard the day before.

Q: People must have been pretty afraid.

James: People were scared to death then.

Nannie: We was just a nervous wreck. It was a terrible time.

James: Whole families would get down with it and you couldn't get nobody to go there and wait on them. Hard to get anybody to go. My daddy went and took care of a family somewhere. I don't think he ever taken it, though.

Nannie: A lot of folks got over it, they didn't die. Every woman who was pregnant who taken that, died. Every one. And if you had any kind of disease, heart disease, and taken it, they didn't get over it. They died. I mean they was laying out dead. Undertakers. That was a horrible time.

James: Sometimes they'd get up, walking around, and drop dead.

Nannie: Yes. Well, it sure did thin out the population at that time.

James: I never did hear how many people died of that in the United States.

Nannie: Thousands in camps in the army died with it. That was the most pathetic thing. It started in the camps. Haul the soldiers out by the truckload. I don't know what they done with them.

James: Right after they fought a war, went into that.

Q: Did they have any special rules around here about going places, traveling? Did businesses close up for a while?

Nannie: No, the businesses didn't close up. But they advised you not to visit these people that had it because it was contagious.

Q: Did the mill close?

Nannie: No, the mill didn't close. Because they come after me while I was working and told me my sister was seriously ill and the doctor called them and said there wasn't no chance for them. My sister had just got out of the hospital. So I got off of work and went and stayed with her until she died. That was a heartbreaking thing. The circle was broken then in the family.

Source: Oral History Interview with James and Nannie Pharis, December 5, 1978; January 8 and 30, 1979. Interview H-0039. Southern Oral History Program Collection (#4007) in the Southern Oral History Program Collection, Southern Historical Collection, Wilson Library, University of North Carolina at Chapel Hill, available at http://docsouth. unc.edu/sohp/H-0039/excerpts/excerpt_7994.html (accessed August 20, 2013). Reprinted courtesy of Carolina Digital Library and Archives.

DOCUMENT 7

Nursing in Chicago

*M*en tended to hold the *"power" positions during the 1918 epidemic—as public officials, medical experts, and military commanders. But when it came to organizing and providing services for flu patients and their families, women played an indispensable role. Besides the nurses who staffed the hospitals and traveled from house to house in the community, thousands of other women functioned as aides, providing routine care in patients' homes and helping stricken families with tasks such as cooking, laundry, and house-cleaning. In addition, female volunteers— often associated with the Red Cross—set up and staffed central referral centers, drove doctors and nurses on their rounds, made gauze face-masks, sewed nightgowns, pajamas, sheets, and pillow-cases for local hospitals, and organized "canteens" where food was prepared for flu-afflicted households.*

In the document below, Edna Foley, the head of Chicago's Visiting Nurse Association (a private charitable organization), reports how these activities were carried out—primarily by women—in her city. She describes the efforts of her own agency, the pooling of resources with Health Department nurses, the participation of aides, the assistance of volunteer drivers, and the canteens that were run by local women's organizations.

Nurses such as Edna Foley worked tirelessly to serve their communities during the epidemic. Yet they were often quite critical of the living arrangements they encountered among those they cared for. For instance, like a number of other nurses, Foley had sharp words about the poor housekeeping she observed in some of the patients' homes. Echoing the views of Florence Nightingale, her report came close to suggesting that better ventilation and cleaner houses could by themselves vanquish future epidemics.

American Journal of Nursing, December 1918

PUBLIC HEALTH NURSING

Edna Foley, Superintendent, Visiting Nurse Association

Illinois.—The influenza epidemic is naturally foremost at this moment in the minds of all public health nurses in America. Local conditions controlled the handling of the situation in most places. Chicago is said to be more fortunate than many other large cities, in that its death rate only rose to 63 per thousand and its epidemic seemed to be of five weeks' duration. The local and state health authorities, ably seconded by the United States Public Health Services, handled the medical and quarantine end. The Visiting Nurse Association, the Tuberculosis Nurses and the Red Cross Teaching Center took care of the home nursing problems in the families.

The experience of the Visiting Nurse Association may be of interest to nurses elsewhere, who have to deal suddenly with epidemics. The average number of daily calls received through the main office in October is from 45 to 60; the average number of daily calls received in September 1918 was 48; consequently an increase to 178 daily calls during the month of October meant an increase of more than 400 per cent in home nursing work, for in addition to its main office, the Visiting Nurse Association maintains nine sub-stations at which calls are received each noon; and these calls represent merely family names and addresses, not the number of patients found when the nurse enters the home.

The epidemic seemed most severe in distinctly localized areas; the congested areas, as usual, suffering most. One district, which is easily handled in heavy seasons by one nurse, required the constant work of four visiting nurses, many aides, and registered 971 calls.

The second and third weeks in October were the busiest and most tragic for they revealed a shortage of everything—physicians, cleaning women, aides, intelligent relatives, clerks, housekeepers, cleaning women, and in a few instances, supplies. The epidemic is said to be revealing an alarming shortage of nurses in the United States. To the nurses in the field, it revealed a great deal more. Whether the prevention of similar epidemics in the future depends upon the production of immunizing vaccines, upon the education of the public in regard to personal hygiene and household sanitation, upon the training of a great many more women as nurses, upon a system of state medical and health insurance, or what not, the fact remains that few communities can get through such an epidemic without feeling that personal and family hygiene are still not understood by the vast majority of our people.

Chicago workers met in conference with the Red Cross on October 11 to discuss the nursing question. It was decided that the Teaching Center of the Red Cross should call on the graduates of its home nursing course, and send out nursing aides; that families able to pay should be referred to registries; that the Visiting Nurse Association would try to cover all families for whom it was impossible to get private duty nurses or aides. So many unnecessary calls were answered by both the Visiting Nurse Association and the Teaching Center in the first twenty-four hours, and so much duplication was found because anxious neighbors, relatives, physicians and friends telephoned for the same family to so many different sources, that the Teaching Center, on the second day, put three investigators into the field. Unless the call for an aide came from a very reliable well-known source, the investigators went to the address first, to see how great the need was.

The [Red Cross] Teaching Center stopped all of its classes, kept open Sundays and evenings, and did an enormous amount of work. Nine hundred families in all were referred to it; 932 volunteers, many of whom asked remuneration, responded to its call. Five hundred and twenty-nine of these were assigned to families; thirty-five practical nurses were secured, and these 564 women were sent out repeatedly. Of course some of the homes to which they were sent were in such bad shape and had so many patients that no one person could remain in them for more than an eight or twelve-hour duty at a time, and frequent changes were necessary, but the volunteers rendered splendid, generous help on very short notice.

Many young women occupied during the day gave up their evenings, Saturdays, and Sundays, and it was hard to turn down the enthusiastic volunteer who had already been at work all day but who insisted that she was able to sit up all night with a sick family, and work the next day.

On the 10th of October, the Health Commission offered the Visiting Nurse Association the assistance of all the tuberculosis nurses in the city, about fifty. Instead of combining the two staffs, at a meeting in the Health Commissioner's office it was decided that all the patients in five zones, the territory lying about the tuberculosis dispensaries, should be turned over to the tuberculosis nurses. . . . After one meeting with the Visiting Nurse Association supervisors, and one day in which to straighten out their own work and secure the supplies required for general work, they took over nearly 500 cases and continued to carry all of the new cases of pneumonia and influenza in those areas for more than two weeks.

By this time the peak of the epidemic had nearly been reached and the nursing resources of the city were taxed to their utmost. Chicago had already given its full quota to the Red Cross, five visiting nurses had been loaned to Waukegan for service around the Great Lakes Naval Training Station, and three others were given for public health nursing services outside of Chicago.

The Visiting Nurse Association had, in addition, the services of about thirty-five aides paid by the Red Cross and advertised for by the Health Department. They were, for the most part, women well over forty, both white and colored, many of them mothers who had never worked outside their own homes. These aides were paid $17.00 a week and served for twenty-four hours, or twelve, as they were able or as the case required.

The city was further districted into small areas, each in charge of a local physician, who had been sworn in as a United States Public Health Service man. When a family needed inspection or free medical service, the case was reported to one of these doctors.

On the 16th of October, the Red Cross Teaching Center, aided by the Women's City Club and nearly every settlement in the city, started an organized canteen service. Up to that time, different settlements had helped out in specific cases, but within forty-eight hours about twenty-five canteen centers were started, from which hot food was sent to hundreds of families.

Conditions in Chicago approximated those in other cities—whole families were stricken. In many instances, the need of food and coal and bedding was most acute, but under ordinary circumstances the families requiring this aid would have been self-supporting and quite able to look out for themselves. The number of orphaned children and the number of children who have lost one parent does not, at first seem so large as has been reported from other cities, and funerals, for the most part, were attended to promptly. The schools were not closed. Theaters and other places of amusement were closed. Public funerals were forbidden.

The illness among the physicians and nurses naturally hampered the work; in fact, in no previous epidemic has the mortality and morbidity of nurses been so great . . . During the month of October [the Visiting Nurse Association] had reported to it 9,200 patients, of whom 1,000 were turned over to the tuberculosis nurses, and to the remainder of whom over 25,000 calls were made . . .

It is gratifying to be able to state that in this emergency, the friends of the Association were never more active. The Illinois Motor Corps and the Red Cross Motor Corps furnished cars for transportation of the nurses, the Board of Directors sanctioned the very liberal use of taxicabs, made thousands of gauze masks, and served in the office and in the sub-stations in numerous ways. When the epidemic first began, it seemed as if all of the usual activities of the Visiting Nurse Association would have to be discontinued in favor of pneumonia and influenza work, but with the assistance of the tuberculosis nurses, and by discontinuing our special work in the after-care of infantile paralysis patients, by visiting uncomplicated maternity cases every second day instead of daily, and by neglecting our poor old chronics until they felt most shockingly abused, we were able to carry all of our acute work, in addition to the work caused by the epidemic.

One very valuable piece of volunteer service was rendered by three friends who came in daily to clip influenza items from newspapers from six others cities, consequently we had on file news from Boston, New York, Philadelphia, Toronto, and other cities. Allowing for occasional inaccuracies, these clippings were extremely helpful in aiding us to avoid the mistakes of other communities, and at the same time to take advantage of all of their good works. We borrowed shamelessly, without taking time to say "Thank you," but we helped our patients, and after all, that was our chief concern.

From the first, the nurses used gauze face masks . . . The nurses carried long-sleeved all-over gowns. Our usual custom is to leave one such gown in every family where there is pneumonia, but as our supply of several hundred quickly gave out, we recalled the gowns, and each nurse carried two aprons, one the usual Visiting Nurse Association crepe apron for non-respiratory disease cases, and the long-sleeved all-over gown wrapped in newspaper, carried outside her nursing bag, for giving care in chest cases.

Nursing care was emphasized in every home entered, even when that care meant only the taking of a temperature and the hasty instruction of a mother, an aide, a husband, or an older daughter, in the bathing and feeding of a patient. In few diseases does nursing care mean more to the patient than in influenza and pneumonia, and in spite of the fact that not all new calls were made on the day received, and that many of our nursing visits were made in less than half our usual time, we tried never to give instructive care only, when actual hand nursing was indicated.

The main office was kept open evenings and Sundays. We did not, however, attempt night visiting nursing. The amount of illness among the nurses and the very heavy amount of work carried by each one during the day, precluded any evening nursing.

It is perhaps too soon to analyze the lesson that such an epidemic teaches us, but in our homes at least, of the middle class, the working class and the destitute class, if such a classification is permissible, the visiting nurses are convinced of two things, that more home nursing must be taught to every woman and girl in Chicago, and that better housekeeping must not only be taught, but insisted upon. We sent aides and nurses into homes where the dirt of months was supposed to be cleaned away by women who kept their own homes in immaculate condition. Surely epidemics of this sort can, in some small measure, be better controlled if we devise not only a scheme for better ventilation of the homes of our people, but if we teach and then require better housekeeping and cleaner homes.

Source: Edna L. Foley, "Department of Public Health Nursing: Chicago," *American Journal of Nursing*, 19 no. 3 (December 1918), 189–193.

DOCUMENT 8

Dealing with the Bodies

*H*owever hard communities worked to control the spread of infection, most of them experienced many weeks of unprecedented death tolls, and the rapid accumulation of bodies frequently overwhelmed local arrangements for dealing with the dead. One common difficulty was a diminishing supply of coffins. Then there was the daunting challenge of keeping up with the need for graves.

No city had more trouble dealing with its dead than Philadelphia, where the morgue became so overwhelmed that many families were forced to keep the bodies of their deceased relatives at home, and then carry them out to the street when municipal wagons came around to collect them.

In the early 1980s, oral historians interviewed a number of elderly Philadelphians at length about their memories of the epidemic. Although by then the events of 1918 were nearly 65 years behind them, the participants vividly recalled those terrible months when death stalked the streets of Philadelphia.

Excerpts: Radio show, WUHY-FM, 1983, Philadelphia, Pennsylvania

"THEY WERE PILING THEM IN THE STREETS," or WHATEVER BECAME OF THE INFLUENZA PANDEMIC OF 1918?

Anna Lavin [*young adult (age unspecified) at the time of the epidemic, living and working in South Philadelphia*]: My aunt died first, they took her to the cemetery. And my father took the 13-year-old boy, who also had the flu, and my father carried him wrapped in a blanket to the cemetery, because he had to say the prayer for the dead . . .

And I nursed over there and nursed at home . . . Doctors couldn't come take care of them. And if a doctor came, he would prescribe the same medicine for everyone, whatever it was that they gave them. In our family there were a number of people in bed, and I was at home during the day and over at my aunt and uncle's at night . . . And the only thing I knew to do was, whoever had fever, to sponge them. Give them a sponge bath.

Mildred Kleeman [*age 18 at the time of the epidemic*]: Yes, my oldest son was born just right then and it was awful.

In 1918, I remember looking out of the window and they were just putting coffins one on top of another and they were taking them out that way. It was really terrible. A terrible thing . . . My mother saw a woman taken out with two babies, they were just born. It was a tragedy. I never want to see anything like that.

Anne Van Dyke [*teenager living with her parents in 1918*]: My whole family had it, except my mother. And my father, he had it. And the doctor said, "Well, I can't come every day." . . . And he said I was going to die, because I had a bad heart, because I had had rheumatic fever. He said I was going to die. Just, when I die they should come over and get a death certificate, it would be alright. But I didn't die . . .

The undertakers just ran, I don't know how many, into their wagons and took them to the cemetery, and that was it. And you had to dig your own grave. I mean, the families had to dig their own graves. Grave diggers were sick and that was the terrible thing . . .

My mother went and shaved the men and laid them out . . . thinking that they were going to be buried, you know. They wouldn't bury them. They had so many died that they kept putting them in garages. That garage on Richmond Street. Oh my gosh, he had a couple of garages full of caskets.

Elizabeth Strupczewski [*28 years old in 1918*]: On Thompson and Allegheny, Schpeda. He used to get the people and take them out and pile them in the garage . . . He'd take the people out of the coffin and put them in the garage and give the coffin to somebody else, and got paid for it. He lost his license and all. The smell would knock you out, it would run down through the alley. So they caught up with him.

People used to die. Oh, they used to die. It was an awful disease.

Louise Abbruzzese [*age 11 in 1918*]: We were the only family saved from the influenza. The rest of the neighbors all were sick.

Now I remember so well, very well, directly across the street from us, a boy about 7, 8 years old died. And they used to just pick you up and wrap you up in a sheet and put you in a patrol wagon. So the mother and father screaming, "Let me get a macaroni box." Before, macaroni—

any kind of pasta—used to come in these wooden boxes about this long and that high, that 20 lbs of macaroni fitted in the box. "Please, please, let me put him in the macaroni box. Let me put him in the box. Don't take him away like that." And that was it.

My mother had given birth to my youngest sister at the time, and then, thank God, you know, we survived. But they were taking people out left and right. And the undertaker would pile them up and put them in the patrol wagon and take them away.

Tony Lombardo [*also age 11 in 1918*]: We had a friend lived on 11th and Carpenter, he had six or seven kids and so this little baby died, maybe 2 years old, I guess, maybe less. So the undertakers couldn't handle them, you know—they were overpowered with work . . . So [the undertaker] says, "If I do get the job," he says, "there's nobody to dig the grave." Nobody wanted to dig any graves. [The father] says, "I'll dig the grave myself." [The undertaker] says, "I can't take your job anyhow." So you know what [the father] does? . . . He went out and hired a horse and a wagon for 75 cents, and he put his little girl in the box in there, and he went off to the cemetery, and he dug the grave, and he put the daughter in the grave.

Source: Excerpted from "'They Were Piling Them in the Streets'; or What Became of the Influenza Pandemic of 1918?" broadcast on WHUY-FM in 1983 as part of the radio series, "I Remember When: Times Gone But Not Forgotten." written and produced by Professor Charles Hardy III. An audio recording of the full show is available at Talking History: Aural History Productions, available at www.talkinghistory.org/hardy.html (accessed August 20, 2013). The longer interviews on which this show was based were conducted by Professor Hardy, Judy Levin, and Mark Gallichio. Excerpt reprinted courtesy of Charles Hardy III.

DOCUMENT 9

The Third Wave Hits Denver

At the height of the influenza epidemic's second wave, in early October 1918, Denver, Colorado—like many American communities—passed regulations requiring masks and limiting public gatherings. These orders were rescinded early in November, as the number of new cases seemed to be declining. But within 10 days, the city was hit by another surge of flu cases. Many communities experienced this "third wave" of the epidemic—probably facilitated (as the newspaper article below suggests) by the massive armistice celebrations, which brought thousands of people into the streets on November 11 to cheer the end of World War I.

Document 9 consists of three news clippings, illustrating how Denver officials responded to the epidemic's third wave. Their first step, on November 23 (CLIPPING 1), was to re-impose the regulations that had just been suspended. However, local businessmen's protests were so intense that within 24 hours (CLIPPING 2), the city rescinded its limitations on public gatherings. It did, however, broaden the requirements for wearing masks. (This reminds us that one of the appeals of the mask as a method of infection control was that it permitted commerce and entertainment to proceed as usual, on the shaky assumption that people wearing gauze masks were protected against infection.)

Just six days later, on November 30, Denver's requirements for public mask-wearing also came to an end (CLIPPING 3). The newspaper article announcing this decision stated that at the same time, quarantine rules had been made stricter, but this only involved limiting visits to the sick. In fact, the time had passed when people's fear of contagion could be depended on to win compliance with any rules as intrusive as those passed at the height of the epidemic. Thus, when a group of ministers pointed out that the epidemic was still far from over and urged the city to keep churches closed for a few weeks longer, the officials took no action, and the newspaper observed: "Indications are that no further regulations will be imposed."

CLIPPING 1

Rocky Mountain News, November 23, 1918

DENVER AGAIN CLOSED TIGHT IN DETERMINED EFFORT TO HALT SPREAD OF INFLUENZA

All Regulations of Previous Orders Become Effective This Morning
Masks to Be Worn as Precaution

Denver is closed again because of Spanish Influenza. Mayor Mills and Manager of Health W. H. Sharpley issued the closing order yesterday, after twelve members of the city medical advisory committee had recommended immediate action. Every regulation that was in effect during the closed period from Oct. 6 to Nov. 11 was put into effect again by the order, and many more were added, the city authorities announcing that all would be enforced rigidly. Churches, schools and all theaters are closed by the order. Lodges cannot hold meetings, and any gathering of people indoors or outdoors is placed under the ban, exactly as was the case during the previous closing order . . .

Vigorous Protests Filed

Managers of all the theaters and big moving picture houses, and employees of these houses, protested vigorously at the closing order. They pointed out that neither New York nor Chicago closed theaters, and both cities stamped out the flu. All were a unit in declaring that they were perfectly willing to observe all regulations, even to giving their patrons masks, but that they considered the order applying to them as discriminating.

The meeting at which the doctors recommended closing the city was held at 12:45 o'clock yesterday afternoon. It had been called to discuss the increase in cases due to the Victory celebration.

No Cause for Alarm

"The people really brought it on themselves, by the Victory celebration, but that couldn't have been prevented, and shouldn't have been," said Dr. Sharpley. "It was certain that with tens of thousands thronging the streets, that there would be hundreds of influenza-infected persons and that infection would be distributed." . . .

The rules that will govern the present ban are far more rigid than under the previous ban.

Visiting Is Taboo

Each member of the advisory committee is created a health officer with power to arrest. All health officers will arrest any person going into or out of a house or apartment where there is a case of influenza. This will include members of the family. This order is made to stop visiting. During the epidemic, the greatest trouble has been to keep relatives and friends from visiting these infected houses and it was decided that the only way to break it up was to arrest the offenders. It was stated that this new rule would be rigidly enforced, regardless of who the offenders might be.

The rule regarding sixty-five persons in a street car also will be enforced to the letter. The conductor must keep tab on the number of his passengers and if he allows more than sixty-five on the car he is liable to arrest at once. If necessary, the conductor will be taken off the car and the car stopped until the tramway company can send a man out to take charge of the car.

Masks Are Compulsory

The committee ordered that all customers entering a store must wear a mask. An employee of the store is to be at the entrance and each customer will be handed a mask to wear while in the store. If the customer refuses to wear the mask then he or she must be forbidden to enter the store.

It is optional with the clerks and store employees in the store if they wear masks. The committee did not order that they should, but recommended that they do so for their own protection.

The wearing of masks of all persons entering a factory is also included, or entering any place of whatsoever nature where there are many people employed or gathered.

Wearing masks on the streets is not compulsory, but optional with the person. However, it is recommended by the committee that these masks be worn, especially on street cars . . .

Dr. Sharpley said that the order against social gatherings would be more rigidly enforced this time than before, and that all such gatherings were strictly forbidden . . .

CLIPPING 2

Rocky Mountain News, November 24, 1918

EPIDEMIC CLOSING ORDER REVOKED; MASKS URGED TO STOP DISEASE SPREAD

Everything Except Schools Allowed to Open
Following Flood of Protests to Mayor;
Visiting Sick Declared Worst Danger

Early yesterday morning delegations from Denver theaters, moving picture houses and other places which were ordered closed, began to file into the city hall and register formal protests with the mayor and manager of health, declaring the action in closing the city worked an unnecessary hardship. Merchants, striving to keep up the morale of the city while the fight against the disease is being made, agreed with the amusement managers and others that the best thing to do was to keep the city open and enforce such rules as would insure the stamping out of the malady. Following these strenuous protests, the advisory committee to the health department, which was responsible for the order of Mayor W. F. R. Mills and Manager of Health W. Sharpley closing the city, issued new instructions which call for the wearing of masks in all public places, except in the streets, the order including factories, stores, places of amusement and street cars . . .

Almost indescribable confusion resulted from the placing of the ban and its lifting shortly afterwards in Denver. There were a score or more of delegations of all kinds that thronged the city hall from 9 o'clock yesterday morning to 4 o'clock in the afternoon to see Mayor Mills and Dr. Sharpley.

The order of Friday and again of yesterday morning calling for masks provoked confusion in all the big Sixteenth Street stores, the Red Cross being unable to furnish the masks and several establishments manufacturing masks being unable to fill orders. The stores reported that they couldn't obey the order to hand a mask to every customer, or even supply their employees.

This resulted in a partial lifting of this order, as its strict enforcement would have meant closing the stores. The Red Cross reported that it was bending every effort to supply masks, but early in the morning it was seen that this could not be done in the stores. In the afternoon the managers of the principal stores saw Mayor Mills and told him they wanted to comply with the order, but couldn't because of the scarcity of masks . . .

The same complaint came from scores of businesses affected by the order. Managers of factories reported they hadn't masks and couldn't obtain any; heads of various industries sent in a similar report, and so did heads of many kinds of businesses. All received the same answer as that given to the managers of the stores—to do the best they could . . .

Medical Advisers Listen

Other delegations of business men called to declare that the closing once more of the city, after six weeks of a closed city, would result in a tremendous loss. The medical advisory committee, meanwhile, had been summoned by Dr. Sharpley and was present to hear all these statements of the immense damage that would be done the city by another closing order.

The outcome of the sessions was that the new order was promulgated. Under the present order there is no closing, but masks are to be worn in all public places and upon street cars, though not on the street, unless the person so desires—and thousands so desire, so that the masked person on the street became a familiar object during the day.

CLIPPING 3

Rocky Mountain News, November 30, 1918

MASK ORDER CANCELLED, BUT QUARANTINE RULES MADE STRICTER

Only Doctors and Nurses May Enter Sick Rooms;
345 New Cases and 22 Deaths Listed;
Pastors Want Churches Closed Again

Under an official decree issued Saturday afternoon, the health rule requiring the face covering is annulled, effective at 6 p.m. Saturday.

The only exception to the cancellation order is that all persons entering rooms where influenza patients are confined must mask.

The quarantine regulations were made more stringent. No one but doctors and nurses will be allowed to enter sick rooms, and all houses must be placarded.

A committee of ministers appearing for the entire clergy of the city have made representations to the mayor and bureau of health that the contagion is unchecked and that the strictest measures possible are demanded for the sake of public health. The ministers asked that all churches be closed until danger is passed. City officials have not given an answer to the request, but indications are that no further regulations will be imposed.

Sources:

Clipping 1, *Rocky Mountain News*, November 23, 1918, 1, 4, posted on *American Influenza Epidemic of 1918–1919: A Digital Encyclopedia*, available at http://hdl.handle.net/2027/spo.7980flu.0003.897 (accessed August 20, 2013).

Clipping 2, *Rocky Mountain News*, November 24, 1918, 1, 4, posted on *American Influenza Epidemic of 1918–1919: A Digital Encyclopedia*, available at http://hdl.handle.net/2027/spo.7090flu.0003.907 (accessed August 20, 2013).

Clipping 3, *Rocky Mountain News*, November 30, 1918, 1, 3, posted on *American Influenza Epidemic of 1918–1919: A Digital Encyclopedia*, available at http://hdl.handle.net/2027/spo.0310flu.0004.130 (accessed August 20, 2013).

DOCUMENTS 10

Lessons Learned

*I*n December 1918, while many American communities were just beginning to recover from the second wave of the epidemic—and while others were combating the rise of the third wave—the members of the American Public Health Association gathered in Chicago for their annual meeting. Understandably, the agenda focused primarily on influenza, as the members reviewed what they had learned from the crisis of the past several months.

The most ambitious document to come out of the conference was a plan for dealing with future epidemics, entitled "A Working Program Against Influenza."

This remarkably detailed plan was developed by a committee of the Association, discussed at the annual meeting, and subsequently published in the American Journal of Public Health. It acknowledged the medical uncertainties still facing the public health community, but its focus was on what could actually be done, in a state of imperfect knowledge, to deal with future flu epidemics. The Working Program is of interest, both because of what it tells us about public health leaders' thinking at the time, and because it outlines steps that we ourselves might need to consider in the event of a future pandemic, during the months before adequate supplies of vaccines and antiviral medications become available.

American Journal of Public Health, January 1919

A WORKING PROGRAM AGAINST INFLUENZA

Editorial Committee of the American Public Health Association

Introductory Statement

The present epidemic is the result of a disease of extreme communicability. So far as information available to the committee shows, the disease is limited to human beings . . .

There is no known laboratory method by which an attack of influenza can be differentiated from an ordinary cold or other inflammation of the mucous membranes of the nose, pharynx, or throat.

There is no known laboratory method by which it can be determined when a person who has suffered from influenza ceases to be capable of transmitting the disease to others . . .

Evidence seems conclusive that the infective microorganism or virus of influenza is given off from the nose and mouth of infected persons. It seems equally conclusive that it is taken in through the mouth or nose of the person who contracts the disease, and in no other way, except as a bare possibility through the eyes, by way of the conjunctive or tear ducts.

Prevention

If it be admitted that influenza is spread solely through discharges from the noses and throats of infected persons finding their way into the noses and throats of other persons susceptible to the disease, then no matter what the causative organism or virus may ultimately be determined to be, preventive action logically follows the principles named below and, therefore, it is not necessary to wait for the discovery of the specific microorganism or virus before taking such action . . .

I. Breaking the channels of communication

    (a) By preventing droplet infection. The evidence offered indicates that this is of prime importance.

    (b) By sputum control. The evidence offered indicates that the danger here is due chiefly to contamination of the hands and common eating and drinking utensils.

    (c) By supervision of food and drink. Evidence offered does not indicate much danger of infection through these channels . . .

II. Immunization and vaccines. In the present epidemic vaccines have been used to accomplish:

    1. The prevention or mitigation of influenza *per se.*

    2. The prevention or mitigation of complications recognized as due to the influenza bacillus or to various strains of streptococci and pneumococci.

In relation to the use of vaccines for the prevention of influenza, the evidence which has come to the attention of the committee as to the success or lack of success of the practice is contradictory and irreconcilable. In view of the fact that the causative organism is unknown, there is no scientific basis for the use of any particular vaccine against the primary disease. If used, any vaccine must be employed on the chance that it bears a relation to the unknown organism causing the disease.

    The use of vaccines for the complicating infections rests on more logical grounds, and yet the committee has not sufficient evidence to indicate that they can be used with any confident assurance of success. In the use of these vaccines the patient should realize that the practice is still in a developmental stage.

    The committee believes that when vaccines are used experimentally for the purpose of determining their preventive or curative value, the following conditions should be complied with:

1. The groups of vaccinated and unvaccinated persons should be the same in number.

2. The relative susceptibilities of the two groups should be equal, as measured by age and sex distribution, previous exposures to infection without development of influenza and a previous history as to recent attacks of the disease.

3. The degree of exposure in each group should be practically the same in duration and intensity.

4. The groups should be exposed concurrently during the same stage of the epidemic curve.

III. Increased natural resistance of persons exposed to infection.
Physical and nervous exhaustion should be avoided by paying due regard
to rest, exercise, physical and mental labor and hours of sleep. The
evidence is conclusive, however, that youth and bodily vigor do not
guarantee immunity to the disease . . .

The committee has found it impossible . . . to lay down any rules for
the guidance of all health officials alike in preventive measures. The most
it has been able to do has been to state certain general principles that in
its judgment should underlie administrative measures for the prevention
of influenza. The application of these principles to the needs of any
particular community must be left for determination by the officers of that
community who are responsible for the protection of its public health.

The preventive measures recommended by the committee are as follows:

A. Efficient organization to meet the emergency, providing for a
   centralized coordination and control of all resources.
B. Machinery for ascertaining all facts regarding the epidemic:

   1. Compulsory reporting.
   2. A lay or professional canvass for cases, etc.

C. Widespread publicity and education with respect to respiratory
   hygiene, covering such facts as the dangers from coughing, sneezing,
   spitting, and the careless disposal of nasal discharges; the advisability
   of keeping the fingers and foreign bodies out of the mouth and nose;
   the necessity of hand-washing before eating; the dangers from
   exchanging handkerchiefs; and the advantages of fresh air and general
   hygiene . . . The public should be made acquainted with the danger
   of possible carriers among both the sick and the well and the resultant
   necessity for the exercise of unusual care on the part of everybody
   with respect to the dangers of mouth and nasal discharges.
D. Administrative procedures:

   1. There should be laws against the use of common cups, and
      improperly washed glasses at soda fountains and other public
      drinking places, which laws should be enforced.
   2. There should be proper ventilation laws, which laws should be
      enforced.
         Since the disease is probably largely a group or crowd
      problem, the three following sub-heads are especially important.
   3. *Closing.* Since the spread of influenza is recognized as due to the
      transmission of mouth and nasal discharges from persons infected
      with influenza, some of whom may be aware of their condition

but others unaware of it, to the mouths and noses of other persons, gatherings of all kinds must be looked upon as potential agencies for the transmission of the disease. The limitation of gatherings with respect to size and frequency, and the designation of the conditions under which they may be held must be regarded, therefore, as an essential administrative procedure.

Non-essential gatherings should be prohibited. Necessary gatherings should be held under such conditions as will insure the greatest possible amount of floor space to each individual present, and a maximum of fresh air, and precautions should be taken to prevent unguarded sneezing, coughing, cheering, etc. . . .

Schools: As to the closing of schools there are many questions to be considered.

(a) Theoretically, schools increase the number and degree of contacts between children. If the schools are closed, many of the contacts which the children will make are likely to be out of doors. Whether or not closing will decrease or increase contacts must be determined locally. Obviously, rural and urban conditions differ radically in this regard.

(b) Are the children in coming to and going from school exposed to inclement weather or long rides in overcrowded cars?

(c) Is there an adequate nursing and inspection system in the schools?

(d) Is it likely that teachers, physicians and nurses can really identify and segregate the infected school child before it has an opportunity to make a number of contacts in halls, yards, rooms, etc. We suggest that children suspected of having influenza and held in school buildings for inspection should be provided with and required to wear face masks.

(e) Will the closing of schools release personnel or facilities to aid in fighting the epidemic?

(f) If schools are kept open, will the absence of many teachers lower the educational standards?

(g) If a number of pupils stay at home because of illness or fear, will they not constitute a heavy drag upon their classes when they return?

(h) If schools are closed, is there likely to be an outbreak in any case when they are reopened?

Churches: If churches are to remain open, services should be reduced to the lowest number consistent with the adequate discharge of necessary religious offices, and such services as are held should be conducted in such a way as to reduce to a minimum, intimacy and frequency of personal contact.

Theatres: As regards theatres, movies, and meetings for amusement in general, it seems unwise to rely solely or in great part upon the ejection of careless coughers. In the first place it is difficult to determine who is a careless cougher, and after each cough, danger has already resulted. It seems, too, that the closing of theatres may have as much educational value as their use for direct educational purposes, etc. Discrimination as to closing among theatres, movies etc., on the basis of efficiency of ventilation and general sanitation, may be feasible.

Saloons, etc.: The closing of saloons and other drinking places should be decided upon the basis of the probability of spread of the disease through drinking utensils and the conditions of crowding.

Dance halls, etc.: The closing of dance halls, bowling rooms, billiard parlors and slot-machine parlors, etc., should be made effective in all cases where their operation causes considerable personal contact and crowding.

Street cars, etc. Ventilation and cleanliness should be insisted upon in all transportation facilities. Overcrowding should be discouraged. A staggering of opening and closing hours in stores and factories to prevent overcrowding of transportation facilities may be cautiously experimented with. In small communities where it is feasible for persons to walk to their work it is better to discontinue the service of local transportation facilities.

Funerals: Public funerals and accessory funeral functions should be prohibited, being unnecessary assemblies in limited quarters, increasing contacts and possible sources of infection.

4. **Masks**. The wearing of proper masks in a proper manner should be made compulsory in hospitals and for all who are directly exposed to infection. It should be made compulsory for barbers, dentists, etc. The evidence before the committee as to beneficial results consequent upon the enforced wearing of masks by the entire population at all times was contradictory, and it has not encouraged the committee to suggest the general adoption of the practice. Persons who desire to wear masks, however, in their own interests, should be instructed as to how to make and wear proper masks, and encouraged to do so.

5. **Isolation**. The isolation of patients suffering from influenza should be practiced. In cases of unreasonable carelessness, it should be legally enforced most rigidly.

6. *Placarding*. In cases of unreasonable carelessness and disregard of the public interests placarding should be enforced.

7. *Hospitalization*. The theory of complete hospitalization is that, if all the sick were hospitalized the disease would be controlled. In certain somewhat small communities where hospitalization of all cases was promptly inaugurated the disease did come quickly under control. It must be recognized, however, that unless every infective person can be detected and identified as such and removed to the hospital before he has infected others, hospitalization cannot be depended upon to eliminate the disease.

    In general, home treatment is to be advocated where medical, nursing and other necessary facilities are adequate, and where home treatment is not directly contra-indicated by the danger of infecting others. The hospitalization in any case, mild or severe, should be undertaken only when facilities for home treatment are inadequate with respect to medical and nursing care or otherwise. The objection to routine hospitalization of mild cases lies in the fact that patients not already suffering from secondary infections may acquire them by exposure to hospital cases already so infected. The objection to the routine hospitalization of severe cases lies in the danger to the patient necessarily incident in the transfer from home to the hospital.

8. *Coughing and Sneezing Laws* regulating coughing and sneezing seem to be desirable for educational and practical results.

9. *Terminal Disinfection*. Terminal disinfection for influenza has no advantage over cleaning, sunning and airing.

10. *Alcohol*. The use of alcohol serves no preventive purpose.

11. *Sprays and Gargles*. Sprays and gargles do not protect the nose and throat from infection . . .

Special Report: Sub-Committee On Administrative Measures For Relief

I. *General Rules*. [*Summarizes points covered in the main report*]
II. *Preliminary Measures*.

1. The listing and distribution of resources, including physicians, nurses, social workers, nurses' aids, clerks, domestics, laundresses, automobiles, chauffeurs, mask makers and volunteers of all kinds.

    All available publicity channels should be used to promote volunteer service.

An appeal should be made for voluntary donors of human blood serum from convalescent influenza patients, to be held in readiness for use in treatment.

2. The centralization of resources, under one control, with central and branch headquarters, the city being districted for medical, nursing and other work . . .

3. The service should be maintained on a 24-hour basis, and a system of outgoing and incoming telephone service is essential.

4. The local authorities should get and keep in touch with state and national agencies.

III. *Current and Continuous Analysis of Case Situation.*
In the smaller communities a canvass should be made of all physicians, soliciting information . . . regarding the need for emergency nursing and medical service, and should be acquired as fully as possible in larger communities, through various agencies . . .

IV. *Analysis, Augmentation and Organization of Principal Facilities.*

A. *Field Nursing.*

1. Ordinarily nursing facilities utilized in general public health work should be diverted to meet the epidemic situation, and should be used on a district basis, with all other available facilities, under one supervision.

2. Nursing assistants, volunteers, etc., should be used wherever possible in homes and institutions, under expert supervision, after classification and assignment on a basis of minimum standards as to fitness, and such intensive training in the care of influenza and pneumonia patients as may be feasible.

3. From the standpoint of the patient, home treatment is to be advocated, if medical, nursing, disease preventive and other facilities are adequate.

4. Restriction so far as possible through the pressure of public opinion should be brought against the unnecessary use of private nurses.

5. Automobile transportation should be provided, and the nursing service used to encourage isolation and education.

6. Special record forms are essential for this and the medical work
. . .

7. Provision as to housing and care should be made for out of town nurses.

8. We recommend further training with reference to influenza for all graduates of Red Cross home nursing courses and more extensive use of their services . . .

B. *Emergency Medical Service.*

    1.   The medical service should be handled through the central office, the physicians being responsible to the central office, though perhaps assigned to district offices.

    2.   In this emergency service there should be utilized all available physicians such as school and factory physicians, volunteers, practitioners on a paid basis, fourth year medical students, etc.
       . . .

    3.   The emergency medical service should be used to select cases needing hospital care.

    4.   It may be feasible to institute a central clearing house in certain districts for private physicians' calls.

    5.   An arrangement should be made through the medical licensing board for the granting of temporary permits to practice to reputable physicians from out of the state, at the request of the Central Influenza Committee.

    6.   In some localities it may be feasible to district the local practitioner . . .

    7.   Certain of the relatively non-essential specialties should be discouraged, and the physicians in those specialties urged to volunteer for emergency district work . . .

    8.   Presumably some effort should be made, through an authoritative medical commission, to suggest standard methods of treatment, and wise limitations as to therapeutic procedure.

C. *Hospital Facilities.*

    1.   It is essential that the facilities, if possible, be kept ahead of the demand. A daily canvass should be made and data collected regarding available beds, medical and nursing needs, domestics, food, cots, supplies, etc. . . .

    2.   Under most conditions a central clearing house, covering most if not all of the hospitals, is advisable for the admission of cases . . . In any event the hospitals, if facilities are inadequate, should be impressed with the necessity for admitting only the most severe or needy cases, pay or free. Special hospital arrangements should be provided for pregnant women.

    3.   It is advisable to add wards or tents or new equipment to existing institutions rather than to establish entirely new emergency hospitals. If practicable, certain hospitals may be urged to handle influenza cases exclusively.

4. Non-emergency surgical and chronic medical cases amenable to home treatment should be de-hospitalized.

5. A convalescent home, if adjacent to the hospital, may serve for the care of mild and convalescent cases, thereby increasing the space in the hospital for acute cases, obviously involving an increase in the nursing facilities.

6. A canvass of ambulance facilities should be made, ambulances being requisitioned with payment, or hired by contract, if necessary. Automobiles and motor trucks should be potentially mobilized for this purpose. Frequently military equipment may be used if accessible.

V. *Social and Relief Measures.*

1. The central office should keep the family advised regarding the patient, thereby saving telephone calls, trolley fares and worry on the part of the family, and thereby increasing the willingness for hospitalization.

2. Volunteer workers such as Red Cross volunteers, teachers, relatives, etc., should be placed in care of families where the responsible members are dead or hospitalized, this service being under expert social supervision, and the families in touch with the supply system. Supervision of placed out children is also necessary.

3. Homes should be investigated before patients are discharged into them, when destitution or other untoward circumstances are apparent.

4. Precaution should be taken that institutions and families too busy with the influenza situation to look after their own needs, are covered by the general relief measures.

5. Ordinary charitable relief should be handled through the routine agencies, the service coordinated with the other epidemiological measures. Churches lodges, etc., should be urged to handle their own cases, in order to relieve the pressure on the central agency. Aid should be immediate, without protracted investigation . . .

VI. *Food.*

1. Available central cooking facilities should be used so far as is necessary, such as the dietetic equipment in high schools, normal schools, colleges, etc., with a delivery system to families and institutions in need.

2. Individual families should be encouraged to cook additional amounts, the same to be delivered to central diet kitchens for

distribution, a standard list of prepared foods needed being devised and advertised, with recognition of racial customs and preferences.

3. It may be necessary to establish canteens in sections of the city.

VII. Laundry.

1. A special collection and distribution system may be essential both for homes and institutions.

2. It may be necessary to take over a public laundry with compensation, or a private non-medical institution laundry.

VIII. Provision for Fatalities.

1. Death reporting should be prompt (24 hours) and a record kept so as to insure prompt disposal of bodies.

2. A daily canvass of available coffins should be made, labor assured for construction, and possibly no coffins sold without the permit of the Influenza Administration Office.

3. If morgue facilities are inadequate a central place should be provided, with embalming facilities, for the temporary disposal of bodies.

4. A canvass of hearses should be made and regulations issued prohibiting unnecessarily long hauls, insisting on maximum capacity loads, etc. A central control will prevent unnecessary duplication as to routes, etc.

5. A reserve supply of trucks and automobiles should be at hand for use in various ways in connection with the handling of fatal cases.

6. The number of graves required should be estimated and labor released from public works or secured through other channels (possibly military) for digging. Possibly temporary trench interment may be necessary.

IX. Education, Instruction and Publicity.

Literature and special instructions will be necessary on many phases, including the following:

1. Instructions to physicians as to reporting, facilities available, district arrangements, etc.

2. Advice to physicians regarding treatment standards and suggestions.

3. Instructions for families, to be distributed by nurses, physicians, social workers, druggists, etc., covering the problems of care during the physician's absence.

4. Instructions to the public as to where aid may be secured, to be printed in various languages, and distributed by druggists, displayed in street cars, used in the press, etc.

5. Instructions for families on "What to do till the doctor comes."

6. Instructions to physicians, factory managers, school superintendents, etc., urging the necessity for immediate home and bed treatment at the first sign of respiratory disease.

7. Popular literature on the essentials of adequate care, the danger of returning to work too soon, etc. Popular press space is worth paying for, if it cannot be secured otherwise.

8. Popular publicity as to legitimate medical, nursing, undertaker, drug, and other charges, to prevent profiteering.

X. *Miscellaneous*.

1. The cooperation of pharmaceutical agencies should be secured to insure an adequate supply of drugs and druggists.

2. Influenza victims and their families should have "first call" on fuel deliveries.

3. While follow-up procedures are not legitimately a factor in the epidemic situation, their consideration is essential to an adequate meeting of the entire problem. This means adequate provision for medical examination and nursing care, relief measures, industrial employment problems, the follow up of special sequelae such as cardiac affections, tuberculosis, etc.

4. It is finally suggested that Health Department draw up a program based on the above outline, holding it in reserve for future use, if not immediately needed, and modifying the proposal to fit the size and other characteristics of the particular community . . .

In view of the probability of recurrences of the disease from time to time during the coming year, health departments are advised to be ready in advance with plans for prevention, which plans shall embody the framework of necessary measures and as much detail as is possible. Laws plainly necessary should be enacted and rules passed now. Emergency funds should be held in reserve or placed in special appropriations, which appropriations can be quickly made available for influenza prevention work . . .

Source: "A Working Program Against Influenza," prepared by an editorial committee of the American Public Health Association, based upon papers, committee reports, and discussions presented at the meeting of the Association, Chicago, Illinois, December 9–12, 1918, *American Journal of Public Health* 9, no. 1 (January 1919), 1–13.

NOTES

1. "Liner Had 5 Deaths Due to Influenza," *New York Times* (August 18, 1918).
2. "Influenza Spreads: 150 New Cases Here," *New York Times* (September 25, 1918).
3. Edwin O. Jordan, *Epidemic Influenza: A Survey* (Chicago, IL: American Medical Association, 1927), 101.

Bibliography

RECENT PUBLICATIONS

Alcabes, Philip, *Dread: How Fear and Fantasy Have Fuelled Epidemics from the Black Death to Avian Flu* (New York, NY: Public Affairs, 2009).

Almond, Douglas, "Is the 1918 Influenza Pandemic Over? Long-term Effects of In Utero Influenza Exposure in the Post-1940 U.S. Population," *Journal of Political Economy* 114 no. 4 (August 2006), 672–712.

Almond, Douglas and Bhashkar Mazumder, "The 1918 Influenza Pandemic and Subsequent Health Outcomes: An Analysis of SIPP Data," *American Economic Review* 95 no. 2 (May 2005), 258–262.

Almone, Francesca, "The 1918 Influenza Epidemic in New York City: A Review of the Public Health Response," *Public Health Reports* 125, supp. 3 (2010), 71–79.

Balinska, Maria and Caterina Rizzo, "Behavioural Responses to Influenza Pandemics: What Do We Know?" *PLoS Current* 1 (September 9, 2009), RRN1037, available at www.ncbi.nlm.nih.gov/pmc/articles/PMC2762764 (accessed August 13, 2013).

Barrett, Ronald, Christopher W. Kuzawa, Thomas McDade, and George J. Armelagos, "Emerging and Re-emerging Infectious Diseases: The Third Epidemiologic Transition," *Annual Review of Anthropology* 27 (1998), 247–271.

Barry, John M., *The Great Influenza: The Story of the Deadliest Pandemic in History* (New York, NY: Penguin Books, 2004, 2005).

Barry, John M., Howard Markel, Harvey B. Lipman, Julian Alexander Navarro, Alexandra Sloan, Joseph Michalsen, Alexandra Minna Stern, and Martin S. Cetron, "Nonpharmaceutical Interventions Implemented During the 1918–1919 Influenza Pandemic," Letter to Editor and Reply, *Journal of the American Medical Association* 298 no. 19 (November 17, 2008), 2260–2261.

Belling, Catherine, "Overwhelming the Medium: Fiction and the Trauma of Pandemic Influenza in 1918," *Literature and Medicine* 28 no. 1 (Spring 2009), 55–81.

Blakely, Debra E., *Mass Mediated Disease: A Case Study Analysis of Three Flu Pandemics and Public Health Policy* (New York, NY: Lexington Books, 2006).

Bloom-Feshbach, Kimberly, Lone Simonsen, Cécile Viboud, Kåre Mølbak, Mark A. Miller, Magnus Gottfredsson, and Viggo Andreasen, "Natality Decline and Miscarriages Associated with the 1918 Influenza Pandemic: The Scandinavian and United States Experiences," *Journal of Infectious Diseases* 204 (October 15, 2011), 1157–1164.

Bootsma, Martin C. J. and Neil M. Ferguson, "The Effect of Public Health Measures on the 1918 Influenza Pandemic in U.S. Cities," *Proceedings of the National Academy of Sciences of the United States* 104 no. 18 (May 1, 2007), 7588–7593.

Bristow, Nancy K., *American Pandemic: The Lost Worlds of the 1918 Influenza Epidemic* (New York, NY: Oxford University Press, 2012).

Byerly, Carol R., *Fever of War: The Influenza Epidemic in the U.S. Army During World War I* (New York, NY: New York University Press, 2005).

Byerly, Carol R., "The U.S. Military and the Influenza Pandemic of 1918–1919," *Public Health Reports* 125, supp. 3 (2010), 82–91.

Chowell, Gerardo, Cécile Viboud, Lone Simonsen, and Mark A. Miller, "Measuring the Benefits of School Closure to Mitigate Influenza," *Expert Reviews in Respiratory Medicine* 5 no. 5 (2011), 597–599.

Crosby, Alfred W., *America's Forgotten Pandemic: The Influenza of 1918*, 2nd ed. (New York, NY: Cambridge University Press, 2003).

Davies, Pete, *The Devil's Flu: The World's Deadliest Influenza Epidemic and the Scientific Hunt for the Virus that Caused It* (New York, NY: Henry Holt, 2000).

Davis, David A., "Forgotten Apocalypse: Katherine Anne Porter's 'Pale Horse, Pale Rider,' Traumatic Memory, and the Influenza Pandemic of 1918," *Southern Literary Journal* 43 no. 2 (Spring 2011), 55–74.

Dehner, George E., *Influenza: A Century of Science and Public Health Response* (Pittsburgh, PA: University of Pittsburgh Press, 2012).

Duffy, John, *The Sanitarians: A History of American Public Health* (Champaign, IL: University of Illinois Press, 1990).

Eyler, John M., "The State of Science, Microbiology, and Vaccines Circa 1918," *Public Health Reports* 125, supp. 3 (2010), 27–36.

Fanning, Patricia J., *Influenza and Inequality: One Town's Tragic Response to the Great Epidemic of 1918* (Amherst, MA: University of Massachusetts Press, 2010).

Foley, Paul Bernard, "Encephalitis Lethargica and Influenza" (Parts I, II, and III), *Journal of Neural Transmission* 116 (2009), 143–150, 1295–1321.

Galishoff, Stuart, "Newark and the Great Influenza Pandemic," *Bulletin of the History of Medicine* 43 no. 3 (May/June 1969), 246–258.

Gamble, Vanessa Northington, "'There Wasn't a Lot of Comforts in Those Days': African Americans, Public Health, and the 1918 Influenza Epidemic," *Public Health Reports* 125, supp. 3 (2010), 114–122.

Garrett, Laurie, *The Coming Plague: Newly Emerging Diseases in a World Out of Balance* (New York, NY: Farrar, Straus, and Giroux, 1994).

Gernhart, Gary, "Forgotten Enemy: PHS' Fight Against the 1918 Influenza Pandemic," *Public Health Reports* 114 no. 6 (November 1999), 559–561.

Goldberg, Myla, *Wickett's Remedy: A Novel* (New York, NY: Anchor Books, 2006).

Hatchett, Richard, Carter E. Mecher, and Marc Lipsitch, "Public Health Interventions and Epidemic Intensity During the 1918 Influenza Pandemic," *Proceedings of the National Academy of Sciences of the United States* 104 no. 18 (May 1, 2007), 7582–7587.

Hume, Janice, "The 'Forgotten' 1918 Influenza Epidemic and Press Portrayal of Public Anxiety," *Journalism and Mass Communication Quarterly* 77 no. 4 (Winter 2000), 898–915.

Iezzoni, Lynette, *Influenza 1918: The Worst Epidemic in American History* (New York, NY: TV Books, 1999).

Johnson, Niall P. A. S. and Juergen Mueller, "Updating the Accounts: Global Mortality of the 1918–1920 'Spanish' Influenza Pandemic," *Bulletin of the History of Medicine* 76 (2002), 105–115.

Jones, Marian, "The American Red Cross and Local Response to the 1918 Influenza Pandemic: A Four-City Case Study," *Public Health Reports* 125, supp. 3 (2010), 92–104.

Kamradt-Scott, Adam, "Changing Perceptions of Pandemic Influenza and Public Health Responses," *American Journal of Public Health* 102 no. 1 (January 2012), 90–98.

Keeling, Arlene W., " 'Alert to the Necessities of Emergency': U.S. Nursing During the 1918 Influenza Pandemic," *Public Health Reports* 125, supp. 3 (2010), 105–112.

Kelso, Joel K., George J. Milne, and Heath Kelly, "Simulation Suggests that Rapid Activation of Social Distancing Can Arrest Epidemic Development Due to a Novel Strain of Influenza," *BMC Public Health* 9 (April 29, 2009).

Kennedy, David M., *Over Here: The First World War and American Society* (New York, NY: Oxford University Press, 1980).

Kilbourne, Edwin D., "Influenza Pandemics of the 20th Century," *Emerging Infectious Disease*, 12 no. 1 (January 2006).

Kolata, Gina, *Flu: The Story of the Great Influenza Pandemic of 1918 and the Search for the Virus That Caused It* (New York, NY: Simon & Schuster, 1999, 2005).

Krause, Richard, "The Swine Flu Episode and the Fog of Epidemics," *Emerging Infectious Diseases* 12 no. 1 (January 2006), 40–43.

Kraut, Alan M., "Immigration, Ethnicity, and the Pandemic," *Public Health Reports* 125, supp. 3 (2010), 123–133.

Langford, Christopher, "Did the 1918–1919 Influenza Pandemic Originate in China?," *Population and Development Review* 31 no. 3 (September 2005), 473–505.

McCall, Sherman, Joel A. Vilensky, Sid Gilman, and Jeffery K. Taubenberger, "The Relationship Between *Encephalitis Lethargica* and Influenza: A Critical Analysis," *Journal of Neurovirology* 14 no. 3 (May 2008), 177–185.

Markel, Howard, Harvey B. Lipman, Julian Alexander Navarro, Alexandra Sloan, Joseph R. Michalsen, Alexandra Minna Stern, and Martin S. Cetron, "Nonpharmaceutical Interventions Implemented by US Cities During the 1918–1919 Influenza Pandemic," *Journal of the American Medical Association* 298 no. 6 (August 8, 2007), 644–654.

Morens, David M. and Jeffery K. Taubenberger, "1918 Influenza, a Puzzle with Missing Pieces," *Emerging Infectious Diseases* 18 no. 2 (February 2012), 332–335.

Morens, David M., Jeffery K. Taubenberger, and Anthony S. Fauci, "The Persistent Legacy of the 1918 Influenza Virus," *New England Journal of Medicine* 361 no. 3 (July 16, 2009), 225–229.

Mullen, Thomas, *The Last Town on Earth* (New York, NY: Random House, 2006).

Murray, Christopher J., Alan D. Lopez, Brian Chin, Dennis Feehan, and Kenneth H. Hill, "Estimation of Potential Global Pandemic Mortality on the Basis of Vital Registry Data from the 1918–1920 Pandemic: A Quantitative Analysis," *Lancet* 366 no. 9554 (December 23, 2006–January 5, 2007), 2211–2218.

Osterholm, Michael T., "Preparing for the Next Pandemic," *New England Journal of Medicine* 352 no. 18 (May 5, 2005), 1839–1842.

Oxford, John S., Armine Sefton, R. Jackson, William Innes, Rod S. Daniels, and Niall P. A. S. Johnson, "World War I May Have Allowed the Emergence of 'Spanish' Influenza," *Lancet Infectious Diseases* 2 (February 2002), 111–114.

Pettit, Dorothy A. and Janice Bailie, *A Cruel Wind: Pandemic Flu in America 1918–1920* (Murfreesboro, TN: Timberlane Books, 2008).

Phillips, Howard and David Killingray, Eds., *The Spanish Influenza Pandemic of 1918–1919: New Perspectives* (New York, NY: Routledge, 2003).

Public Health Reports 125, supp. 3: "Influenza Pandemic in the United States," Ed. Alexandra Minna Stern, Martin S. Cetron, and Howard Markel (2010), entire issue.

Quinn, Tom, *Flu: A Social History of Influenza* (London, UK: New Holland Publishers, 2008).

Rosenberg, Charles E., *Explaining Epidemics and Other Studies in the History of Medicine* (New York, NY: Cambridge University Press, 1992).

Rosner, David, "Spanish Flu, or Whatever It Is . . .," *Public Health Reports* 125, supp. 3 (2010), 38–47.

Schaffer, Ronald, *America in the Great War: The Rise of the War Welfare State* (New York, NY: Oxford University Press, 1991).

Schoch-Spana, Monica, "'Hospital's Full-Up'; The 1918 Influenza Pandemic," *Public Health Reports* 116, supp. 2 (2001), 32–33.

Schoch-Spana, Monica, "The 1918–1920 Influenza Pandemic Escape Communities Digital Document Archive," *Bulletin of the History of Medicine* 81 no. 4 (Winter 2007), 863–865.

Spellman, Paul N., Ed., "'A Million Kisses': Love Letters from a Doughboy in France," *Southwestern Historical Quarterly* 114 no. 1 (July 2010), 37–54.

Stern, Alexandra Minna, Mary Beth Reilly, Martin S. Cetron, and Howard Markel, "'Better Off in School': School Medical Inspection as a Public Health Strategy During the 1918–1919 Influenza Pandemic in the United States," *Public Health Reports* 125, supp. 3 (2010), 63–70.

Stern, Alexandra Minna, Martin S. Cetron, and Howard Markel, "Closing the Schools: Lessons from the 1918–1919 U.S. Influenza Pandemic," *Health Affairs* 28 no. 6 (2009), w1066–w1078.

Stohr, Klaus, "Avian Influenza and Pandemics—Research Needs and Opportunities" (Editorial), *New England Journal of Medicine* 352 no. 4 (January 27, 2005), 405–407.

Taubenberger, Jeffery K. and David M. Morens, "Influenza: The Once and Future Pandemic," *Public Health Reports* 125, supp. 3 (2010), 16–26.

Taubenberger, Jeffery K. and David M. Morens, "1918 Influenza: The Mother of All Pandemics," *Emerging Infectious Diseases* 12 no. 1 (January 2006), 15–22.

Taubenberger, Jeffery K., Ann H. Reid, Raina M. Lourens, Ruixiue Wang, Guozhong Jin, and Thomas G. Fanning, "Characterization of the 1918 Influenza Virus Polymerase Genes," *Nature* 437 no. 7060 (October 6, 2005), 889–893.

Tomes, Nancy, "'Destroyer and Teacher': Managing the Masses During the 1918–1919 Influenza Pandemic," *Public Health Reports* 125, supp. 3 (2010), 48–62.

Tumpey, Terrence M., Christopher F. Basler, Patricia V. Aguilar, Hui Zeng, Alicia Solorzano, David E. Swayne, Nancy J. Cox, Jacqueline M. Katz, Jeffery K. Taubenberger, Peter Palese, and Adolfo Garcia-Sastro, "Characterization of the Reconstructed 1918 Spanish Influenza Pandemic Virus," *Science* 310 no. 5745 (October 2005), 77–80.

van Hartesveldt, Fred R., Ed., *The 1918–1919 Pandemic of Influenza: The Urban Impact in the Western World* (Lampeter, Wales: Edwin Mellen Press, 1992).

WEBSITES

Escape Communities: The 1918–1920 Influenza Pandemic Escape Community Digital Document Archive, Center for the History of Medicine, University of Michigan. http://chm.med.umich.edu/research/escape-communities.

Influenza Encyclopedia: The American Influenza Epidemic of 1918–1919—A Digital Encyclopedia (University of Michigan). www.influenzaarchive.org/about.html.

"Spanish Influenza, 1918–1919," Historical Views of Diseases and Epidemics website (Harvard University Library). http://ocp.hul.harvard.edu/contagion/influenza.html.

U.S. National Archives and Records Administration, "The Deadly Virus: The Influenza Epidemic of 1918." www.archives.gov/exhibits/influenza-epidemic/index.html.

U.S. Department of Health and Human Services, "The Great Pandemic: United States, 1918–1919." www.flu.gov/pandemic/history/1918.

VIDEOS

"American Experience: Influenza 1918" (Documentary, 2005)
"We Heard the Bells" (Drama, 2010)
"1918" (Drama, 1985)

FIRSTHAND COMMENTARY (1918–1960)

American Public Health Association, "Working Program Against Influenza," *American Journal of Public Health* 9 no. 2 (February 1919), 1–13.

Baldwin, Florence C., "The Epidemic in Joliet, Ill.," *Public Health Nurse* 11 no. 1 (1919), 49–51.

Colon, Anne L., "Influenza at Cedar Branch Camp," *American Journal of Nursing* 19 no. 8 (May 1919), 605–607.

Davies, Elizabeth J., "The Influenza Epidemic and How We Tried to Control It," *Public Health Nurse* 11 no. 1 (1919), 45–47.

Delano, Jane A., "Meeting the Spanish Influenza Situation," *American Journal of Nursing* 19 no. 2 (November 1918), 108–111.

Deming, Dorothy, "Influenza—1918: Reliving the Great Epidemic," *American Journal of Nursing* 57 no. 10 (October 1957), 83–85.

Doty, Permelia Murnan, "A Retrospect of the Influenza Epidemic," *Public Health Nurse* 11 no. 12 (1919), 949–957.

Foley, Edna L. "Department of Public Health Nursing," *American Journal of Nursing* 19 no. 3 (December 1918): 189–195.

Frost, Wade Hampton, "Epidemiology of Influenza," *Public Health Reports* 34 no. 33 (August 15, 1919), 1823–1836.

G. R. "Experiences During the Influenza Epidemic," *American Journal of Nursing* 19 no. 3 (December 1918), 203–204.

Gribble, Beulah, "Influenza in a Kentucky Coal-Mining Camp," *American Journal of Nursing* 19 no. 8 (May 1919), 609–611.

Howard, Col. Deane C., "Influenza—U.S. Army," *Military Surgeon* 46 (1920), 522–548.

"Influenza Outbreak" (Editorial), *Journal of the American Medical Association* 71 no. 14 (October 5, 1918), 1138.

Jordan, Edwin O., *Epidemic Influenza: A Survey* (Chicago, IL: American Medical Association, 1927).

Keegan, John J., "The Prevailing Pandemic of Influenza," *Journal of the American Medical Association* 71 no. 13 (September 28, 1918), 1051–1055.

Lent, Mary E., "Public Health Nursing in the Extra-Cantonment Zone," *American Journal of Public Health* 9 no. 3 (March 1919), 193–195.

McCarthy, Mary, *Memories of a Catholic Girlhood* (New York, NY: Harcourt Brace, 1957).

Nicoll, Matthias, Jr., "What We Really Know About the Epidemic," *American Journal of Public Health* 9 no. 1 (January 1919), 43–44.

Nuzum, John W., Isadore Pilot, Fred H. Stangl, and Barnet Edward Bonar, "Pandemic Influenza and Pneumonia in a Large Civil Hospital," *Journal of the American Medical Association* 71 no. 19 (November 9, 1918), 1562–1565.

O'Neill, R. A., C. St. Clair Drake, and Julius O. Cobb, "The Work of the Illinois Influenza Commission," *American Journal of Public Health* 9 no. 1 (January 1919), 21–24.

Pearl, Raymond, "On Certain General Statistical Aspects of the 1918 Epidemic in American Cities," *Public Health Reports* 34 no. 32 (August 8, 1919), 1732–1783.

Porter, Katherine Anne, *Pale Horse, Pale Rider* (New York, NY: Harcourt Brace, 1939).

"Report of an Epidemic in Chicago Occurring During the Fall of 1918," in *Octennial Report of the Department of Health, City of Chicago, 1911–1918* (Chicago, IL: Chicago Department of Health, 1919), available at www.epimodels.org/midas/catdoc.do?methodToCall=view&catalogDocId=594&mode=view (accessed August 23, 2013).

"Spanish Influenza" (Editorial), *Journal of the American Medical Association* 71 no. 8 (August 24, 1918), 660.

Sydenstricker, Edgar, "The Incidence of Influenza among Persons of Different Economic Status During the Epidemic of 1918," *Public Health Reports* 46 no. 4 (January 23, 1931), 154–170.

U.S. Bureau of the Census, *Mortality Statistics 1918* and *Mortality Statistics 1919* (Washington, DC: Government Printing Office, 1920), available at www.cdc.gov/nchs/products/vsusl.htm (accessed August 13, 2013).

Westphal, Mary E., "Influenza Vignettes," *Public Health Nurse* 11 no. 2 (1919), 126–132.

Winslow, Charles-Edward Amory and J. F. Rogers, "Statistics of the 1918 Epidemic of Influenza in Connecticut: With a Consideration of the Factors Which Influenced the Prevalence of This Disease in Various Communities," *Journal of Infectious Diseases* 26 no. 3 (March 1920), 185–216.

Index